The
Tibetan
Nun
Mingyur
Peldrön

The Tibetan Nun Mingyur Peldrön

A WOMAN OF POWER AND PRIVILEGE

Alison Melnick Dyer

UNIVERSITY OF
WASHINGTON PRESS
Seattle

The open-access edition of *The Tibetan Nun Mingyur Peldrön* was made possible in part by an award from the James P. Geiss and Margaret Y. Hsu Foundation.

This publication was also supported by grants from the Chiang Ching-kuo Foundation for International Scholarly Exchange and the Bates College Faculty Development Fund.

Copyright © 2022 by the University of Washington Press

Parts of chapter 2 are adapted from Melnick Dyer, "Female Authority and Privileged *Lives*: The Hagiography of Mingyur Peldrön," published in the *Journal of the International Association of Tibetan Studies* (2018).

Composed in Alegreya typeface designed by Juan Pablo del Peral

26 25 24 23 22   5 4 3 2 1

The digital edition of this book may be downloaded and shared under a Creative Commons Attribution Non-Commercial No Derivatives 4.0 international license (CC-BY-NC-ND 4.0). For information about this license, see https://creativecommons.org/licenses/by-nc-nd/4.0. This license applies only to content created by the author, not to separately copyrighted material. To use this book, or parts of this book, in any way not covered by the license, please contact University of Washington Press.

UNIVERSITY OF WASHINGTON PRESS
uwapress.uw.edu

Library of Congress Cataloging-in-Publication Data
Names: Melnick Dyer, Alison, author.
Title: The Tibetan nun Mingyur Peldrön : a woman of power and privilege / Alison Melnick Dyer.
Description: Seattle : University of Washington Press, 2022. | Includes bibliographical references and index.
Identifiers: LCCN 2021050724 (print) | LCCN 2021050725 (ebook) | ISBN 9780295750354 (hardcover) | ISBN 9780295750361 (paperback) | ISBN 9780295750378 (ebook)
Subjects: LCSH: Mi-'gyur-dpal-sgron, Smin-gling Rje-btsun, 1699–1769. | Buddhist nuns—Tibet Region—Biography. | Yoginis—Tibet Region—Biography. | Lamas—Tibet Region—Biography. | Buddhism—Tibet Region—History.
Classification: LCC BQ972.I347 M45 2022 (print) | LCC BQ.I347 (ebook) | DDC 294.3/657092 [B]—dc23/eng/20220223
LC record available at https://lccn.loc.gov/2021050724
LC ebook record available at https://lccn.loc.gov/2021050725

♾ This paper meets the requirements of ANSI/NISO Z39.48-1992 (Permanence of Paper).

Contents

vii	Acknowledgments
xi	Note to the Reader
xiii	Chronology
1	Introduction
30	Chapter One. A Privileged Life
67	Chapter Two. Authorizing the Saint
104	Chapter Three. Multivocal *Lives*
140	Chapter Four. Mingyur Peldrön the Diplomat
162	Chapter Five. The Death of Mingyur Peldrön and the Making of a Saint
179	Tibetan Glossary
185	Notes
205	Bibliography
215	Index

Acknowledgments

This book has been in process so many years, with the help of so many people, that it might be impossible to thank all those who have helped it come into being in one way or another. Initial research for the project was funded by a Fulbright grant, and gratitude goes to Paromita Datta, Neeraj Goswami, and Vinita Tripathi for their support of the Fulbright grantees in India. My translation of Mingyur Peldrön's *gur* was supported by a Tsadra Foundation grant to participate in the 2018 Lotsawa Translation Workshop in Boulder, Colorado. Thanks to Marcus Perman and Tracy Joosten for supporting the Tsadra workshop and to Sean Price for his tireless efforts compiling Mingyur Peldrön's collected works. Later stages of research were conducted with funds from Bates College.

It is hard to convey the impact that great mentors can have on a scholar's trajectory and process. I am infinitely grateful to three people whose scholarly support has most significantly benefited me in the creation of this book. Thanks to Kurtis Schaeffer, Andy Quintman, and Holly Gayley, whose good humor, profound kindness, brilliant guidance, and unwavering advice have been the fulcrum for this project.

For getting into the linguistic nitty-gritty (and other things) with me, thanks to Ben Nourse, Catherine Hartmann, Christie Kilby, David DiValerio, Dominic Sur, Gareth Sparham, Gedun Rabsel, Jampa Samten, Jann Ronis, Jue Liang, Khenpo Sherab Konchok, Natasha Mikles, Nick Trautz, Pemba Tashi, Tseten Chonjore, Yaron Bahir, and Yeshe Namgyal Choenzom. I appreciate your patience and willingness to talk all things Tibetan.

For helping me navigate the research process, thanks to Alex Gardner, Amy Holmes-Tagchungdarpa, Anna Johnson, Betsy Napper, Erica Prochaska, Dan Melnick, Dipitman Roybardhan, Gauri, Kalsang Tshering Thendup, Kalzang Dorjee Bhutia, Kumkum Roybardhan (of blessed memory), Pema Namgyel Ringutsang, Sara Lewis, Shashi Panicker, Sucheta Panicker, Swati

Chawla, Viji Melnick, Wangyal Bhutia, and Yap Tshering Bhutia. Much of the initial work for this project was conducted at Songtsen Library, Dehradun, and later at Pemayangtsé Monastery, Pelling, Sikkim—two communities whose warmth and interest in this project helped it fly.

As thought partners along the way, thanks to Amy Paris Langenberg, Ann Gleig, Brenton Sullivan, Chris Bell, Chris Hiebert, Colleen Laird, Dominique Townsend, Elena Pakhutova, Erin Nourse, George Archer, Ipsita Chatterjea, Julie Regan, Karen Lang, Joe Leach, Nicole Willock, Shreena Gandhi, Suzanne Bessenger, Tasha Kimmet, and Ulrike Roesler. Thank you for reading and discussing drafts, offering critique, and suggesting improvements at different points in the development of the book.

Among my wonderful colleagues at Bates College, those who helped with this book in direct and fundamental ways include Anelise Hanson Shrout, Beth Woodward, Bridget Fullerton, Brittany Longsdorf, Christy Adams, Cynthia Baker, Dan Sanford, Darby Ray, Erica Rand, Francisca Lopez, John Strong, Justine Wiesinger, Karen Melvin, Katie Dobkowski, Keiko Konoeda, Lauren Ashwell, Lisa Gilson, Margaret Creighton, Stephanie Kelley Romano, Stephanie Pridgeon, Stephanie Wade, and Tiffany Salter. Thank you for drafts read, writing groups organized, ideas bounced, and everything else.

Editorial support takes many forms. Thanks to Lorri Hagman for her enthusiasm and insight and to the editorial team at the University of Washington Press, including Elizabeth Gratch and Joeth Zucco, for all that they have done to bring the project along. Great thanks to Meredith Carroll for helping me navigate the early stages of the publication process. For her thoughtful comments and suggestions, thanks to Madeline Korbey. Infinite gratitude to the anonymous readers whose critique and feedback were vital to improving this work.

To complete a book in the midst of a pandemic is no easy thing, and in this case it was bolstered by a loving community. Thanks especially to Amy Bunker, Andy Harrington, Andy Hegle, Angelique Pilon, Ciaran Fullerton, Jessica Eschman, John Bowker, Karla Harrington, Khenmo Drolma, Laura Trumbull, Megan Goodwin, Michelle Greene, Rick Fullerton, Sarah Shotwell Wallace, Sita, and my family, who all helped me stay grounded and connected with the living world when it was needed most.

This book would not have come into being without the unwavering love, compassion, and support of Eric Dyer, whose confidence was the bedrock of the project and whose contributions, if fully recounted here, would occupy a whole other volume. Thank you for believing it was possible, for working through ideas together, and for helping make it happen in a million different ways. This book is dedicated to Eric.

Note to the Reader

Most Tibetan names and terms in the main text are rendered *phonetically* in the roman alphabet, as they are pronounced in a Lhasa dialect. Corresponding *transliteration* of written Tibetan forms according to the Wylie system is provided in notes and in the "Tibetan Glossary."

Likewise, in the main text, titles of Tibetan literary works are given in English translation, with a note linking to the corresponding romanized Tibetan title.

Throughout this book the many translated passages from *A Dispeller of Distress for the Faithful*, the biography of Mingyur Peldrön authored by her disciple Khyungpo Repa Gyurmé Ösel, are in a different font to distinguish them from quotations from other sources.

Chronology

1699	Birth
1710	Commencement of studies with Terdak Lingpa
1714	Terdak Lingpa dies
1714	Commencement of studies with Lochen Dharmaśrī
1716	Retreat
1717–18	Civil war
1717	Flight to Sikkim
1718	First public teaching
1719	Return to Mindröling and monastery reconstruction
1720	Illness and recovery
1720	First meeting with Polhané and the Seventh Dalai Lama
1723	First meeting with Gyurmé Ösel
1726	First meeting with the Fifth Lelung, Jedrung Rinpoche
1727	Khangchenné assassinated, war in Gyantsé begins
1728	Cease-fire of the war in Gyantsé
1730–35	Seventh Dalai Lama exiled in Kham
1732	Teaching tour in central Tibet
1736	Second meetings with Polhané and the Fifth Lelung
1737–38	Mass teachings at various locations in central Tibet
1739	Retreat
1740	Mass teachings in central Tibet
1742	Gyurmé Ösel begins writing *A Dispeller of Distress for the Faithful*
1743	Mass teachings in central Tibet
1744	Beginning of three-year retreat
1747	Polhané dies
1751–66	Pilgrimage and teachings at Shauk Taggo
1766–69	Mass teachings at Mindröling
1769	Death

The
Tibetan
Nun
Mingyur
Peldrön

Introduction

THE driveway to Pemayangtsé Monastery rises at a steep grade, as do most of the roads in this part of Sikkim. Off to the right, level with the bottom of the hill and just inside the driveway's entrance, there is a stand where prayer flags flutter like leaves in the wind. Nearby sits what at first appears to be a white pile of rocks. Upon closer inspection, I notice that the dilapidated stone structure has been carefully whitewashed year after year, so that although the rocks have shifted over time, they remain fused together, encased in layers of white paint. The surrounding ground is covered with wild strawberries. There are no signs to mark this structure, which I am told is in fact a throne originally erected for the nun Mingyur Peldrön (1699–1769).[1] It is said that when the young woman arrived here in 1718—a refugee from the Ü region of central Tibet—she was exhorted to give teachings at Pemayangtsé. Although she consented, she refused to enter the monastery itself, citing impropriety that a woman would enter the realm of celibate men.[2] Thinking of this invitation, I look up the hill and wonder wryly if perhaps she had insisted on remaining at the bottom of the mountain to avoid the climb.

Like the stone throne, Mingyur Peldrön's work for the Nyingma community had an influence that has persisted over centuries, even if it is not always immediately identified. Although Sikkim is where this story starts, Mingyur Peldrön only spent a few years there. She was born, educated, and later taught at Mindröling Monastery, located in modern-day Dranang, in Ü, central Tibet, some seventy miles south of Lhasa. Born to Phuntsok Peldzöm (17th–18th CE) and Terdak Lingpa Gyurmé Dorjé (1646–1714), she was one of seven children. As a daughter of Mindröling's founding family, she received an unprecedented religious education, which began early on in her childhood. Terdak Lingpa and his brother, Lochen Dharmaśrī (1654–1717/18), oversaw her education until their respective deaths. Empowered with an encyclopedic collection of teachings, she was raised with the expectation that alongside her brothers she would inhabit the role of religious teacher and carry on the new populist reframing of the Nyingma tradition that her father and uncle had established. She lived her entire adult life as a celibate nun, never marrying or having children. In her role as a religious teacher, she worked for the edification of the Mindröling community, teaching throughout her adult life and authoring works focusing on the Great Perfection (Dzogchen) praxis of the Nyingma school. As a prolific author, she wrote texts throughout her adulthood that spanned a range of genres, including Great Perfection ritual manuals and other instructive texts for her disciples that have been preserved down to the present day. Alongside the work of her brother Rinchen Namgyel (1694–1768), her role as a teacher and an author was centrally important to Mindröling's survival in the eighteenth century.

Of the relatively small extant collection of literary works about the lives of Tibetan Buddhist women, Mingyur Peldrön's hagiography suggests a woman who was unusual for her time and place. Unlike most other Tibetan women whose lives have filtered down to the present day, Mingyur Peldrön was born and raised in the heart of a prominent religious family at the center of the religious elite. Like Khandro Tāre Lhamo, Sera Khandro, and Chökyi Drönma, she was born into the aristocracy. Her family took the unusual step of supporting her religious pursuits and did not pressure her to marry. Her education was directed by the well-known and erudite members of her family (all men), which meant she received an education that would support her rise as a respected religious teacher in Ü. Her story defies some of our received notions of how gender has been treated as a topic in the life stories of Tibetan Buddhist women and complicates how we approach religious women's recorded biographies—their *Lives*. Most significantly, the treatment of her status as a woman—and the implications of her womanhood for her own religious authority—is inconsistent throughout her hagiography. Rather than a uniform narrative about the challenges of living as a woman, her gender is at turns held up as a benefit, and in other moments it is said to hold her back. Likewise, privilege plays a dynamic role throughout her story. She was simultaneously the recipient of multiple forms of high privilege and also experienced great hardship. Different aspects of her lived experience are combined in unexpected ways in her hagiography, and learning about her life story can help us understand more about how the intersectional nature of her identity strengthened and challenged her religious path and her public persona. Her privilege and the support of her family allowed her access to a host of social contexts that would have been otherwise inaccessible and were not even extended to all the women of her family's generation. Meanwhile, their sectarian affiliations would lead to her persecution and exile during the 1717–18 civil war. The effects of these difficulties, and her later relationship to powerful Nyingma and Geluk Buddhist institutions, tell of a woman who was resourceful and determined to achieve soteriological and institutional progress for herself and her community.

Mingyur Peldrön is one of few women of her time and place for whom we have a long and detailed life story. Querying the factors that influenced the decision to memorialize her in a hagiography shows how her life story exemplifies the interrelated nature of privilege and authority, the multifaceted aspects of privilege, and the ways these were negotiated within a gendered context in eighteenth-century Tibet. Mingyur Peldrön's life offers an example of how these themes of gender and privilege function in the creation of the public persona of a saint who happens to be a woman, an eldest daughter, and a celibate nun.[3]

Hagiography and *Namtar*

This study takes as its central source the life story of Mingyur Peldrön, which was written by her disciple Khyungpo Repa Gyurmé Ösel (b. 1715) and completed in 1782. Titled *The Life of Mingyur Peldrön: A Dispeller of Distress for the Faithful* (hereafter referred to as *Dispeller*),[4] it is one of the extant life stories of Tibetan Buddhist women, which all told comprise about 1 percent of the approximately two thousand extant hagiographies of Tibetan Buddhist saints.[5] The scholarship for this study is based upon three different editions of *Dispeller*. The version referred to in the notes as "*Dispeller* ms. 1" is a 237-folio edition reproduced by the National Library of Bhutan in 1984. "*Dispeller* ms. 2" was published in 2015 by the Sichuan Minzu Language Press as part of a multivolume series of Tibetan women's lives.[6] Finally, "*Dispeller* ms. 3" consists of Mingyur Peldrön's life story as well as a collection of works (*sungbum*) written by her. It was compiled by Sean Price, from texts housed at Mindrolling Monastery in Clement Town, India,[7] with support from Eric Columbel and the Tsadra Foundation. Apart from some spelling and grammatical differences, these three versions of her story are much the same in content and organization. There are also other, shorter life narratives of her, which are referenced throughout the book and identified based on the collections in which they are found.

Understanding the life story of Mingyur Peldrön means understanding its author. We know very little about Gyurmé Ösel beyond what is found in *Dispeller*, but the text does offer some clues as to his own trajectory. In addition to composing the text, we know that he hailed from Shang, in the Tö region of Tibet. We also know that he first met Mingyur Peldrön when he was about eight years old. He became her disciple and joined her community as a child, leaving the home of his grandmother for Mindröling. He became a monk at some point, although the details of his ordination are unclear. We also know he did not finish writing *Dispeller* until some thirteen years after Mingyur Peldrön's passing.[8] In addition to *Dispeller*, Gyurmé Ösel is not known to have authored any other works, although he did act as scribe for at least one piece that Mingyur Peldrön wrote. This work was the result of a request he made, asking that she explain one of Terdak Lingpa's treasures focusing on the Highest Yoga (Atiyoga) teachings of the Great Perfection.[9] The result was her text *Elaborations on the Awareness-Empowerment Methods for the Ati Zabdön, Profound Unsurpassable Meaning of the Great Perfection*.[10]

Dispeller falls into the Tibetan literary genre of *namtar*, a ubiquitous form of Tibetan life writing that includes a variety of narrative styles. These life stories of religious practitioners vary widely in focus, tone, and style, although they do constitute a loosely associated genre.[11] Broadly speaking, *namtar*, which literally translates as "complete liberation,"[12] portray the lives of historical and semihistorical figures and have been received as examples of successful paths to enlightenment. The ostensible purpose of these texts is to provide soteriological guidance by recounting the exemplary lives of saintly figures. The central subject of the text is often depicted in miraculous terms, and the texts include accounts of spiritual realization, visions, and thaumaturgy woven together with worldly activities and the historical accounts of mundane life. Miracles occur, deities and demons appear and interact with humans, and prophecy and revelation are par for the course. Namtars often include devotional language, references to dreams and visions, and prophecy. Engaging the Buddhist concepts of samsara and reincarnation, namtars also include accounts of the subject's previous lives. In some cases the texts are composed by the disciples of the main subject, as is the case for *Dispeller*.

Significant work has been done to highlight the ways that the genre of namtar intersects with and diverges from the various North American and Western European genre groupings of saintly *Lives* and semihistorical narratives.[13] While the relationship between the namtar and its potential non-Tibetan equivalents is not necessarily a one-to-one correlation, Tibetan life narratives often reflect a similar approach to life writing, crossing the boundaries between the broadly defined genres of biography and hagiography, according to the intentions of the author. In the case of Mingyur Peldrön's namtar, the most relevant Eurocentric genre is that of hagiography. While similar to namtar in diversity and range, generally speaking, the term *hagiography* refers to texts that are focused on the life of a saint. In particular, these life narratives tend to provide accounts supporting the subject's identity as a saint that include miracles, trials overcome, and other signs of virtuous activity. In addition to proving an individual's saintliness, they depict exemplary behavior for readers and hearers to emulate, ostensibly for the goal of soteriological benefit. *Hagiography* will here be loosely defined as narratives of the life of the saint, written for devotional and/or historical purposes, which include a combination of miraculous and historically traceable events.

As several European medievalist scholars have shown, *hagiography* is a term that encompasses a range of literary styles and approaches.[14] It is a modern word that developed out of studies of medieval European saints and the diverse corpus of writing by and about them. As such, it has been applied to a variety of texts that contemporary medievalists argue would be more accurately differentiated into separate genres. The concept of hagiography can be approached not as a bounded category but, rather, as what scholar Anna Taylor describes as a "horizon of expectations" about style, form, and content.[15] This corrective offers flexibility in understanding the role of narratives of saintly lives in the contexts of both European and Tibetan life writing. In the same way that hagiography can be applied to a multifaceted set of texts, namtar can apply to a broad range of Tibetan saintly *Lives*. Both genres can be taken as polythetic in their scope.

Much has been written on the namtar genre and its relationship to European medieval hagiography and spiritual instruction manuals, and methods for approaching this have been well established. Scholars have variously translated *namtar* as "biography," "hagiography," and the more neutral "Life" or have chosen to retain the Tibetan term rather than hazard a translation, all depending on the specific context of a given *Life* and the circumstances of its authorship. Hagiography is not a direct translation of *namtar*, so we must tread lightly and acknowledge that the overlap of the two terms will not necessarily be comprehensive. Nevertheless, using a modern English term to make sense of a long-standing Tibetan genre can be useful insofar as it helps situate namtar in a comparative intercultural context of soteriologically minded life writing about eminent religious figures. In cases like Mingyur

Peldrön's *A Dispeller of Distress for the Faithful*, *namtar* is best translated as "hagiography," rather than "biography." This is because it better describes the *Life* of the saint that is soteriologically grounded, imbued with the miraculous, and diverges from European post-Enlightenment concepts of a narrative bounded by the subject's birth and death. Applying the term *hagiography* to Tibetan sources also helps to draw connections between the devotional textual traditions of disparate parts of the world, allowing for equivalencies to be drawn between Buddhist and Christian religious literature in ways that are useful for understanding the works of both traditions.

Hagiography is useful for differentiating Mingyur Peldrön's life story from what we might think of as biography. While *namtar* is sometimes translated as "biography," this term conjures up notions of European post-Enlightenment accounts of historical figures presented in an etic and allegedly objective manner, to act as a window into the lives of individual people. Whether or not such objectivity is actually possible, biography indicates a factual representation that neither claims to excessively elevate nor to apotheosize the subject. Because it suggests some modicum of objectivity and the assumption that all accounts reflect world-bound historically verifiable events, *biography* is ill suited as a term to use for some namtars, including Mingyur Peldrön's. Referring to namtar as biography indicates that the post-Enlightenment goals of objective reporting were in place for the authors of these texts and that miraculous events, stories of previous incarnations, and so forth would be excluded. For her *Life*, and with so many other *Lives* of Tibetan heroes and saints, this is simply not the case. The term *hagiography* is a more appropriate reference than *biography* with these works because it indicates that the person will be depicted as a saint, their life serving as an example of enlightened activity with the story a lesson for soteriological benefit.

Given the similarities between Mingyur Peldrön's namtar and the genre of hagiography (broadly defined), the two terms are used interchangeably here. Throughout this study the terms *namtar*, *hagiography*, and *Life* are all used to refer to the genre of miraculously imbued Tibetan life writing, specifically *Dispeller*. This is not meant to simplify the genres but, rather, to emphasize the author's visible effort to assert the sanctity of the subject, especially as it relates to the context of her spiritual authority.[16] In the case of *Dispeller*, the text sits squarely in the hagiographic realm, much closer to the European *Lives* of Christian saints than it is to the post-Enlightenment biographies of the Euro-West. In contradistinction, while *Dispeller* contains biographical attributes, and some sections reflect the conventions of biography, in general it is not written in the European post-Enlightenment biographical tenor.

Mingyur Peldrön's life story weaves miracle with historical occurrence and represents her life as the exemplary model of a highly realized religious practitioner. It includes miraculous accounts, stories of spiritual realization, and narrations of the extreme hardships endured by the saint along her path. Like other namtars, *Dispeller* also includes accounts of her previous lives. And perhaps most important, it was written by her devotee Gyurmé Ösel, whose goal appears to be elevating her in the eyes of their community. *Dispeller* also follows a format that is common in namtar. It begins with an opening homage to buddhas and bodhisattvas, followed by a description of the subject's previous lives. After this discussion of her pre-lives, the text goes on to discuss her life *as* Mingyur Peldrön. It ends with a description of her death and closes with a colophon that gives the details of the text's composition.

Tibetanists and European medievalists alike have explored the ways that the abundant hagiographies of these respective religious communities can be used in conjunction with other sources to better understand significant moments in religious history and, to a lesser extent, the lived experience of those who are memorialized in these works. While the historical and religious contexts are different, continued dialogue between the two fields of scholarship could help advance both. Hagiographic texts are best understood within a broader literary and historical context. Tibetan literature differentiates between these saintly *Lives* and actual histories (*logyü*), and looking at them together can be a fruitful exercise. In contrast with namtar, logyü recount specific moments in political and religious institutions, naming the actors involved, the dates of occurrence, and the outcome of these engagements.

In comparison, it is clear that namtar are not meant to be read solely as histories, but if read thoughtfully and alongside other sources, they can be beneficial in terms of how we understand the mores and historical events of a specific moment. These works are often best read alongside related texts, including histories, liturgies, songs, rituals, letters, and even other hagiographies, to get a better sense of the context of the hagiography's creation and the world in which the author was situated.[17] Taken alone, one text cannot offer a coherent religio-historical context but, read in conjunction with other works, can indicate the significant religious and social implications of the material found within a given hagiography. Thus, hagiography can give some insight into the cultural and religious indicators functioning in the time and place where a text was produced. While they are not "windows" into a historical moment, when contextualized they can give clues about what was important to both author and readers in the time of the text's creation. Taken contextually, hagiography provides a complicated source of information for meeting historical and imagined figures through literary means.[18] Hagiography can be mined to understand society and the saint by understanding the literary and historical context in which the text was written.

Avoiding the presumption of objectivity, such an undertaking should be carefully navigated. The scholarship of European medieval scholars Patrick Geary and Jane Tibbetts Schulenburg offer helpful guidance for engaging these works. In reading hagiography, it is important to acknowledge the "propagandistic nature" of the genre and to take into account that hagiographic works have political implications beyond the literary realm.[19] It is particularly useful to keep in mind that hagiographers' "works were panegyrics, conscious programs of persuasion or propaganda, meant to prove the particular sanctity of their protagonists."[20] While these works offer unique insight into their subjects and the historical moment in which they were written, first and foremost they give the reader a sense of the author's goals for elevating a particular historical figure, a set of approaches to religious praxis and doctrine, and the social mores of the moment in which they were writing. In thinking about the creation of the saint, hagiography also gives the reader a sense of what the author considered most important for achieving the goal of elevation to sainthood.

This is all relevant in the Tibetan literary context of the eighteenth century as well. Insofar as Gyurmé Ösel sought to present his female teacher in a saintly light, *Dispeller* tells us a great deal about his particular soteriological and social concerns. These works also need to be read contextually to understand how they do and do not represent the values of a given historical context. Taken together with other contemporary works, hagiography can offer insight into historically embedded ideals and proscriptions as well as some reference to historical events (even if these events are construed ahistorically in some moments in the text).[21] As such, it is also important to note that *Dispeller* was completed more than a decade after Mingyur Peldrön's death. In the colophon of the work, Gyurmé Ösel explains that he had completed it in order to support the newest generation, the future of Mindröling leadership.

As such, it is instructive to read *Dispeller* as reflective of the late-eighteenth-century concerns of the institution, sometimes diverging completely from the concerns on which Mingyur Peldrön focused during her lifetime.

The very aspects that make namtar challenging historical sources also mean that they are compelling literary works and can tell us something of the religious attitudes and conventions of the time, at least in terms of how the author and the author's interlocutors were engaging with their social and historical context. Hagiographers can be seen following certain socially embedded stylistic themes in their literary creations, which often exemplified the social mores and soteriological anxieties of their religious and historical contexts or at the very least represented their own concerns.[22] Especially in this context and when treated in conjunction with other works, hagiography can be helpful for learning about the socioreligious environment of both author and subject. It communicates themes and aspects of sainthood and religious praxis that were considered important to the hagiographer and may have been significant for their community as well. By looking at these works, we can learn what authors thought was ideal behavior, how they viewed the missteps and foibles of the intended audience, and their process of grappling with contemporary issues. By understanding the symbolic, doctrinal, and culturally bound significance of these literary productions, the reader can learn about the intellectual and religious environment of the period.

Incorporating both historical and literary analyses of Mingyur Peldrön and her *Life* is useful for understanding both the life she actually lived and how it was presented in literary form. Engaging both histories and hagiographies helps make sense of her position as a religious leader and practitioner who was also a woman. We can consider the ways in which she is represented in texts and work to glean from this what her lived experience might have been. The themes of gender and privilege are particularly useful for building this understanding, especially when we consider their positioning in her *Life* narrative. Taking an analogy from the fiber arts, in this book the themes of privilege and gender act as the weft. We can ask whether and how they can impact each other when laid side by side in Mingyur Peldrön's life story. Meanwhile, the hagiography *Dispeller* acts as the warp on which these concepts hang. Privilege and gender appear in the text at different moments, impacting the narrative accounts of her experiences and her significance as a religious figure. Considered together, the warp and weft make sense of the whole.

Mingyur Peldrön's namtar includes several accounts of historical events, the result of which is a confluence of history and hagiography wherein history is presented to further the ends of the author's goal of soteriological storytelling. While Gyurmé Ösel's work is useful as an example of hagiography of the period and contributes to our knowledge about hagiographies of women, it also represents a specific historical depiction of her life and legacy. Political, social, and doctrinal clashes are woven into the work to meet the goals of the author. As a source, there is a great deal of generative potential, if the text is read responsibly. To do this, I read *Dispeller* in conjunction with histories, hagiographies, and other accounts from contemporary sources and related institutions, all of which give context to Gyurmé Ösel's presentation of her and eighteenth-century central Tibetan political and religious life. These include histories of Sikkim and Mindröling and hagiographies of her brother and grandmother. *Dispeller* offers an example of the hagiographic text as a rhetorical product. That is, it is a location in which soteriological narrative is used as a literary device to legitimate her and reinforce her goals for the Nyingma community. Gyurmé Ösel drew on and elided gendered norms at turns in his process of elevating his teacher to the level of a saint. His engagement with gender, especially in relation to other aspects of Mingyur Peldrön's identity, is considered in relation to other literary sources in order to show how we can make sense of one woman's rise to an authoritative role in the world of eighteenth-century central Tibet.

Religion and Politics in the Long Eighteenth Century

Historical context can tell us a great deal about the social dynamics that color individual experience. For Mingyur Peldrön the most significant influences were the regional religious and political communities associated with two religious denominations, both the Nyingma (such as her birthplace of Mindröling) and the Geluk. In particular, the religiopolitical machinations of central Tibetan organizations set the stage for the causes and conditions that altered her lived experience, literary representations of her, and her own writing. At the turn of the eighteenth century, Lhasa had become well established as a center of cultural, political, and religious power in Tibet, and there were rumblings of inter-sectarian strife that would ultimately erupt into outright war. Much scholarship has been dedicated to the mid-seventeenth-century contexts, such as the establishment and rise of the

Ganden Podrang government in Lhasa. Likewise, a great deal of work has been done to study the rise of nonsectarian (*rimé*) developments that later centered in nineteenth-century Kham, in eastern Tibet. I categorize the interim between these periods as the "long eighteenth century." Less scholarship has focused on this interim period so that it remains vague in our current understanding. Mingyur Peldrön's hagiography helps to fill this lacuna by linking the rise of the seventeenth-century Ganden Podrang with the nonsectarian developments of the nineteenth century. The long eighteenth century was a time of fluctuating sectarian factionalism, with significant tensions between the Nyingma and Geluk denominations.

In the mid-seventeenth century the Fifth Dalai Lama, Ngawang Lobzang Gyatso (1617–82), had condensed political and religious power into the aforementioned centralized government known as the Ganden Podrang. He founded the Ganden Podrang in 1642, and with it he established an inclusive and far-reaching ecumenical system of governance, which he developed in partnership with his advisor, the Desi Sangyé Gyatso (1653–1705). The sectarian underpinnings of the Fifth Dalai Lama's background are notable in that they significantly impacted Mindröling's beginnings. Although ostensibly a Gelukpa and the head of a predominantly Geluk institution, the Fifth Dalai Lama hailed from a Nyingma family and maintained close ties with the leadership of several Nyingma institutions in the greater Lhasa region, including Mindröling and Dorjé Drak monasteries. In line with his intersectarian affiliations, the Fifth Dalai Lama became a proponent of ecumenism in far-reaching political and religious affairs. The Buddhologist Jacob Dalton addresses this approach as it manifested in the treatment of ritual and sectarian division during the seventeenth century: "The Fifth Dalai Lama and Desi Sangyé Gyatso's new ceremonies brought together (even if by force) all competing political factions beneath the banner of the Ganden Podrang. Everyone was guaranteed a place at the table, so long as they remained seated and followed the proper ceremonial procedures."[23] Mingyur Peldrön and her family were the direct beneficiaries of this ecumenism, at least in the early days when they founded Mindröling. Religious institutions were deeply impacted by regional relationships during the long eighteenth century, including Mindröling Monastery. The Fifth Dalai Lama supported the development and founding of Mindröling, while his ecumenical approach was also a boon for Nyingma communities in general and made way for a Nyingma resurgence in the period.

The Mindröling Project

Mindröling was a Buddhist monastic and tantric community founded in the 1670s by Terdak Lingpa and Lochen Dharmaśrī. These brothers had been raised in a family that was religiously engaged, well-to-do, and highly respected. Their father, Trinlé Lhundrup (1611–62), was a descendant of the Nyö clan and a well-known non-celibate teacher, or *nakpa*, with Nyingma affiliations. His wife, Yangchen Drölma (b. 1624), had been born into a noble family in Yorpo.[24] According to Lochen Dharmaśrī, she was the financial manager of Dargyé Chöding, which had been the family seat prior to Mindröling's founding.[25] From their own position of social and religious standing, the brothers had immediate access to patronage from aristocratic families and religious institutions, which would help their progress as they worked to establish Mindröling. The family moved among the most respected community members of the religious and governing institutions in Ü. Terdak Lingpa was an accomplished and recognized treasure revealer, or *tertön*, and had made a name for himself and for Mindröling through large-scale public rituals resulting in the revelation (and later dissemination) of so-called hidden treasure texts, or *terma*. Over the course of his adult life he would reveal three treasure collections (in 1663, 1667, and 1676), and his renown grew with each successive treasure discovery. As a non-celibate practitioner, he had seven children, several of whom would be actively involved in one way or another in carrying on the family tradition of religious community building. When Terdak Lingpa and Lochen Dharmaśrī founded Mindröling, they began a lifelong project of Nyingma development in central Tibet. While Terdak Lingpa established the foundation for a hereditary lineage system for future generations of Mindröling, Lochen Dharmaśrī began the lineage of monastic ordination at the monastery. He was an ordained monk who upheld the commitment to monastic practice and scholastic study. A prolific author and translator, he also directed the scholarly activities of the monastery.[26] He wrote on a wide array of topics, from canonical exegesis and commentaries to prayers, liturgies, and poetry. He wrote several meditation and reference manuals for Mindröling and wrote down the life stories of his brother and his mother.

The brothers represent the two legitimate streams of practice that have been upheld at Mindröling since its inception. These were dual succession lineages that they established as a means to lead the monastery. Terdak Lingpa acted as the first *trichen*, or non-monastic throne holder.[27]

Lochen Dharmaśrī was the first *khenchen*, or lead holder of monastic vows—a role something along the lines of an abbot. The trichen and khenchen lines have been maintained and persist today. This has ensured a dual power base with foundations in both non-celibate and celibate monastic traditions and allows for generational succession within the family in both celibate and non-celibate lines.

In founding Mindröling, the brothers sought to reinvent the Nyingma tradition in an ecumenical and inclusive light. *Inclusive* here means that they developed a series of practice methods, rituals, and philosophical approaches that were accessible to monastic and non-monastic practitioners and laypeople. Rituals were publicized and made open to the general public, and the aristocratic sons of the Lhasa elite were invited to study religious and nonreligious topics at the monastery. All of these activities resulted in Mindröling reaching a wide-ranging population. In reenvisioning the Nyingma as a "big tent" tradition, they made space for both monastic and non-monastic practitioners under the auspices of Mindröling. As they engaged this rhetoric of inclusion, they grounded it in significant historical research and a new systematization of the canon.[28] In his analysis of the brothers' approach, Jacob Dalton explains that "[Terdak Lingpa and Lochen Dharmaśrī] forged a more inclusive system that provided places for everyone. Together, the brothers remade the Spoken Teachings from the bottom up. They combined extensive historical research with creative innovation to provide a new ritual platform that could be shared across the Nyingma School. Their careful typologies of ritual texts, compartmentalization of ritual procedures, and unprecedented emphasis on public performance produced a Sutra initiation tradition that in many ways mirrored Sangyé Gyatso's political project."[29]

The brothers were successful in rapidly elevating Mindröling to high status among religious institutions. Large-scale publicization and inclusivity were not the only philosophy of the day. For example, Dorjé Drak Monastery, just across the Tsangpo River from Mindröling, took a more exclusive approach, with only a select group gaining access to teachings. But the brothers were inclusive in their approach, which also meant that they incorporated all branches of Nyingma history and practice into their curriculum. Most notably, both the *kama* and *terma* traditions were alive and active at Mindröling.

In the Nyingma tradition, esoteric scriptures have been generally divided into these two types (kama and terma), depending on their provenance. While texts falling into these categories are not specific to the Nyingma, this division is particularly prominent within Nyingma lineages, and it is noteworthy that Mindröling emphasized both of them. As mentioned earlier, *terma* refers to religious materials (in this case, texts) that were said to have been discovered and removed from hiding by a divinely guided spiritual adept. During the tenth to twelfth centuries, terma became increasingly associated with the Nyingma, although they were also present in other traditions. These esoteric texts began to appear in the tenth century and paved the way for further scriptural innovation and development. It is believed that treasure texts had been hidden by religious adepts in ancient times so that they could be rediscovered at an appropriate moment in the future. Guru Rinpoche (Padmasambhava) and Yeshé Tsogyel figure prominently in the narratives of treasure concealment and revelation, and Mingyur Peldrön would come to be considered an incarnation of Yeshé Tsogyel—an association that would be used to reflect and emphasize Mingyur Peldrön's religious authority. Guru Rinpoche and Yeshé Tsogyel were said to have hidden terma in the Tibetan landscape (mountains, for example), where they would remain safe until the appropriate time for their discovery and then protected until they could be used to their highest potential. Then, when the time was right, a suitable individual would reveal the text from its hiding place, translate it from *ḍākinī* script, and then present it to the people. This was often done with the help of ḍākinīs and a tantric consort. As a non-monastic adept (nakpa) with a consort, Terdak Lingpa was the most suitable individual in this case and revealed texts amid great fanfare through a process that established his works as authoritative in the canonical word. Between the years 1663 and 1680, he revealed three terma.[30] These proprietary treasure texts reinforced the validity of the Mindröling project and created the foundation for a new set of teachings to be passed on in the institution and also gave the brothers a textual focus for their specific approach to institutional organization and religious practice.

Likewise, kama refers to the texts and teachings that are said to have been transmitted from teacher to disciple, passed down from person to person throughout history. These texts are considered to be the "Buddha's word" (Sanskrit, *buddhavacana*) and, according to tradition, can be traced all the way back to a specific buddha. In the Tibetan context this refers to scriptures said to have been translated during the imperial period (seventh to mid-ninth centuries CE) and passed down through direct transmission from master to disciple. At Mindröling both kama and terma texts were valued and transmitted to students. Likewise, everything from the nominally secular five sciences (*rikné*) curriculum to the most advanced Great Perfection (Dzogchen) meditative practices were available for study.

In essence the brothers were inventing—or reinventing—a tradition of ritual, praxis, and historical memory, employing methods that were similar in spirit to that of the Fifth Dalai Lama's Ganden Podrang. Terdak Lingpa and Lochen Dharmaśrī were very close to the Fifth Dalai Lama and the Desi Sangyé Gyatso. Indeed, they exchanged teachings back and forth throughout their lives, and Mindröling received support from the Fifth Dalai Lama that helped propel the monastery to its position of being recognized as an institution of learning for the Lhasa elite. With its proximity to Lhasa, Mindröling became an educational center for the sons of the central Tibetan aristocracy. The monastery grew in renown, and the brothers' work ultimately led Mindröling to be recognized as one of the six "mother monasteries" of the Nyingma tradition. It was Terdak Lingpa and Lochen Dharmaśrī who made what appears to have been the somewhat unusual decision that Mingyur Peldrön should receive an advanced religious education. Her position in this institutional context would provide her with a level of religious privilege that was unique in her milieu and fairly unusual for women prior to the twentieth century.

Tibetan Buddhist Women's *Lives*

The majority of scholarship on early modern Tibet from the seventeenth to nineteenth centuries has largely focused on the activities of men and their contributions to the political and religious institutions of the period. Significantly less has been written about the women of the day, including their engagement in powerful political and religious organizations, their soteriological and mundane concerns, or the types of agency they exercised, although correctives are being made to this imbalance. In recent years several scholars have dedicated their work to the lives of Tibetan Buddhist women, and while this has been beneficial for our understanding across a range of topics relating to these women's lives, the work still constitutes a relatively small fraction of scholarship on Tibetan Buddhist history and literature. With this in mind, the presence of Mingyur Peldrön's life story in the Tibetan literary canon is of great significance. Moreover, in a time and place where few women's *Lives* were recorded, hers stands out as a testament to her importance at Mindröling and a means by which we might begin to explore at least one woman's role at the religious and political center of the

Lhasa aristocracy. Mingyur Peldrön's life and work can be best understood in conversation with the life stories of other Tibetan women for whom we have Lives, whose stories range from the fourteenth to the twentieth centuries. In addition to the diverse historical and geographic regions that these women occupied, their relationships to power and religion varied widely. As their stories will be presented for the sake of comparison throughout the rest of the book, here each one will be briefly introduced.

The fourteenth-century non-monastic tantric practitioner Sönam Peldren (ca. 1328–71) is one of the earliest historical women for whom we have a Life.[31] The differences between her and Mingyur Peldrön start with Sönam Peldren's lack of formal training or early contact with religious teachers.[32] Where Mingyur Peldrön had early access to formal religious education, Sönam Peldren largely charted her own path and faced significant barriers to engaging in religious praxis. Unlike Mingyur Peldrön, Sönam Peldren married and never was ordained as a nun. Also, rather than growing up close to the city center of Lhasa (as Mingyur Peldrön did), Sönam Peldren lived out her adult life as part of a nomadic community. In this context she developed her own approach to Buddhist soteriology and tantric practice. The narrative of her life has persisted to the present day in the form of her multiauthored hagiography. This stands in distinction from Mingyur Peldrön's Life, whose colophon asserts that Dispeller was authored by one person.[33] Sönam Peldren's Life, and the related scholarship of scholar of Tibetan Buddhism Suzanne Bessenger, serve as important points of comparison with Mingyur Peldrön, especially in terms of how authorial and subjective voice are used in these literary works.

In comparison with Mingyur Peldrön's Life, the story of the hermitess Orgyan Chökyi (1675–1729) gives a sense of the diversity of women's religious experience in seventeenth- and eighteenth-century Tibetan regions. Although a near-contemporary of Mingyur Peldrön and similar in her religious affiliation and concerns, Orgyan Chökyi's story still differs dramatically in most ways. Born and raised in the region of Dolpo, in Nepal, Orgyan Chökyi's path to religious praxis was marked by suffering and the burdens of domestic responsibility. Like Mingyur Peldrön, she was a nun and a practitioner of the Great Perfection whose teachers were male and who sought the religious life and eschewed the domestic realm.[34] Orgyan Chökyi's Life narrative addresses her struggles to gain access to religious training and to occupy a physical and mental space in which she could engage in rigorous practice. She was born into a family that had hoped for a son and were unhappy with the birth of a daughter, and she was initially obliged to live the life of a herder. But she was able to take ordination and studied the Great Perfection in spite of—rather than supported by—her parents.[35] Orgyan Chökyi lived far from the religiopolitical centers of power and gained little institutional authority during her lifetime. Although she attended public teachings by her teacher in Dolpo and was therefore active in the Dolpo religious community, it seems that she did not gain agency or recognition from these engagements.

The tone of Orgyan Chökyi's *Life* is notably different from Mingyur Peldrön's in part because it is not hagiography but an auto/biographical form of *Life* writing.[36] In writing *Dispeller*, Gyurmé Ösel was interested in emphasizing his teacher's soteriological accomplishments and community prominence and wrote from the perspective of the disciple working to elevate his teacher. Meanwhile, Orgyan Chökyi composed her own *Life* and was presumably restricted by the social norms of the time to not elevate herself overmuch. Instead, she emphasizes the themes of sorrow and suffering and the trials of the impermanent world and depicts mundane life as filled with unwanted interruptions on the path to enlightenment.[37] Where Mingyur Peldrön is elevated, Orgyan Chöyki highlights the physical and emotional suffering that slowed her soteriological progress. Moreover, where Mingyur Peldrön had the full support of her family in pursuing a religious life, taking ordination, and acting as a representative of her family's religious community, Orgyan Chökyi had no formal education in her youth, and her access to religious teachings in her early adulthood was hard-won. Ultimately, Orgyan Chökyi treated her status as a woman very differently from how Mingyur Peldrön's gender is addressed in *Dispeller*. Drawing on Tibetanist Kurtis Schaeffer's scholarship on Orgyan Chökyi, considering the two nuns' experiences and the relationship between their status as nuns and their status as women is useful as it offers intermittent focal points for understanding Mingyur Peldrön and her context.

While Sera Khandro (1892–1940) was like Mingyur Peldrön in that she was a central Tibetan woman from an elite family and a practitioner affiliated with the Nyingma school,[38] her access to and engagement with religion was quite different from Mingyur Peldrön's. The trajectories of the two women show the significance of familial support for religious practice and bodily autonomy and the impact of family expectations on women's lived experience. These women are different in terms of the paths they took toward religious study and the way that the relationships with their natal communities influenced that process. Much like Orgyan Chökyi, Sera Khandro's family disapproved of her longing to become a serious practitioner. For Sera Khandro the path to religious realization meant a divergence from the life of privilege in which she was raised. In the end she ran away from home, leaving the safety of her privileged Lhasa household to join a community of tantric practitioners in Kham. Both Orgyan Chökyi and Sera Khandro wrote autobiographical *Lives* depicting their struggles to practice, the opposition they met from their families, and the hardships they faced in the process of pursuing a religious life as women. After her early struggles to be accepted, Sera Khandro was eventually recognized as a legitimate teacher in the non-celibate community she joined. Unlike Mingyur Peldrön, she was not an ordained nun but a lay practitioner who had a consort relationship with her male teacher Drimé Özer. Tibetan studies scholar Sarah Jacoby has done extensive work on Sera Khandro and her *Life*, which offers an important counterpoint for understanding the breadth of possible trajectories for religious women from elite central Tibetan households.

As an ordained nun and the first abbess of Samding Nunnery, Chökyi Drönma (b. 1422–d. 1455/67) has significantly more in common with Mingyur Peldrön than the other women mentioned here.[39] She existed at the center of her religious institution and took on a prominent leadership role within that organization. She also became a nun and used her family connections to further her religious career. While other women have overlapping similarities, including an aristocratic family of origin, a connection with the Nyingma community, familial support to study the dharma, and the decision to ordain as a nun, all of these traits together are not shared with another woman other than Chökyi Drönma. Aside from her, none of the other women for whom we have life stories reported the particular combination of elite privilege, supportive family, and monastic pursuit that were Mingyur Peldrön's inheritance. For example, while Sera Khandro came from an aristocratic family, her religious pursuits were often at odds with her family's expectations for her.[40] Meanwhile, Chökyi Drönma's family supported religious engagement and offered high social status. Moreover, her monastic inclinations closely resemble those of Mingyur Peldrön. Their positionality is similar insofar as they were born into privileged contexts and were able to develop a religious praxis and public identity while remaining within that community (Chökyi Drönma eventually became the abbess of a nunnery).[41] The work of Tibetan studies scholar Hildegard Diemberger, which focuses on the *Life* of Chökyi Drönma, will be a common point of comparison when considering the life of Mingyur Peldrön.

Although separated by a century and a half, Khandro Tāre Lhamo (1938–2002) also has a great deal in common with Mingyur Peldrön. Both were born into elite religious families with fathers who were treasure revealers. As a result of their social status and supportive families, both had significant access to religious teachings and established institutions for religious study.⁴² Both women were active at the center of the Nyingma religious activities of their day, and traveled widely to exchange teachings with their Nyingma compatriots. Moreover, the reach of their privilege was not infinite, and they lived through war and hardship but survived to witness the revival of their religious communities in a postwar period. Unlike Mingyur Peldrön, Tāre Lhamo was not ordained as a nun. She married Namtrul Rinpoche, with whom she had a consort relationship. Rather than spending time in central Tibet, she lived most of her life in Golok, eastern Tibet, traveling with her husband on pilgrimage and discovering hidden treasure texts together.⁴³ While Tāre Lhamo is quite like Mingyur Peldrön in several ways, Mingyur Peldrön's identity as a nun differs from Tāre Lhamo's role as a non-celibate practitioner. The scholarship on Tāre Lhamo by Holly Gayley—a scholar of Tibetan Buddhism—will be of central importance for exploring Mingyur Peldrön's life.

Comparison with these women helps illuminate the complexity of Mingyur Peldrön's relationship with authority and gender, her privileged social position, how she is represented in *Dispeller*, and how gender as a concept was deployed in the context of hagiography. Specifically, *Dispeller* offers a means for understanding the literary depictions of one woman's life at the center of a powerful institution. Studying Mingyur Peldrön's story in the context of the religiopolitical shifts of the era elucidates her positionality, the challenges she faced in her soteriological and social pursuits, and the opportunities available to her as a woman of privilege. Likewise, her namtar provides some new perspective on a less studied period of Tibetan history (that is, the long eighteenth century), its literary traditions, religious practices, institutional organization, social structure, and family life. While *Dispeller* is not a history, the literary treatment of Mingyur Peldrön's lived experience can tell us a great deal about how her life was narrativized and the perceptions surrounding her as a religious practitioner and leader.

Mingyur Peldrön was literally born into the religious institution in which she would rise to prominence. Empowered from within Mindröling, her assumption of authority as a teacher, author, advanced practitioner, and purveyor of the monastery's highest teachings (in Mindröling's case, the Great

Perfection) simultaneously allowed her to pursue a religious path and perpetuate her family's legacy. This religious position, coupled with her family's support of her religious aspirations, makes Mingyur Peldrön distinctive among Tibetan women of her time, and even within her family, in terms of the amount of privilege she held. For example, whereas the young Sönam Peldren, Sera Khandro, and Orgyan Chökyi had to escape the pressures of marriage in order to pursue their religious goals, Mingyur Peldrön was pushed to study and carry on her family's tradition of religious knowledge and leadership and rejected proposals of consort relationships.

The suffering of female existence is attested in many arenas of broader Buddhist history and literature and appears in different contexts in various ways.[44] Focusing specifically on the early modern and premodern *Lives* of Tibetan Buddhist women, a rhetoric of marginality exists across these texts that establishes women as beneath men in a hierarchy of gender that applies to both monastic and non-monastic people. It is also present to some extent in *Dispeller* and was applied in complex ways to Mingyur Peldrön. This rhetoric of marginality is best exemplified in the trope of the "lesser female birth," a concept that was functioning alongside and reinforcing the gender hierarchy. The phrase *lesser female birth* is a translation of the Tibetan *skye dman* or *skye lus dman* and notes women's positionality in relation to that of men.[45] In eighteenth-century central Tibet there was a functioning normative gender binary that collapsed gender and sex and assumed that one was either a woman or a man. While there were different implications for how this binary impacted monastic and non-monastic people, the samsaric effects of one's gender were assumed to exist in one or another of these two camps. Scholars of Tibetan women's *Lives* have pointed to the multiple ways in which the rhetorical engagement that laments birth as a woman as worse than that of men is present frequently and in a variety of ways in these texts.[46] Women are depicted as inferior to men in spiritual capability, nuns are described as beneath monks within the monastic hierarchy, and the status of being born a woman is attributed to negative past karma.[47] This lesser status was directly connected with women's bodies, bodies that in turn became representative of the round of samsara (the cyclic existence of birth, death, and rebirth).[48]

In this context, to pursue a life of religious practice was considered especially challenging for women and directly related to their embodiment, which was in turn correlated with assumptions that nuns were inferior to monks in their learning and in their position within the larger religious society. This rhetorical system had real-world consequences for nuns, who in many cases would have been considered inferior "fields of merit" than their monk counterparts, making it harder for them to receive enough lay patronage to survive. Being a "lesser field of merit" meant it was likely that laypeople would donate less to nuns, believing that they would earn less merit than they would if their donations went to monks.[49] This meant that the life of a nun was considered to be one of significant hardship, in comparison with perceptions about a monk's life. These notions reinforced each other, exacerbating the challenges that nuns faced. A similar gendered hierarchy also existed for non-monastic women, with the exception that wealthy aristocratic laywomen sometimes acted as lay patrons for religious organizations and gained status through this patronage.[50] In each Tibetan woman's *Life*, the question arises as to how the woman (or her hagiographer) will engage with (and potentially refute) this trope. For some it becomes a narrative divide whereby they are able to overturn the ignorant view of samsara; for others it is a means by which they are able to express their frustrations with the world and their situation.[51]

For all her privilege, Mingyur Peldrön was still linked with other female figures through her status as a woman, and social assumptions about the lesser female birth would likewise create challenges for her lived experience and her literary depiction. No doubt her gender impacted her life in numerous ways, and they will be considered within their historical and religious context. It is noteworthy that when compared with the other women mentioned here, the lesser female birth trope scans differently onto Mingyur Peldrön's life story. Specifically, it diverges from other women's *Lives* in its representations of her gender identity as positive while continuing to engage social concerns about gender and authority and bifurcated opinions about the gendered implications of soteriological pursuits. Other women's stories are shot through with traditional Buddhist depictions of the suffering of human existence, especially that of a life lived in a female body.[52] Meanwhile, Mingyur Peldrön's relationship with her gender is depicted as sometimes fraught and sometimes positive. Her status as a woman is used variably as a tool to elevate her in *Dispeller*, and elsewhere in the text womanhood is emphasized to underscore the woes of women. The hagiography fluctuates between positive and negative depictions of female birth, offering a complex approach to gender identity and its impact on lived experience. Like a few of the women mentioned here, she was also set apart from laywomen by virtue of being a celibate nun. Her nunhood had a significant impact on her life, especially her role in the community outside Mindröling. When compared with previously studied women, some aspects of Mingyur Peldrön's *Life* will be very familiar. For example, her *Life* follows common stylistic patterns, describing her religious praxis and biographical details, some of the challenges she faced, moments of soteriological attainment and realization, and so forth. However, her positionality diverges from that of most other previously studied women and so offers a different perspective on women's approaches to and experiences with religious praxis.

Themes of Privilege, Authority, Gender, and Dialogue

Four themes are at the center of this study: privilege, authority, gender, and dialogue. It is useful to trace them throughout *Dispeller* and also to apply them to a contextualized understanding of the hagiography within its historical milieu. It is important to point out that these concepts originated in the twentieth-century Euro-West and are here being used to elucidate a context found in eighteenth-century Ü. When engaging theoretical modes in a different cultural and historical context, one must tread lightly. With this sort of cross-historical engagement, there is the danger of imparting contemporary assumptions onto a completely different historical and cultural moment. In order to avoid falling into anachronism, we must consider the ways in which assumptions that are intrinsic to or joined with these concepts in twentieth- and twenty-first-century Euro-Western contexts might impact our reading of how privilege, authority, gender, and dialogue played out in Mingyur Peldrön's milieu and consider how the concepts were actually functioning in her arena. These themes are useful for unpacking the eighteenth-century central Tibetan context at the same time that twentieth- and twenty-first-century concerns are at risk of skewing our reading. The cultural-historical tensions involved in using this terminology thus require some attention.

First, this project seeks to highlight the ways that systems of privilege and disadvantage have informed personal and public representations of women through their life stories. This project draws on the work of several scholars of privilege to better understand its roles in Mingyur Peldrön's context. As a scholar of privilege, Peggy McIntosh defines privilege as "unearned advantages with regard to race, gender or sexuality" and explains that such advantages and disadvantages are used in perpetuating systemic injustice.[53]

Here McIntosh's definition is deployed to reflect the eighteenth-century Tibetan context, including the unearned advantages that would have been especially salient during Mingyur Peldrön's lifetime. These include advantages gained from birth into a wealthy household, a powerful family (regardless of whether that power is gleaned through social, political, or religious status or some combination of the three), or a community that affords other benefits through association with it. Religious affiliations could lend someone privilege (for example, being born into a family closely associated with the prominent Geluk denomination in its ascendency), as could factors of family wealth or political connections.

Sociologists B. Ethan M. Coston and Michael Kimmel treat privilege as "distributed along a range of axes" rather than a "zero-sum quantity," such that one who might be marginalized with one status that they hold (such as gender) might have privilege with another status (wealth, for example).[54] Rather than treating privilege as monolithic, this approach allows for a variety of personal, institutional, and social markers to impact the privilege status of a group or individual. It applies directly to Mingyur Peldrön's context and offers a means for understanding her relationship with privilege and other aspects of how she was situated. Likewise, Eline Severs, Karen Celis, and Silvia Erzeel have adopted Kimberlé Crenshaw's concept of intersectionality as it relates to power, privilege, and disadvantage in order to better understand the relational nature of power in contexts of uneven privilege, especially in institutional contexts. This is not meant to detract from Crenshaw's original focus in using intersectionality to point to the ways in which Black women have been specifically oppressed in the United States justice system. Rather, their work offers a helpful entry point for tracing connections between different parts of identity at the individual and community level (including gender identity, monastic status, education, wealth, and religious authority). From here intersectionality is a salient means for parsing socially embedded privilege in historical religious institutional contexts and pointing to the ways that these contexts converge and alter individual agency at the hands of powerful institutions. This book draws on the work of these scholars in its conceptualization of privilege and its relationship to how power functions in religious institutional and social contexts.

Privilege, while important as a notion in the contemporary "West" and present throughout human society, has not been directly applied as a theoretical tool to Tibetan Buddhist history or literature. Although Tibetanists have touched upon questions of class and social status in discussions of the lives of prominent religious figures, a more sustained focus on the phenomenon of privilege will provide a nuanced understanding of the multivalent social influences on individuals whose lives are discussed in the historical record. Mingyur Peldrön's hagiography provides a clear example in that she was born into extreme religious and social privilege, which bolstered her role as a leading figure in her community. But in spite of privilege in some areas of her life, she was decidedly unprivileged in others. These markers of privilege and non-privilege impacted her trajectory significantly, depending on the historical context in which she was working at the time. Elsewhere, scholars of women's *Lives* have addressed specific aspects of privilege and lack of privilege as they relate to specific women's contexts, such as a woman's birth into an elite aristocratic family (Sera Khandro), women who received religious training within their families (Tāre Lhamo), the ways that women incorporated their gendered identity into their religious personas and how that related to their privileged or unprivileged status (Sönam Peldren), and the influence of a lack of privilege on women's access to religious teachings (Orgyan Chökyi). Like some of these women, Mingyur Peldrön was born into a family that was not only elite and aristocratic but was also a family with a cache of religious power. Additionally, and perhaps most unusually when compared with other women, Mingyur Peldrön's family went so far as to urge her to adopt a role of religious leadership and allowed her to forgo marriage and become a nun.

In reading privilege back into the historical and hagiographic records, a few challenges arise. The first is whether to adhere to Tibetan usage of terms that might be translated as *privilege* or whether to impose the concept externally. The twenty-first-century North American renderings of the concept described earlier connect to historically situated social constructs and hierarchies that would have meant an increased ability to decide one's own educational and vocational fate in eighteenth-century Ü. Privilege is treated at the individual level and at the level of social groups, including one's position in family and larger social units based on gender, institutional affiliation, wealth, and so forth. Also, to understand privilege in a historical context, we need to point to the specific systems of power that determined which aspects of social standing would imbue an individual or group with privilege. In the context of Mingyur Peldrön's life, privilege was supported by power structures that favored high aristocratic standing, elite family membership, and monetary wealth. But it was an umbrella that also spread wider than these advantages. Privilege was also determined by education, gender, and political connections. Religious authority was drawn from religious access, such as the ability to receive empowerments (*wang*) and other training, the financial ability to offer patronage to religious organizations, and the physical and social proximity to prominent religious centers. At the personal level Mingyur Peldrön's privilege was also impacted by her birth order, her religious propensities, her bodily autonomy, her status as a nun, and her age when civil war broke out. Thinking of privilege markers with a capacious definition of privilege creates space for how we think about its many signifiers and how they influence power and authority, both separately and in concert, in Mingyur Peldrön's lifetime. Moreover, the broader notion of privilege highlights how a variety of cultural constructs can be assigned positions of value in overarching systems of power. Reading privilege back into the historical record and into hagiography requires an investigation of the social signifiers that were indicative of a privileged or disadvantaged positionality in a specific time and place and the varied effects of positionality on individual and group experience in a specific historical moment.

There are multiple types of authority functioning in *Dispeller* that imply systems of social and religious power that were specific to Mingyur Peldrön's historical context. As with most hagiographies, her *Life* is in part an argument in favor of her authoritative position at Mindröling, an argument that uses several forms of authority to establish her legitimacy. Three significant threads of authentication are woven throughout the *Life*, and all rely heavily on her privileged position. Twentieth-century definitions of authority and power are useful for elucidating the dynamic connections between public persona, gender, and types of authority that Gyurmé Ösel used to elevate Mingyur Peldrön when these concepts are developed to reflect her sociohistorical environment.

In Mingyur Peldrön's hagiography, privilege and authority imbue her with legitimacy, and the vagaries of socialized gender dynamics influence the tone of Gyurmé Ösel's assertions about his teacher's authority and legitimacy. A tripartite delineation of modes of authority were present and active in Mingyur Peldrön and Gyurmé Ösel's worlds. These modes of authentication are: emanation authority gleaned from identification with female divinities;[55] institutional authority, which draws on institutional connections to establish legitimacy; and educational authority, which was developed through an individual's religious training. Mingyur Peldrön's role as a lineage holder for Mindröling meant that it was important for her to be perceived as authoritative in her ability to pass on the monastery's teachings. This is not to say that *Dispeller* is dedicated solely to the legitimation of her authority. It is a fully developed life narrative that presents her as a highly realized religious practitioner and a key contributor to the perpetuation of Mindröling. Moreover, it provides details of an important historical moment and her role in that moment and gives one example of the lived experiences of a prominent eighteenth-century female Buddhist practitioner. With that said, a key component of Gyurmé Ösel's goals as author appears to be establishing her position as authoritative. The three ways in which he establishes this authority tells us a great deal about how authority functioned in their particular context.

The theme of gender—and Mingyur Peldrön's identity as gendered—plays a central role in *Dispeller*. As with other themes, we must take care not to heedlessly impart twenty-first-century assumptions about gendered identity onto the eighteenth-century context. The treatment of gender in *Dispeller* follows Buddhologist Amy Langenberg's caution that we approach the subject of gender in Buddhist historical and literary contexts with a modicum of critical self-reflexivity, to ensure that we do not impose contemporary Euro-Western concerns or assumptions where they did not exist previously.[56] To avoid anachronistic assumptions, textual and historical analysis will be paired throughout my treatment of Mingyur Peldrön's gendered position, in order to situate her in her historical context, rather than imposing twenty-first-century ideals upon her or her arena. For example, I eschew the term *feminism* completely while leaving room for discussions about how and where Mingyur Peldrön furthered women's religious education and individual agency. This approach follows the work of Tibetanists Padma'tsho and Sarah Jacoby, who have sought to elucidate twenty-first-century Tibetan Buddhist nuns' engagement with "pro-women activities" that have been established "in and on Tibetan terms" by nuns in the twentieth and twenty-first centuries.[57] As my focus is an eighteenth-century text reflecting the life story of a woman in that era, my goal is to avoid twenty-first-century presumptions, or the culturally contextualized implications attributed to terms such as *feminism* in contemporary Tibetan contexts. It is worth noting that gender and sexuality are collapsed in the text, rather that delineated as separate constructs, an approach that was normative in Mingyur Peldrön's context. Gender plays an important role in *Dispeller*, and at places it overlaps, and elsewhere diverges markedly, from presentations of gendered identity in the *Lives* of other premodern Tibetan women. For other women, gender is often listed as an obstacle preventing women from pursuing religious and spiritual development, a challenge at odds with their soteriological goals and sometimes their bodily autonomy. The topic is treated with more variation in Mingyur Peldrön's case in such a way that *Dispeller* offers a more complex reading of how gender impacted Mingyur Peldrön's lived experience and also how gender could be conceptualized in writing about women.

Whereas Orgyan Chökyi, Sera Khandro, and Sönam Peldren all had to fight against the gendered expectations of their families and communities, Mingyur Peldrön's position as a woman within her family is not recorded as a *consistent* soteriological hindrance in her *Life*. Whereas other women's Lives report gender-related battles over marriage (whether or not to marry, whom to marry, whether to choose marriage over monasticism), Mingyur Peldrön's hagiography does not report her family pushing her in one direction or another. This suggests that she either had a higher level of bodily autonomy or that her hagiographer had other reasons to depict her as an autonomous and celibate woman. However, Mingyur Peldrön's gender is rarely cited by Gyurmé Ösel as an impediment to educational or religious pursuits; it is implied as a barrier for her sister's freedom of choice in marriage and thus her bodily autonomy. Nevertheless, Mingyur Peldrön's gender still plays a significant role in representations of her status and authority in the community and the challenges she faced. It is clear that gender played out differently for individual women, even within the Mindröling family. With that said, gender remains an important piece of Mingyur Peldrön's narrative, marking moments of triumph and despair and being frequently evoked as a means of elevating her in some places and barring her from access in others. Notably, the gendered language that is used to refer to her changes depending on the importance of the moment. In less significant accounts she is named using androgynous appellations, while at highly significant moments the language used to reference her also emphasizes her position as a woman. Sexuality and Mingyur Peldrön's decision to eschew sexual relationships and adopt monastic celibacy are also significant factors in the text. Her identity as a woman informs the proposals for consort relationships that she received from male adepts and the difficulty she had in rebuking these proposals, although she was ultimately able to dismiss them successfully.

While it was not always troublesome, in some places her womanhood *is* referenced as a source of consternation for her and something to be changed in her next life, even though it was not consistently a direct impediment to her religious pursuits. While these moments are few in the text, they still act as reminders of the ways gender impacted her lived experience and how it continues to influence her literary representation. Rather than being fully negative or positive, her identity as a woman is one among several important factors that influenced her supposed lived experience and so is discussed prominently in her literary narrative. It served as benefit and detriment at different moments in her life. Gender is a central theme in a complex conversation written into *Dispeller* and is used to underscore the disparity in how Mingyur Peldrön interacted with her male and female students and the expressions of her concern about tantric and monastic forms of praxis.

Alongside these other themes, a study of the role of gender in Mingyur Peldrön's *Life* reveals a rich and complex narrative about how she navigated her particular context and how this context was inherently gendered. Simultaneously working for gender equity in Nyingma religious education and praxis and arguing for the supreme role of celibacy in all religious pursuit, she viewed monastic life as the preferable way forward for a community previously known for both non-monastic and monastic paths. Although raised in a community that supported both non-celibate religious practice—as her father's student, she indeed benefited from this in her own access to religious education—her staunch pro-monastic approach suggests a change in the religious institutional landscape of central Tibet during her lifetime, or at least in terms of her own views and those of Gyurmé Ösel.

Another recurring theme in this project is that of dialogue. As a literary work, *Dispeller* exemplifies the dialogic potential of hagiography. Although ostensibly authored by one person—a point that is reaffirmed frequently throughout the text—extensive quotations attributed to Mingyur Peldrön herself work to establish the text as a site of dialogical engagement in which contemporary concerns are negotiated between multiple-voiced perspectives. *Dispeller* can be read as a constructed dialogue between author and subject. "Voice" plays a role in hagiographic narratives, and the same elements are at play here.[58] Moreover, the subject's identity is developed in conversation with the world around her.[59] Reiterating the dialogic nature of the Tibetan life story does not mean conflating the auto/biographical literary voice with the multiple "voices" found in Gyurmé Ösel's work, although there is overlap insofar as multivocal dialogue in these texts offers a sense of the subject's identity, her world, and the concerns of that world.[60] With that said, Gyurmé Ösel's *Dispeller* offers a literary style markedly different from auto/biography. For example, the former often engages methods such as the "self-humbling strategies" of the first-person voice, in which the author engages in self-effacement. Meanwhile, the latter idealizes the voice of the subject in a way that perfects her presentation as an enlightened being. Mingyur Peldrön's voice as it is represented in *Dispeller* has been subject to the hagiographic idealization of the devoted disciple-turned-author that is described in the latter example. The notion of hagiographic tenor and devotion in women's *Lives* is useful for exploring this, in particular the ways in which female protagonists are idealized and divinized to elevate them above the faults of mere mortal women.[61] Hagiographic tenor and devotion in women's *Lives* are also relevant to the literary impact of Gyurmé Ösel's authorial choices in giving his beloved teacher a voice in her own life story. Beyond this, hagiography can act as a ground on which contemporary anxieties and concerns are negotiated and discussed. In particular, the civil war and subsequent unrest in Ü at the beginning of the eighteenth century had a significant impact on Mingyur Peldrön's community, shaping her lived experience as well as later representations of her activities during this time. The stresses and anxieties of this period likewise appear in the hagiography.

Given the political and religious developments of the time, *Dispeller* intimates a particularly fraught period for central Tibetan Nyingma practitioners. In this context it describes the views and concerns of the community through dialogic representations of specific issues and concerns (such as celibacy and women's roles in religious institutions). The four themes of privilege, authority, gender, and dialogue are threaded throughout the book with varying degrees of frequency, intersecting in some moments and in others standing alone. They serve as a means for understanding Mingyur Peldrön's *Life* as a literary creation, the historical contexts and events that she experienced, and how we might best understand their depiction in *Dispeller*.

Chapter One

A Privileged Life

> There is great hope for you. Will you lead many accomplished men and women to the Pure Land?
>
> —Terdak Lingpa

In the year 1699 Mindröling Monastery was in its heyday. After nearly three decades of institutional development, Terdak Lingpa and Lochen Dharmaśrī had established a well-known and highly regarded center of learning in Ü. They had built their reputation as the educators of Lhasa's aristocratic elite and purveyors of a new inclusive form of Nyingma religious training that made room for a range of practitioners. However, trouble was in the air. The brothers were close enough to the Gelukpa-led Ganden Podrang government that when the Fifth Dalai Lama died, in 1682, they participated in the thirteen-year cover-up of his death.[1] The regionally stabilizing force of the Fifth Dalai Lama's influence began to deteriorate after his passing, quickly fraying the inter-sectarian ties that he had made with institutions like Mindröling. The discovery of the Fifth Dalai Lama's death not only left the Nyingma community without a champion in the Ganden Podrang; it also left the Ganden Podrang to fall into a state of barely controlled chaos that would continue throughout the life of the Sixth Dalai Lama.[2] During this time political uncertainty and infighting increased both within and beyond the government leadership, with some factions coalescing around policies of pro-Geluk protectionism. At the same time, foreign leaders jockeyed for influence in Tibet. This led to widespread unrest and the rise of bias against non-Geluk institutions amid a complex and contentious ever-shifting political terrain. For people affiliated with non-Geluk religious communities (including Nyingmapas), this meant institutional instability and external persecution at the hands of powerful Geluk factions and their supporters. Active proponents of the Nyingma in central Tibet were at times supported by the government in Lhasa, and in other years entire monastic complexes were destroyed. The cycle of oppression, destruction, and revival repeated itself several times over the course of the long eighteenth century. Scholar Trent Pomplun sums up the messy factionalism of central Tibetan religious leadership: "The tangled affairs of early eighteenth-century Tibetan politics are impossible to describe in a single chapter. The Geluk monastic order that dominated the central government was divided into several competing factions, each with complex and ever-shifting alliances with various Tibetan aristocrats, Manchu nobles, and Mongol chieftains. Between the regent Sangyé Gyatso and the secular 'king' Lhazang Khan in central Tibet—and the Manchu Empire and Zünghar̄ia beyond its borders—these factions bound Tibet to its increasingly unstable neighbors as they battled for control within the Lhasa government."[3]

For Mindröling the Geluk-dominant religious and political environment of Ü began with inter-sectarian support in the mid-seventeenth century but degenerated into persecution by the second decade of the eighteenth century. The situation reached its nadir with the 1717–18 civil war, when pro-Geluk Dzungar Mongols laid waste to non-Geluk institutions, including Mindröling. This was followed by a slow recovery and tentative collaboration between some members of each denomination, but relations remained uncertain and fractious until the early nineteenth century. The shifting political and institutional landscape of central Tibet in the long eighteenth century had a significant effect on Mingyur Peldrön and her prominent Nyingmapa family. The political and historical context of Mingyur Peldrön's early years is largely Geluk-centered and Geluk-centric, and this background is reflected in *Dispeller*. This may in large part have been because it was a period of increasing Geluk dominance throughout central Tibet. As such, the political histories of non-Geluk organizations (such as Mindröling) were dictated by the historical arc of the dominant group, even as they became the target of inter-sectarian tension. The events of Mingyur Peldrön's life must be viewed in this historical context, while the details of these events are based largely on hagiographic reports. Keeping in mind Patrick Geary's caution against assuming that hagiography should be read as history,[4] some details of *Dispeller* are best read alongside information gathered from historical sources. Rather than assume that these events necessarily occurred, this gives a sense of the narrative arc of Mingyur Peldrön's *Life*, and it becomes easier to understand the narrative within its own literary context and to connect it with relevant historical context.

Birth and Childhood

In the year 1699 the political and religious unrest of the early eighteenth century was still only brewing, and Mindröling remained an important center of learning for the Lhasa aristocracy. It is here that our story begins. On the twenty-fifth day of the tenth month of the Female Earth Hare year, a daughter was born to Phuntsok Peldzöm and Terdak Lingpa;[5] she was the fourth of seven children. In *Dispeller* the child's birth story is recounted with all the traditional fanfare of a Tibetan saint's birth. Terdak Lingpa and Lochen Dharmaśrī spent the days surrounding her arrival by performing rituals for the baby's safety; meanwhile, several women attended Phuntsok Peldzöm in labor. Gyurmé Ösel references their account in *Dispeller*:

> Just like that, she came forth from her mother's womb. She roared a little "HUM!" sound and went directly into a squat. Everyone in the room—mother, attendants, all—were able to conquer their fear. This was reported by the mother's attendant Lhakyi Peldzöm, and the others who were fortunate enough to be present at the birth, including Gyurmé Chödron. Thus, I assume this is in keeping with visions of *Dzogchen Trekchö*.[6]

According to Gyurmé Ösel, this birth story is an oral history that was passed on to him by the women who themselves were present at the child's birth. The account was relayed by women who were invested in a record of Mingyur Peldrön and her importance and who related the story to support the hagiographer's efforts in recording the saint's life. Including this firsthand account of her unusual birth lends weight to Gyurmé Ösel's narrative, offering the gravity of eyewitness "proof" to the author's larger argument about Mingyur Peldrön's sacrality. The newborn's first cry of "HUM!" replaces the cries of an infant with a sacred syllable, suggesting that she emerged from the womb already enlightened. Her sudden movement into an upright squat echoes the surprising mobility of Siddhartha Gautama (later called Shakyamuni Buddha), who was said to have taken seven steps upon his birth.[7] The story reports that the women's fears were quelled, but it is unclear what those fears actually were. Was it concern surrounding the liminal life-and-death event of childbirth? Or perhaps they found the child's strange behavior particularly frightening? While these questions must go unanswered, it is clear that Mingyur Peldrön's birth was reported in saintly terms and with a great deal of drama.

Gyurmé Ösel also makes sure to relate Mingyur Peldrön's birth story to the institution into which she was born by connecting it with high-level Great Perfection practices. In the last sentence of the excerpt about her birth, he mentions "Dzogchen Trekcho." This refers to the Great Perfection teachings called Trekchö (variously translated as "Cutting Through," "Breakthrough," or "Cutting Through Solidity"). The phrase would have brought to mind Trekchö and the subsequent Thögel ("Crossing the Crest" or "Leap Over") teachings, two subcategories of the Nyingtik genre, in the "Instruction Class" (Menakdé) category of Great Perfection literature. Thus, in mentioning it, he correlates the unusual circumstances of her birth with high-level practices taught at Mindröling, drawing an overt connection between her and well-known practices that would indicate to the reader that Mingyur Peldrön's abilities from birth were very advanced indeed.[8] Here the moment of her birth foregrounds the emphasis on her role as a practitioner and purveyor of advanced teachings within Mindröling simultaneously.

The themes of a miraculous and saintly life—in keeping with the stylistic parameters of namtar—continue as the hagiography presents Mingyur Peldrön's early life and the significant signs and portents that attended her at every turn. In several cases Gyurmé Ösel draws direct connections to her previous lives as well as to her familial and institutional lineages. According to *Dispeller*, as the infant grew into a toddler, the auspicious signs continued piling up:

> Furthermore, right after her birth she began to grow quickly, even though she would only take a little of [her mother's] milk each day. She naturally displayed a superior nature [and] good [qualities]. In particular, from previous lives she remembered the saints of her tradition, including The Great Master of Oddiyana [Padmasambhava], Kunkyen Drimé Özer, and Sangdak Trinlé Lhundrup. To them she showed one-pointed devotion. Going to each of their statues in turn and venerating them, she was able to recognize and identify them without any assistance. She made supplication to them as though this present life were founded on previous incarnations, with no difference between the two. It's said that this predisposition is due to her having previously been a disciple of Kunkyen Longchen Rabjampa.[9]

Here the narrative implies that it was Mingyur Peldrön's profound compassion that led her to only take a little of her mother's milk each day. In spite of this, she managed to grow quickly (another sign of her unusual capabilities). Her ability to identify important religious leaders of old without anyone's help is meant to signify both her high level of realization and her connectedness with several religious institutions.

Each of the figures mentioned represent different nested communities. If we think of them in terms of Mindröling's institutional positioning, they affirm three levels of Nyingma organizational connectivity. Padmasambhava (here the "Great Master of Oddiyana") represents an early imperial connection with the Nyingma school, broadly defined, and also points to the treasure revelation tradition of her treasure revealer father. Mindröling was established with the dual institutions of treasure revelation and scholarly prowess, and treasure revealers have remained important throughout its history. "Kunkyen Drimé Özer" and "Kunkyen Longchen Rabjampa" are references to Longchenpa (1308–64), who represents the codification of the Nyingma denomination during the fourteenth century. He is mentioned twice in the excerpt, reinforcing Mingyur Peldrön's connection to the Nyingma with the suggestion that this early behavior was an indicator that in a previous life she had been one of his students. Finally, Mingyur Peldrön's grandfather, the Nyingma master Trinlé Lhundrup, represents a combined spiritual and genetic connection to the Nyö clan of Terdak Lingpa's heritage. The depiction of the young girl recognizing these three statues on sight and toddling off to visit them on her own gives the reader the sense that she was born with an innate and extraordinary devotion to the Nyingma lineage holders, and in particular the Mindröling tradition, coupled with highly devout behavior for someone who was barely old enough to walk.

> In childhood, although it was playtime, she was able to differentiate between saṃsāra and nirvana far beyond the reach of ordinary children. Sometimes she would sit cross-legged in meditation, maintaining a fixed gaze. Then there was that time with the cloth. When she was quite small, she had a green cloth that was used for polishing ornaments. To her nursemaid Gyurmé Chödron she said "You're my closest disciple! When we two have to go out to the barbaric borderlands in the future, we can use this as our food pot." She took very good care of the cloth. Thus, she was able to clearly see important future events, unobscured by saṃsāra. I learned this directly [from her]. Later, after the reverend father had departed for the Pure Land, when the Hong Taiji's army had unspeakably destroyed some of the essential teachings, she had to go to Sikkim to protect her life and

that of the teachings. Having listed these many examples, the argument [of her divinity] is certain.¹⁰

In traditional namtar style, Mingyur Peldrön's supposed supernatural abilities are centered in the discussion of her childhood, from an unusual penchant for contemplative practice (forgoing playtime to sit in meditation) to supernatural precognition and clairvoyance and other strange behaviors (fretting over and preparing for an exile years in the future). Here the young girl helps to prepare the adults around her for the strife that would eventually befall Mindröling, exhibiting an early concern for her family and their institutional tradition. It also foregrounds the deep impact that the events of the civil war would have on Mindröling. Reverberations of this impact would last well into the 1780s, when Gyurmé Ösel actually completed *Dispeller*. The anxieties surrounding the events are expressed throughout Mingyur Peldrön's *Life*, pointing to this moment as a major juncture in her lived experience.

As a hagiography, in *Dispeller* Gyurmé Ösel uses moments of supernatural activity to paint Mingyur Peldrön as an enlightened being from her very birth. As such, his focus on her childhood is centered not on mundane events but on the miraculous. Ordinary activities are not mentioned, and in their place he reports accounts of her performative devotion, her astounding dedication to meditative practices, and gives the reader an image of a girl who emerged from the womb ready to fight for the dharma. Most notably, the girl was born into a familial context in which, according to her hagiography, she was immediately received as an important member and future contributor. There is no discussion of an unwanted girl-child in this part of the narrative, no disappointment on the part of the parents or the rest of the family. Rather, as the story is written, she is received as an enlightened future participant of the family. The signs and portents of this section of *Dispeller* then give way to a less miraculous discussion of her childhood and adult years.

At Mindröling, Mingyur Peldrön's generation eventually grew to include seven children. Her eldest brothers were Gyurmé Pema Tenzin (1677–?) and Yizhin Lekdrup (1679–1718). Not much is mentioned about them in *Dispeller*, although we know that Yizhin Lekdrup did become a teacher at Mindröling and died in 1718 (presumably during the civil war). The next eldest brother was Pema Gyurmé Gyatso (1686–1717/18), who would become the second trichen of Mindröling, after their father died of illness in 1714. He was important for

Mindröling's survival after their father's death, and he passed on teachings to his younger siblings and had been expected to lead the monastery prior to his own untimely death in the civil war. In *Dispeller* he is described in his role as one of Mingyur Peldrön's early teachers and in his position as trichen. Mingyur Peldrön was closest in age to her brother Rinchen Namgyel, who was five years her senior. The two would become coleaders of Mindröling in their adulthood and frequently traded teachings with one another. His extant hagiography, *The Namtar of the Bodhisattva Rinchen Namgyel, Dispeller of Longing for the Fortunate*,[11] is comparable in style and length to *Dispeller* and thus offers helpful information for comparing the upbringing, religious training, and activities of the two siblings.

The male children were all active participants in the family project of educating monastics, non-monastics and the sons of aristocratic families at Mindröling. In *Dispeller* Mingyur Peldrön's elder brothers also educated her in the transmission lineages of their father's treasure texts and multiple other systems of religious training, helping to prepare her for similar leadership positions. Depictions of Rinchen Namgyel in *Dispeller* include him receiving teachings from Mingyur Peldrön, and the two are shown as having a collaborative relationship in terms of religious education. They are depicted as equals, exchanging teachings to reinforce one another's education. However, in his namtar the flow of education is unilateral, with him teaching Mingyur Peldrön and her remaining always in the role of student.[12] He is described as having studied with many people in his childhood—far more than Mingyur Peldrön in fact—but they are all men, and renowned elder teachers, rather than anyone from his immediate age group. In Rinchen Namgyel's namtar he is also depicted in his role as a religious teacher and political advisor to the military general Polhané Sönam Tobgyé (1689–1747). This pattern is mirrored in *Dispeller*, in which Mingyur Peldrön takes on the role of an advisor to and confidante of important political figures—often the very same people described as having received advice from her brother in his namtar. While the hagiographies of each of the two siblings represents their individual subjects as the sole political advisor, both texts corroborate that the sister and brother did work together in Mindröling's leadership. These two namtars contain many parallels. For example, both works exhibit a focus on recounting how each sibling taught large groups of people. Likewise, they both report that Rinchen Namgyel did indeed share his education with Mingyur Peldrön by passing on teachings to her where he could (although in her telling, she repaid him in kind with teachings of her own). The story of Mingyur Peldrön's childhood is largely one of her education and is best understood in conversation with Rinchen Namgyel's educational narrative, given their proximity in age and later co-leadership of the monastery in adulthood. Like *Dispeller*, his hagiography also includes a section describing his early education, and a comparison reveals significant similarities as well as important distinctions between the two.

Among these siblings Mingyur Peldrön also had two younger sisters, generally referred to as "Lady Peldzin" and "Lady Drung" in *Dispeller*. Lady Peldzin was born in or shortly after 1701 and is mentioned slightly more frequently than Lady Drung, who only makes passing appearances. While Lady Peldzin was recognized as an incarnation of her grandmother Yangchen Drölma, we have little information about whether or not she received a formal religious or secular education along the lines of Mingyur Peldrön or Rinchen Namgyel. Generally, the sisters are mentioned in *Dispeller* as accompanying Mingyur Peldrön and their mother on pilgrimages and also occasionally participating in religious ceremonies. According to the namtars of both Mingyur Peldrön and Rinchen Namgyel, the younger sisters attended a few large group teachings alongside Mingyur Peldrön in their youth. Likewise, in adulthood they were present for teachings from both their elder sister and brother.[13] However, these younger sisters had no lengthy accounts written about their lives and appear only sporadically in their siblings' namtars. We know little about their early years or education. Based on the brief moments where they are mentioned, it seems that they may have had access to religious teachers (especially those within their family), but no information suggests an education nearly as extensive as Mingyur Peldrön's. Nor do we have much information about whether or not they were encouraged or allowed to engage in religious training as children. We know that Lady Peldzin remained a laywoman, although she accompanied Mingyur Peldrön on pilgrimage journeys and into exile in Sikkim. Lady Peldzin shows up in *Dispeller* and in Rinchen Namgyel's namtar most prominently in brief accounts of her short-lived marriage to the king of Sikkim, which can also be found in Samten Gyatso's *History of Sikkimese Monasteries*.[14] The absence of a discussion about these other daughters' education is in stark contrast to the descriptions of the training bestowed on their elder siblings and as recounted in the namtars of Rinchen Namgyel and Mingyur Peldrön.

How Mingyur Peldrön came to inhabit the role of community leader and religious teacher while her sisters did not is an essential question. Her early instruction meant that later in life she could rely on her religious knowledge to gain support in times of need, whereas Lady Peldzin and Lady Drung may have had to rely on their family connections alone. The best example of this incongruence is when the sisters and their mother fled into exile during the civil war. Upon arrival in Sikkim, Mingyur Peldrön was hailed by the Sikkimese royal family as a revered teacher who was able to share her training, bestowing teachings on the monastics at nearby Pemayangtsé Monastery and offering mass teachings for the Sikkimese laity. The discrepancy between Mingyur Peldrön's experience in exile and that of Lady Peldzin is notable. While the elder sister was hailed as an important religious teacher, the younger was bound in a marriage alliance to the king of Sikkim for the duration of their time in the kingdom. It turns out that Lady Peldzin's marriage did not last long, and the sisters and their mother would ultimately return to Ü together. The *History of Sikkimese Monasteries* also mentions a little about their mother, Phuntsok Peldzöm, including that she was generous with gifts, which she distributed widely.

Mingyur Peldrön's religious training was one of the most important aspects of her upbringing and denotes a status of privilege. In the context of the twenty-first-century reader, one might be inclined to point to this as evidence of a dramatically pro-woman stance. However, it is not useful to impose a uniform sense of pro-woman education throughout the family, as we have little evidence that Mingyur Peldrön's education mirrored that of her sisters. Rather, the literature suggests an uneven educational experience within the family itself. When comparing her education to that of her two closest siblings (Rinchen Namgyel and Lady Peldzin), inconsistencies arise. She received far more involved training than Lady Peldzin, but as we shall see, she was still excluded from some teachings that Rinchen Namgyel received. The impact of gender and the dynamics at play in the respective siblings' access to religious training are obscured in *Dispeller* and raise the question of how gender and privilege were interconnected in Mingyur Peldrön's case specifically and in the family more generally. Her education indicates access to religious training beyond that of her sister but not as extensive as what her brother enjoyed. This may have had to do with birth order, acumen, interest, or any number of other, unknown factors. Thinking specifically about her case, even with hierarchies in place within the family, in the wider scope of religious education of the time, she had relatively direct access to an array of teachings that were within her grasp because of her position of birth in the Mindröling family and parents and teachers who supported her education. Her training was not necessarily accessible (or of interest) to all the girls in the family and may have been completely inaccessible to many other girls beyond this inner circle. It is notable that she had the fortitude to engage these trainings throughout her adulthood and would ultimately use them to her benefit in establishing her role as a leader. This raises a question about what her access to religious training says about her individual positionality and the power structures that informed privilege in her context.

The details of Mingyur Peldrön's educational narrative in *Dispeller* largely center around her close relationship with her father, Terdak Lingpa. Accounts of the two suggest a warm and affectionate relationship focused on her religious education and preparation to take on a significant educator's role in the family. To establish this connection, Gyurmé Ösel points to the fortunate karmic predispositions that he argues led to her high birth:

> Furthermore, past prayers ripened at the right time, the result of which was that by her birth she formed a master-disciple connection with the Great Terton King, Tamer of All Beings Terdak Lingpa. Thus, she was born the child of her father's pure and wondrous line of ancestral fathers and mothers. And so, she became the remedy, breather of life into the definitive Secret Vajragarbha. When she was young, she held the three vows without contradiction, she was protector and friend to all teachings and living beings, and received the highest scriptural transmissions.[15]

As predictable as it is for this genre, the karmic explanation of her origins highlights the single most important privilege she enjoyed: birth into a family that supported her religious education (even if the educational support among her generation was potentially uneven). In keeping with the concept of karmic retribution, birth into this family is described as the result of good karma from having engaged in devout activities in earlier lives. The mention of the Three Vows would also become relevant to Mingyur Peldrön's later monastic position. Taking into consideration that *Dispeller* was composed long after her death, Gyurmé Ösel created an image of a baby who was immediately identified as an important figure for high-level practices in the Mindröling community and raised with the anticipation that she could become an eminently successful teacher. This teleological reading stands as his explanation for why she received an education directed by her father: from her very birth it was anticipated that she would step into a role of leadership.

In *Dispeller* Mingyur Peldrön's relationship with her father is based entirely on her potential contributions to the family institution. Whereas other women escaped their households to pursue a religious life or faced off over marriage prospects, Terdak Lingpa's primary concern for Mingyur Peldrön was apparently that she would become a teacher and liberator of suffering beings who was adept at the monastery's Dzogchen teachings. The phrase *great hope* is repeated five times in the discussion of her education, and each time it is reportedly uttered by Terdak Lingpa.[16] A few examples of the phrase's occurrence will shed some light on its importance. The account of Mingyur Peldrön receiving her religious name from her father in 1710 goes like this:

> Then, if I'm to give a true account about her name, [here it is]. It happened in her twelfth year—the iron tiger year—in the fifth month, on the tenth day ceremony for the Great Guru of Oddiyana, the Lake-Born Vajra [that is, Padmasambhava], at the time when the *ḍākinīs* assembled, in the Samantabhadra Palace that is the residence of the Great Orgyen Mindroling family. In the center of the immeasurable self-arisen vajra palace sat her own father—the master of the secret doctrine Dharmavajra—perched atop the indestructible throne in the guise of a human. That tamer of beings and knowledge-bearer, the Great Tertön Dharma King Terdak Lingpa, the Vajra-Holder of Oddiyana,[17] conferred [her name] on her. He cut her hair with the razor of wisdom of the true nature of reality, and she took the name Mingyur Peldrön. At that moment flowers of consecration blew about. A rainbow stood like an arrow over the roof of Mindröling. Then the Great Tertön himself showed minor signs of fatigue, and outside many rainbows stuck out like arrows. There was worried talk that maybe this was a sign that his lordship's feet had become infirm [and that his life would be cut short]. At the same time, in the center of the Samantabhadra palace, the water in the vase in the arranged mandala of Lord Amitabha began to bubble a bit! The reverend father said, "Girl, what great hopes do I have for you? This is a sign that you have the right karmic connections to be a holder of the essential teachings. Now, quickly drink the water from the vase!" Additionally, in *The Revealed Treasure of the Empty Plain* it says, "The master and disciple remained inseparable." It's also said that flowers were scattered. From then on, she stayed close to her reverend father and attained spiritual maturity by the steam of the Four Empowerments in the mandala of the Profound Teaching of the Rigdzin Tuktik.[18]

In this account of Mingyur Peldrön's first refuge ceremony, it is clearly important to Gyurmé Ösel that the reader believes the account to be true in spite of (or because of) the signs and portents so typical of hagiography that proliferate and render the scene miraculous.[19] What we can tell from the account is that in 1710, the eleven-year-old Mingyur Peldrön (twelve by Tibetan age calculations) took refuge with Terdak Lingpa at their home in Mindröling. In the refuge ceremony her father expressed his hope for her future engagement with religious training. The account makes heavy use of symbolism that renders the house and participants as Buddhist deities, existing in the ultimate reality of a Buddha-field. The family home becomes the palace of the primordial Buddha Samantabhadra, who is considered to be the progenitor of the Great Perfection. Her father is depicted as Dharmavajra and Padmasambhava as they participate in the ceremony in which she will become officially linked to him for her religious training. In hagiographic fashion the rainbows standing like arrows outside the house, the flowers flying about in the air, and the water spontaneously bubbling in its vase, all cloak the narrative in a sense of the miraculous. Some signs are positive, while others are not. The rainbow arrows are interpreted alongside Terdak Lingpa's slight fatigue to portend his early demise (he would die only a few years later). However, when the vase of water in the Amitabha mandala begins to bubble, this is considered a good sign. He exclaims that he has great hopes for Mingyur Peldrön and orders her to drink the bubbling water and thereby seal her karmic connection to the "essential teachings."[20] With the use of miraculous language, the moment establishes her as inextricably linked to Terdak Lingpa as his religious disciple, and to Mindröling and its teachings, lending weight to his declaration that he has great hopes for his daughter's future. Practically speaking, the account also tells us that Mingyur Peldrön began studying in earnest with her father when she was eleven years old and had no other teachers until his death, that he held an expectation that she would be successful in her religious study and practice, and that this would position her optimally for a leadership role in the family's religious institution. As a point of comparison, Rinchen Namgyel was reported to have begun his studies at the age of four and to have studied with a wide range of renowned teachers throughout his childhood, although he did also spend time studying with his father. Here the familial relationship of father and daughter is combined with teacher and student, bringing together the realms of religious and natal families, which in many parts of Tibetan history have been separated. For the family at Mindröling, and especially for Mingyur Peldrön, these relationships were completely enmeshed.

Gyurmé Ösel reports that Mingyur Peldrön herself told him about her early education. He claims that she requested these initial empowerments and began with the preliminary practices, following Terdak Lingpa's instruction diligently until she had signs of realization.[21] Terdak Lingpa repeatedly expressed his goals for Mingyur Peldrön and the future of Mindröling as well as her own spiritual development. Accounts of the early years of her studies include repetition of this theme, with Terdak Lingpa patting her affectionately and saying things like "There is great hope for you. Will you lead many accomplished men and women to the Pure Lands?"[22] Sometimes the phrase was uttered in commands to her, such as "Now, [you] must earnestly meditate on the Three Classes of the Great Perfection. In the future you must explain [it] to others. I have great hope for you!"[23] These words solidified Mingyur Peldrön's resolve to be diligent in her studies and reinforced for her and others the idea that she was brought up to be a Dzogchen teacher. Even if Mingyur Peldrön had had other ideas about what her future held, these specific expectations were established for her early on. At different moments the phrase *a great hope* acts as a positive reinforcement that buoys the young girl during her education, while in other places it is a reminder to fulfill the nonnegotiable expectations of her father.[24] It seems this method worked. She was reportedly a diligent student, studying hard in each stage of her training. Mingyur Peldrön's own hopes and desires, however, are never discussed. While she received strong support for her education and was urged to pursue elevated religious practice and become adept in it so as to be able to pass the practice on as a teacher, it is also possible that the weight of familial expectations had little to do with her own interests. There is never any inquiry in *Dispeller* about what Mingyur Peldrön herself wanted to do with her life or what she would be interested in. In addition to these anecdotes, her childhood and early youth are distilled down to *senyik*, or lists of teachings, initiations, and empowerments that she received from Terdak Lingpa and later from other important Mindröling figures, all of whom were men.

Dispeller reports that Mingyur Peldrön's early years were occupied with religious study, and life at Mindröling continued somewhat uninterrupted until her father died in 1714, her fifteenth year. One can imagine that the death of her father would have been jarring and sad for her, both in terms of her personal relationship with her father and root teacher but also in that it threw the monastic community into uncertainty at a time when she was still in her youth. After Terdak Lingpa died, she studied closely with her uncle Lochen Dharmaśrī, also receiving teachings from her elder brothers Pema Gyurmé Gyatso and Rinchen Namgyel. Pema Gyurmé Gyatso took up the role of trichen at this time. The interim between the beginning of Mingyur Peldrön's study with Terdak Lingpa and the onset of the civil war is depicted through more long lists of the teachings she received from each of these men. These senyik are interspersed with a few brief vignettes that emphasize her close relationship with Terdak Lingpa. After his death Mingyur Peldrön's educational program was directed by Lochen Dharmaśrī, with most training coming from him and a handful of teachings from her elder brothers.

Mingyur Peldrön's religious training is the most prominent topic of her childhood discussed in *Dispeller*, and so the story of her youth becomes synonymous with that of her education. The narrative of this period is not given in prose. Rather, ages eleven to eighteen are depicted as chronological lists of the texts and teachings that made up her educational curriculum and the empowerments, initiation, and instructions that she received attendant with them, with a few vignettes interspersed throughout. This section of the hagiography models the style of senyik, the records of teachings received, mentioned previously. These lists appear frequently in Tibetan life writing and can range in length and detail. For example, the Institut für Indologie und Tibetologie's collection of senyik for nine Sakya practitioners from the sixteenth century range in length from 5 to 81 folios.[25] In comparison, the section of Mingyur Peldrön's namtar that reads like a senyik covers 9 folios (18 folio sides) of the 236 folios sides (117.5 folios) that compose the namtar. This amounts to approximately 7.5 percent of the namtar.

The senyik section—while not terribly engaging as a narrative choice—conveys important information about the nature of Mingyur Peldrön's education, including the weight of her religious credentials. These lists are impressive not only in their sheer length but also in the range and diversity of trainings they represent. They point to the importance of her religious training as fundamental to her depicted identity as well as for the larger narrative concerns of Gyurmé Ösel's *Dispeller*. Including this record in the hagiography trains the reader's attention on the broad scope of her religious education. The nearly (but not quite) exhaustive collection of teachings comprising her education suggests that she was sufficiently prepared for her future role of religious practitioner and educator for Mindröling. The section establishes her religious authority by pointing out her comprehensive training in her father's revealed treasure texts and in high-level Atiyoga (Highest Yoga) and Anuyoga (Subsequent Yoga) Great Perfection teachings. It also indicates a curriculum that overlaps with her brothers in some places, and diverges in significant ways. Terdak Lingpa gave her the reading transmissions, practical guidance, explanatory transmissions, and empowerments for a host of texts and teachings. According to Gyurmé Ösel, she received training in the works of the "famous treasure revealers" of the time.[26] She studied *The Heart Essence of Vimilamitra* and Longchenpa's commentary on it as well as Machik Labdrön's *Severance* (*Chöd*) and teachings from the earlier and later Northern Treasure tradition (Jangter).[27] Terdak Lingpa taught and transmitted to her all of his revealed treasure texts, including his ritual instructions on *Dredging the Depths of Hell* (for which Mingyur Peldrön would later compose an instruction manual). The concern was whether his corpus would continue to be passed down after he was gone, and passing the teachings to her along with her brothers meant that these works were that much more likely to be preserved.[28] Finally, Mingyur Peldrön received an extensive education in an array of Great Perfection texts and teachings. These included teachings that originated in each of three divisions treating approaches to understanding the primordial state of existence, the Semdé (Mind Section), Longdé (Space Section), and Menakdé (Instruction Section).

Dzogchen transmissions are especially highlighted in the senyik. The list reflects a significant part of the collection of high-level Nyingma teachings, generally only accessible to those who have undergone significant training and received initiation into the practices and the empowerments to perform them from authorized teachers. Indeed, Mingyur Peldrön and Rinchen Namgyel were the only two in the younger group of siblings to receive transmission for Mindröling's cycle of Atiyoga teachings, which heightened the significance of Mingyur Peldrön's role as a religious teacher after the civil war.[29] By receiving these teachings and transmissions, including the authorization to pass them on, Mingyur Peldrön established herself as a repository of knowledge from the prior generation and an important link in the transmission of the Mindröling to future generations. The extensive nature of these lists also reinforces the expectation that she would enthusiastically carry on the family tradition of being a public religious practitioner.

As the sibling closest in age to Mingyur Peldrön for whom we also have a namtar, her brother Rinchen Namgyel serves as the best comparison in terms of access to education and treatment within the family during the years when they were children. Pema Gyurmé Gyatso and Yizhin Lekdrup were already young men by the time their younger siblings were born. While Mingyur Peldrön's education is reported as having begun at age eleven, Rinchen Namgyel began school when he was a mere four years old. His education began much earlier than his sister's and was more far-reaching in scope as well. Both siblings' educations were directed by their father. However, the content of their training was different, and his was far more thorough. He received an extensive education in the five sciences (*rikné*), while she was barred from studying them. He studied with many well-known tutors and teachers, while she studied almost exclusively with senior male family members such as her father and later with her uncle and Pema Gyurmé Gyatso.[30] Whereas Mingyur Peldrön's education was centered on training that she could acquire at Mindröling, Rinchen Namgyel also received initiations from the Fifth Dalai Lama and leaders of the Drikung Kagyu and Sakya denominations.[31] His formal education was such that he would have been familiar with a range of approaches to religious praxis, logic, and secular topics.

While the list of Mingyur Peldrön's educational credentials is impressive and surprisingly extensive, there is one key training module that was omitted—that of Mindröling's foundational rikné curriculum. Sometimes glossed as the five "arts and sciences" or "texts of the cultural sciences," rikné consisted of five areas of study: plastic arts, medicine, language, logic, and "inner knowledge."[32] According to Buddhologists José Cabezón and Roger Jackson, "In modern parlance, the term *rig gnas* is frequently employed as the equivalent of the English word *culture*, referring in some instances to culture in general, in others to classical culture in particular. There is, however, a sense in which the term *rig gnas* means 'cultural science,' as in Sa skya Paṇḍita's enumeration of the ten *rig gnas* that must be mastered by a 'great pandit.'"[33] Mindröling was well known for a curriculum bearing the same title. Rikné was not studied at the Geluk monasteries in and around Lhasa and had in fact been discouraged during the reign of the Fifth Dalai Lama but remained present at Mindröling. While Rinchen Namgyel studied rikné extensively in his childhood,[34] Mingyur Peldrön was denied this training.

According to *Dispeller*, in 1712 Terdak Lingpa and Lochen Dharmaśrī had a conversation about whether or not Mingyur Peldrön should train in rikné, in which Terdak Lingpa made it clear that he felt there was no need for her to do so. Two questions arise here. Why was she excluded from studying rikné? Also, why does Gyurmé Ösel choose to discuss this decision in the hagiography? *Dispeller* asserts that Terdak Lingpa found rikné to be unworthy of Mingyur Peldrön's time. He thought her to be a bright and intelligent student who learned quickly and for whom studying rikné would be unnecessary. Terdak Lingpa also suggests that since Rinchen Namgyel had already begun his study of rikné, he should continue it and use it for his future leadership. Meanwhile, Mingyur Peldrön could focus on other things. Gyurmé Ösel's discussion of the matter in *Dispeller* suggests that he expected his readers to wonder why she had not trained in rikné. He sought to make clear that it was due to external reasons, such as dividing up the children's expertise, not wasting Mingyur Peldrön's time with unnecessary training (she had started her studies significantly later in life than her brother had), and so forth. Gyurmé Ösel makes it clear that her father explicitly decided she need not spend time in study that he considered redundant for both her educational program and the institution. Rinchen Namgyel would need rikné for his future role as trichen of Mindröling, and besides, he had begun studying it earlier in his life than his sister was when her studies began. If he focused on rikné, there was no institutional need for her to also occupy her time in this pursuit.

The focus in the decision to forgo rikné training for Mingyur Peldrön is notably twofold. Her educational needs are mentioned, but the needs of Mindröling as an institution take precedent. As a result of Terdak Lingpa's decision, Mingyur Peldrön received high-level Great Perfection trainings (in fact, the highest teachings in her tradition) while being barred from an entry-level foundational set of teachings. Ultimately, she received less education than Rinchen Namgyel did. While it is not stated explicitly, it is possible that this was a case of gender exclusion. Dominique Townsend's work on Terdak Lingpa and his correspondence with women has uncovered a complex relationship with women's training. While he did maintain correspondence with female rulers, patrons, and practitioners, it seems that he tended to offer women less pragmatic, more idealistic advice for their religious pursuits.[35] We cannot assume that his approach to his daughters' education was uniform for all of them, nor can we assume that it was equal to that of his sons. Nevertheless, he is portrayed in *Dispeller* as having a clear concern that Mingyur Peldrön receive religious training. There is also the possibility that as he aged he was more concerned that the Great Perfection be transmitted to the next generation and so sought to make sure she was trained up in the teachings as soon as possible. In the hagiography Mingyur Peldrön's education is described as something intentionally crafted to situate her as an authorized purveyor of the Great Perfection and prepare her for the life of a religious educator. This is notable as it further emphasizes her position of high privilege in the household while simultaneously explaining why she was denied a basic foundation of the Mindröling education (that is, rikné).

There are important gender implications in the records of Mingyur Peldrön and Rinchen Namgyel's educational histories and the absence of any such account for Lady Peldzin. It is unclear whether or not Lady Peldzin received any training—secular or religious—or what the nature of the training might have been. Since we have no namtar for her and she is little mentioned in other histories and narrative accounts, her educational experience has been largely lost to history. It is also worth noting that none of Mingyur Peldrön's teachers were women. Both Mingyur Peldrön and Rinchen Namgyel studied exclusively with men during their childhood. This could suggest that either Gyurmé Ösel did not perceive her as having learned anything of significance from women or that she simply did not have any female teachers to work with. Given the emphasis that he applies to her role as a teacher of women during her late teenage years, it is likely that he *was* interested in accounting for women's education and that he would have mentioned Mingyur Peldrön's study with women if such events had occurred. This tells us that there were no female role models of institutional religious engagement from whom Mingyur Peldrön could learn during her early years at Mindröling. Thus, it seems likely that she was the first woman at the monastery to take on the roles she adopted. This is not at all unusual—the presence of a female teacher is the exception rather than the norm in this specific sociohistorical context. In this section of *Dispeller* Gyurmé Ösel draws on Mingyur Peldrön's religious education to position her as a fully authorized religious teacher of Mindröling. Given his concern that she be recognized as an important religious teacher, it would have been especially important for Gyurmé Ösel to establish her educational background as a means of legitimating her role in the community. Another foundational aspect of Mingyur Peldrön's identity as it is portrayed in *Dispeller* was her position as a nun.

Becoming a Nun

Unlike her sisters, Mingyur Peldrön was a nun, and that status defined her religious identity as much as her position as a daughter of Mindröling. The theme of monasticism is persistent throughout *Dispeller* and is discussed from the earliest section of the text, among stories of her previous lives. The depictions of women's previous incarnations in Tibetan life writing have served to create profound links between the main subject of a *Life* and inspirational women of the past.[36] The importance of these pre-life narratives will be discussed in further detail in the next chapter, but here it serves to show how the initial representations of Mingyur Peldrön's previous lives foreshadow important themes for her story, including that of celibacy. Interestingly, her celibacy becomes intertwined with her persona as an incarnation of Yeshé Tsogyel. For example, at one point in a description of Yeshé Tsogyel found in *Dispeller*, the iconic figure is described quite differently from how she is usually portrayed. In this hagiography she is a celibate woman who never married, never took a consort, and never had children. "I am a nun," Yeshé Tsogyel declares in *Dispeller*, "unblemished by *saṃsaric* defects."[37] The theme of monasticism and celibacy is so strong in this text that famous consorts are made celibate in order to reinforce the image of Mingyur Peldrön as a staunchly celibate woman from her early years until her death. The emphasis on monasticism in these early stories of previous lives reverberates into the sections of the text that describe her own life as Mingyur Peldrön.

While Mingyur Peldrön lived her entire adult life as a nun, her namtar includes no account of her ordination, a noteworthy omission for a text that frequently reinforces her role as a nun in other ways. While her refuge ceremony with Terdak Lingpa is described in fine detail, any actual ordination that she may have had is relegated to a single brief phrase and a collection of strong hints scattered throughout the *Life*, including accounts of her vocal advocacy for monasticism. The only place in *Dispeller* where Mingyur Peldrön's actual ordination is explicitly and unequivocally described is in the account of her fifteenth year:

> There was a time between [the period] when the reverend father departed from life, when his form body was established in the expanse of peace, and [the time] when she fled the Hor soldiers. During that interim she was mostly in retreat. During that time she also received all kinds of [teachings] from Lochen Dharmaśrī. Having taken monastic vows, she then received the Precious Word Empowerment of the reverend father's *New Treasure*[38]—along with instructional reading and clarification—from Lochen [Dharmaśrī] Rinpoche. This resulted in a thorough transmission of the texts.[39]

This passage, which is followed by a senyik of the teachings that she received from Lochen Dharmaśrī, suggests either that Mingyur Peldrön had been ordained by Lochen Dharmaśrī or that, having been ordained by someone else, she was able to receive the listed initiations from him. This is the most concrete evidence of her ordination. Prior to this moment, there is also an important but brief discussion of how in her twelfth year she was established as both a nun and tantric practitioner. This is implied in the statement "As a youth, [she] *concentrated on the Three Vows without contradiction*, and so acted as protector and friend to the teachings and all beings, and received the highest transmissions."[40] This language is common in Three Vows literature and indicates that she was simultaneously a dedicated monastic and tantric practitioner.[41] The statement is repeated in Mindröling's collected *Lives* of the monastery's lineage holders, *The Lives of the Orgyen Mindröling Lineage Succession: A Festival of Victorious Conquerors*.[42] There it reads, "When she was the appropriate age [of twelve], she practiced the Three Vows without contradiction."[43] These moments simultaneously establish her as a nun and tantric practitioner and a Three Vows expert who was able to maintain her celibacy while taking up tantric praxis. This evidence of how she could continue practicing and disseminating high-level tantric teachings while remaining a nun offers the secondary implication (or perhaps assumption?) that she was in fact a nun, and thus maintained celibacy.

There is no discussion in *Dispeller* about whether or not Mingyur Peldrön had any agency in the decision to become a nun and study with Lochen Dharmaśrī or whether or not it was something that she actually wanted. Most other women's *Lives* in this genre talk about a woman's decision to become a nun and her reasons for doing so. While the early impetus for Mingyur Peldrön becoming a nun is unclear, throughout *Dispeller* she is portrayed as arguing truculently for the superiority of the monastic life, over and above that of the non-celibate path.[44] This was a rhetorical stance that was at least partly political in nature and directly related to her affiliation with the Nyingma denomination in an age of Geluk ascendency. In *Dispeller* there are several dramatic scenes establishing her eventual rejection of the famous Fifth Lelung Jedrung Losang Trinlé (1697–1740), who proposed that they establish a tantric consort relationship. She rejected him on the grounds that earlier in life her father had told her she would have to remain celibate if she was to successfully train in higher Dzogchen practices.

The emphasis on Mingyur Peldrön's position as a nun continues throughout *Dispeller* until her final days, when she supposedly expressed a desire to be born a man in the next life and to become "fully ordained."⁴⁵ This is the first and only moment when her level of ordination is mentioned throughout the whole of the text. *Dispeller* frequently refers to her as a *tsünma*, which in the context of this text is best translated as "nun,"⁴⁶ but this is a general term and does not designate her level of ordination. We will unpack the full meaning of Mingyur Peldrön's statement in later chapters, but in the context of her position as a nun, it suggests that she was perhaps not fully ordained, in spite of having lived her entire life as a nun at a major religious center.

Women's status in the Buddhist monastic community, their roles and their relationship to different levels of ordination, has been raised as a topic of discussion among scholars and practitioners in recent years. In academic circles, scholars of Mahayana and Vajrayana Buddhist traditions have begun addressing the nun-laywoman divide and the social and religious ramifications of this division. In place of this dyad, Buddhologist Jessica Starling has pointed to a "spectrum of ordination practices and an active negotiation of ritual authenticity" among female religious professionals that illuminates the range of possible ways that women could participate in religious life.⁴⁷ Whether or not one was ordained would have different ramifications for woman's access to religious practice depending on the time and place in which she lived. For those who sought to ordain as nuns, a host of causes and conditions were required for a woman to be allowed to take all the vows of her ordination lineage and be recognized as a *bhikṣuṇī*. This title would distinguish one from novice nuns and probationary postulants and within the monastic world would establish a woman in a different place in the social hierarchy.⁴⁸ The details of ordination rules vary from one denomination to the next, and their rules (and significance) are as culturally embedded as any other aspect of Buddhist tradition. While there is recourse to the *vinaya* for grounding ordination rules in a legalistic framework, the interpretation of ordination rules has been historically and geographically rooted.

The complexity of how religious women are labeled according to vows and lifestyle pertains to Tibetan Buddhist religious contexts and the ways that women navigate their roles within the tradition. Tibetan Buddhism has valorized non-celibate paths, and these were frequently available to women seeking a serious religious practice.⁴⁹ In Tibet the path of the non-celibate *yogini* (*neljorma*) was in many cases more readily available to women than was the male-dominated monastic realm.⁵⁰ Historically, in Tibet the life of a nun was not the sole choice for religious pursuit. However, nunhood was certainly an option, and conversations about ordination were present in Tibet long before the twentieth century.[51] The status of ordination would not necessarily determine a woman's access to religious training, nor were specifics of ordination status always obvious to the general population beyond the monastery walls. As Janet Gyatso and Hanna Havnevik have explained, in Tibet and elsewhere in the Buddhist world, "terms for female renunciates in Tibet are employed loosely to refer to various lifestyles and levels of ordination, although there are few references to the fully ordained *bhikṣuṇī* (Tib. *dge-slong-ma*)."[52] In some Tibetan contexts a woman's level of ordination was not necessarily considered as important in the larger social world when compared with whether or not she was a nun. Public perspective on nuns does not seem to have been dependent on level of monastic ordination. Instead, the fact of living as a nun would have the most significant implications for a woman and the social perceptions about her and her gender, regardless of her ordination status. These gendered implications were based on a woman's relationship to householder life. With that said, gendered perceptions of monastic men and women are highly variable depending on the historical and geographical context.[53] Likewise, every aspect of ordination—from its symbolic and social importance to the ritual requirements for ordination to occur—was context dependent.[54] While there is a trend within Tibetan history that social perceptions about women would shift depending on their engagement with the gendered and sexed expectations of being part of the family unit (for example, as a wife and/or mother), those perceptions might change depending on time and place. Janet Gyatso and Hanna Havnevik echo Charlene Makley in explaining that "the mere fact of leaving householder status and shaving one's head is already enough to 'perform' most of the gender-bending that the taking of monastic vows accomplishes in public perception—a bending that has been used deliberately by individual women to escape their conventional gendered roles as wives and mothers."[55] While the relationship between gender identity and monastic identity continues to be a point of discussion, it is clear that women presenting as ordained (with shaved head and monastic robes) convey to the wider community a different social status than non-monastic women, regardless of their exact level of ordination.

This is not to elide the importance of full ordination for women who sought out the life of a nun and hoped to establish themselves within the larger religious institutional structure, for reasons soteriological, social, or otherwise. There are hints that full ordination was possible for women in Tibetan history—at least in the eleventh, twelfth, and fifteenth centuries. Likewise, some nuns who were fully ordained rallied to ordain others and argued for the benefits of full ordination. We have no evidence that Mingyur Peldrön herself received full ordination, although we do know that she was a nun. There are no indications that her level of ordination had an impact on her religious education or social role, although before she died she is reported to have expressed a strong desire for full ordination (and birth as a man) in her next life. We can also understand the impact that becoming a nun had on her socioreligious position.[56] *Dispeller* is written from the basic assumption that, if sufficiently supported, the nun's life had the potential to allow her the freedom to focus on and develop her religious practice. This is borne out in other nuns' contexts as well. For example, Chökyi Drönma was compelled to choose between either acting as a ruler, or becoming a nun and pursuing enlightenment.[57] Her narrative arc echoes that of the *Life of Shakyamuni* and includes her renunciation of the householder life after having married and had children. Chökyi Drönma was herself fully ordained and argued for the benefits of full ordination. While her context was different from Mingyur Peldrön's in some ways, the potential that nunhood could be liberatory was emphasized for both, and the decision to become a nun while retaining a privileged status was as feasible and within reach.

Although the possibility would be raised in her adult life, Mingyur Peldrön did not take the path of the non-celibate yogini. And today she remains a woman of indeterminate ordination status who lived life as a nun. While Mingyur Peldrön's level of ordination is not discussed in detail, her social position as a nun is frequently reiterated throughout *Dispeller*. Rather than inhabiting a liminal place on the spectrum of monasticism and lay life, she is depicted as fighting against suggestions that she (or anyone else) engage in consort relationships, arguing that her path was one of celibacy. While there is little discussion of her actual ordination, her dedication to the life of a solitary nun is made most prominent in *Dispeller*. Whatever the lived reality, in her story the rejection of the householder life is emphasized in her early adoption of monasticism before she was old enough to consider establishing her own household. Mingyur Peldrön's expected path of supporting her family's religious institution could potentially have been pursued in either the monastic or non-monastic setting. In her community marriage did not preclude involvement in religious leadership. As such, the status of full ordination may not have been as significant, given that she could access the religious teachings of her community without becoming a fully ordained nun. While Mingyur Peldrön's level of ordination is unclear, it makes sense to refer to her as a nun because that is how she referred to herself. Setting aside her level of ordination, what is significant is the practical impact of her choices to live life celibately, even to the extreme of causing tension between Mindröling and Lelung Monasteries, her frequent urgings that women take up ordination, and her own identity as a nun.

While becoming a nun was a goal for some women, in many cases the most well-known religious women in Tibetan history and myth have been non-monastic. Being a nun was actually somewhat unusual among the Tibetan women for whom we have *Lives*. Whereas Tāre Lhamo, Sera Khandro, and Sönam Peldren were all obliged to marry and Chökyi Drönma left her marriage to take monastic vows, Mingyur Peldrön's celibate life was supported—if not actively urged—by her family. Like Mingyur Peldrön, Chökyi Drönma was literally born into a family of high privilege. She married in her youth but soon voiced a desire to take monastic vows. She had to go to extremes to be released from her marital duties, going so far as to tear out her hair in front of her in-laws, before her husband would grant her permission to end her marriage.[58] For her the pursuit of religious life and the duties of marriage were mutually exclusive.

Among recent English-language scholarship, Orgyan Chökyi (1675–1829) and Shugsep Jetsün Rinpoche (19th–20th c.) are the only other Tibetan women who have *Lives* and who also became nuns without having ever married at all. While Orgyan Chökyi was in no way supported by her family in this endeavor, Shugsep Jetsün Rinpoche came from a family of little means, but her parents encouraged her to pursue a religious path.[59] Of the three women, Mingyur Peldrön alone came from a family of high status both in terms of wealth and religious position. Mingyur Peldrön's role as a nun sets her apart from many other exceptional women and suggests a different narrative arc for both her religious life and activities. Later chapters address how Mingyur Peldrön's status as a nun influenced her social position and augmented her particular access to religious, institutional, and social authority.

CIVIL WAR AND EXILE IN SIKKIM

Mingyur Peldrön's life was upended by the civil war that broke out in the winter of 1717–18. This event was the result of previously mentioned intersectarian tension that was exacerbated by instability in the Ganden Podrang government after the death of the Fifth Dalai Lama.[60] Two external competing factions sought inroads to political ascendency in central Tibet, and the region eventually broke into all-out warfare.[61] Representing one interest was Lhazang Khan, a Qoshot Mongol supported by the Qing emperor Kangxi (r. 1662–1722). The second was the Dzungar Mongol leader Tsewang Rabten, who had assumed leadership of the powerful expansionist Dzungars between 1690 and 1697.[62] These two men and the groups they represented vied for influence in the region, at times supported by different factions of the faltering Ganden Podrang and at times going so far as to assassinate members of the government leadership. Lhazang Khan took control of Lhasa in 1705 with the support of the Qing imperium.[63] Following the death of the Sixth Dalai Lama in 1706, the different factions within and beyond the Ganden Podrang sought the installment of their preferred candidate for Seventh Dalai Lama.

In the midst of widespread unrest, there arose a pro-Geluk sentiment that was undergirded by antipathy toward all non-Geluk organizations (including Mindröling). Concerned about Lhazang Khan's rulership and the increasing Qing influence in the region, Tsewang Rabten aligned himself and his Dzungar army with the pro-Geluk faction. In the winter of 1717–18, he sent a Dzungar army of six thousand troops to remove Lhazang Khan's forces from power in Lhasa. In December 1717 growing sentiment against non-Geluk organizations and individuals reached a tipping point, and Dzungar troops began first arresting and then executing prominent non-Geluk religious leaders. Known for their opposition to the Fifth Dalai Lama's relatively ecumenical relations, the Dzungars also destroyed many non-Geluk institutions in central Tibet.[64] According to Petech, they acted like a raiding party as they moved through the region, laying waste to monasteries and villages and taking food and fuel, with little regard for the needs of local people.[65]

Lhazang Khan and most of his ministerial cabinet were killed, and Tsering Döndrup issued summonses to all provinces, calling for them to pay homage to him.[66] Whatever local popularity the Dzungars had established before the occupation, their behavior afterward led to a decline in enthusiasm for them. As time went on, the Dzungars failed to deliver a legitimate Dalai Lama to Lhasa, and the trust of their Geluk supporters waned.[67] While this period was a nadir marked by unrest in the early eighteenth century, the occupation would last until 1720, and regional instability and inter-sectarian strife would continue throughout the 1720s.[68]

Central Tibet's political environment had a jarring impact on Mingyur Peldrön's life, probably more so than the death of her father a few years earlier. The persecution of non-Gelukpa people and organizations was particularly marginalizing for Mindröling, which had long been the recipient of Ganden Podrang patronage during the reign of the Fifth Dalai Lama. Mindröling's inhabitants were the victims of significant sectarian violence against non-Gelukpa people and religious sites. The destruction of Mindröling during the civil war of 1717–18 was formative for their institutional narrative, as it forced a dramatic shift in the trajectory of the monastery and the lives of those who had been part of it. The Dzungar destruction would take center stage in the collective memory of the events of the eighteenth century.

When Terdak Lingpa died, in 1714, he left the leadership of Mindröling to Lochen Dharmaśrī and Pema Gyurmé Gyatso. The Dzungar army occupied Lhasa three years later, and the general Tsering Döndrup called for the arrest of non-Geluk leadership, including both men. On the day that Mingyur Peldrön's uncle and brother were taken to Lhasa, it became clear that Mindröling would not be spared from the sectarian violence.[69] Fearing for her safety, the family decided that Mingyur Peldrön should flee the monastery that very night. She was pulled out of her retreat, exchanged her retreatant's clothes for the disguise of a layperson, and ran up into the mountains behind the monastery with four attendants, intending to travel to Sikkim and take refuge there.[70] At the same time, Rinchen Namgyel fled to Bhutan. Shortly after they left, the Dzungar army descended upon the monastery. Gyurmé Ösel recounts the event in *Dispeller*, mentioning the traumatic experiences of Mingyur Peldrön's sisters at the hands of the Dzungars (who are here referred to as "Horpas" and "Sokpos"):

> At that time both Lady Drung and Lady Peldzin tried to avoid being harassed by some of the lewd Horpas, and faced great hardship. Out of their mother's mouth slipped [the words] "I have a daughter—Mingyur Peldrön—who acts just like a nun." As a consequence of these words, just like the roll of thunder thrills the peacock's heart, the Hor army halted all travel to and from Sikkim. When Terdak Lingpa's daughter was mentioned in this way, it would be unacceptable if the logical consequence were borne out [and she were caught]. What would have happened? She would have been taken to Lhasa, and day and night she would have been harmed. Since the Western Sokpos brought down suppression in this place of violence, Depa Wangdu

offered beer to the Sokpos in order to skillfully confuse them, and the Lama herself was invited to leave by a rope through a window. Hoping to spot her, Zhunggyu Dumpo Tashi spent the entire night in Dranang, and went to her maternal uncle's place. These days, we talk about the Hor Sokpos' destruction on that day. The Zhabdrung Zhenpen Wangpo also skillfully confused the Hor Sokpos with beer, [and] drew them from Ngön Gé Zhelkar to Martak Shur. Then [the escapees] hid among the boulders in the rocky upper part of Lungring valley for two days and two nights. Four helpers dressed as householders by day, and went in disguise to Menji Monastery. In this way they took turns making food, and delivering it by night. Then the Sokpos came to the spot in that rocky part of the Lungring valley [where she hid], and wandered back and forth past the head of the master herself. She told me "That moment I thought 'I am finished!' and my heart became fevered with an awesome fear." Due to the [Three] Jewels in general, and more specifically the compassion of the glorious master Padmasambhava, father and son, as well as the merit that the [escapees] had accumulated in their training as disciples, the Hor Sokpas were unable to see them, and having completely lost hope, the [Hor Sokpas] left. The group [of escapees] then proceeded to the learned yogini's place at Menji. After rising the next morning, they went to Dol Khangpa Gye, where they hid in one of the wives' kitchens.

At that time, the elder monks—Bumrap Jampa Orgyen Kelsang, Zhabdrung Gyurme Zhenpen Wangpo, Gelong Rabten, and others—were all consulting. Bumrap Jampa said, "Isn't this girl the very essence of Terdak Lingpa? She mustn't be squandered. Now, what to do? Which way to go?" Gelong Orgyen Rabten said, "You are all very wise and knowledgeable, so whichever way you think we should go, we will go. We must make an effort to establish a monastery. I will protect this girl from being spoiled, and once again she will give instructions to you all." Talking thus, they came to a harmonious decision. The monk[s] said, "The Precious Lama will go to Khang Gyang." As was predicted in the revered father's prophecy, the next morning they crossed the mountains, and went to Sikkim by way of Yardrok and the Karo pass. Graced with a vision of Pakri, they went in that direction. Moreover, normally she went about with a slow gait, or rode a horse. But at this time, dressed as a beggar, she had to walk continuously day and night. She became weak and exhausted, and kept going.[71]

Mingyur Peldrön's harrowing journey to safety was racked with danger and the threat of assault and death and was likely the most traumatic event of the young woman's life. Fear and urgency are palpable in this account, as are the conditions of uncertainty and the very real threat of physical violence and assault that Mingyur Peldrön and the other women in her community faced during this time. Here we get a sense of what today we would think of as the trauma that they experienced in the course of their exile into Sikkim. As Phuntsok Peldzöm and her other daughters are being harassed by the Dzungar troops, the mother accidentally alerts them to the existence of her other daughter. This sets in motion the lockdown and search for Mingyur Peldrön, erasing any hope for an easy escape. While the Dzungars are plied with beer until they are too drunk to function, Mingyur Peldrön escapes by climbing down out of a window. Given the danger she faced, it is no wonder that she made the grueling journey, hiding amid boulders and in the homes of friendly well-wishers as she made her exhausting walk to Sikkim. Her mother and sisters followed her there. Along the way she received word of her uncle's and brother's executions and the extent of the destruction of Mindröling. This news was of course terribly upsetting and also highlighted the necessity that her own escape and that of Rinchen Namgyel be successful. If the teachings were to be disseminated in the future, these two had to survive. At this time Mingyur Peldrön was eighteen years old. The *History of Sikkimese Monasteries* also recounts her escape to Sikkim:

> In the year 1717—the [year of the] fire bird—during the time of the Sokpo Dzungar's unrest, she reached her nineteenth winter. Having just come out of retreat, without having taken the time to cut away the long plaits that had grown (during her retreat), she donned a woolen dress. So, taking on the guise of a householder, she carried a small statue of her father on her back. The helpers Gyurmé Chödron and the kitchen maid Gyurmé Yangzom, the monks Tashi Wangchuk and Gendun Tsampel—five people altogether—carrying the bare necessities of provisions, fled in secret. Leaving through a secret door, they fled over the mountain behind the family home. The master came here, to Glorious Sikkim. She was welcomed with marvelous processions honoring her, and she settled at Sangnak Choeling Monastery. She dwelt there five years. The Dzogchenpa and the Dharma King [received] transmissions, and all the living beings of this land—high and low—were lucky to benefit from being near the *jetsünma* and receiving her advice.[72]

In Sikkim, Mingyur Peldrön's identity as a member of the Mindröling family meant that she received a warm reception. The Sikkimese royal family were supporters of Nyingma institutions, and some of the high-level teachers there had been trained at Mindröling, including Jikmé Dorjé, an expert in the Great Perfection.[73] Thus, two generations of Mindröling women became guests at the royal palace at Rabdentsé. Generally speaking, foreigners were not allowed to teach the Sikkimese populace, but Mingyur Peldrön was granted a special royal dispensation to do so and began instructing everyone—royalty and commoner, layperson and monastic, alike. It was unprecedented to have a woman, and a non-Sikkimese woman at that, teach Buddhism in Sikkim. However, Terdak Lingpa was well known by monastic leaders in the kingdom, and it was considered a great opportunity to have one of his trained close disciples giving instruction.

Phuntsok Peldzöm and her other daughters arrived shortly after Mingyur Peldrön and began their own diplomatic engagements. As representatives of the Mindröling family, they had important roles to play. Phuntsok Peldzöm dispensed gifts widely throughout the realm, to royalty and commoners, developing a reputation for her generosity.[74] During this time Mingyur Peldrön also brokered a marriage match between her sister Lady Peldzin and the King Gyurmé Namgyel (1707–33). The unhappy marriage only lasted until they returned to Mindröling but was politically important for cementing positive relations between the two houses, especially during their stay in Sikkim.[75] It is significant that Mingyur Peldrön arranged the marriage. In terms of her apparent concern for political expediency, it shows that she was actively thinking about creating strong connections with their hosts. It also exemplifies that she had relative bodily autonomy in comparison with that of her sister, as she was able to determine her own autonomy but also the fate of her sister. It is noteworthy that as a woman, she was willing to do what was necessary to convince her sister to marry the king. Finally, this moment conveys her own authority in the larger context of political and religious exile. As a refugee, she sought important political relationships for her family and their religious institution. It was also during their time in Sikkim that Mingyur Peldrön began her own teaching career, disseminating the teachings that she had brought with her from Mindröling.

In Sikkim she exchanged teachings with several people and acted as a religious advisor to King Gyurme Namgyel.[76] One person she regularly met to exchange teachings with was Jikmé Dorjé, who had studied with Terdak Lingpa at Mindröling in his youth. Their meetings during this period of exile reinforced the connections between the Sikkimese Nyingma community and the monastery in Ü. Mingyur Peldrön was also invited to teach the community of monks at nearby Pemayangtsé Monastery. According to the traditional narrative of Pemayangtsé, Jikmé Dorjé invited her there and requested she ascend their highest throne and offer instruction for the assembly. But she refused to enter the gates of the monastery grounds, stating that because she was a woman, it would in fact be dangerous for the monks.[77] To accommodate her, they built a stone throne for her just outside the gates of Pemayangtsé, where it remains today. It is noteworthy that after this first teaching, she was reported to have taught large crowds of monks from this spot and eventually also the laity. She initially resided nearby at Sangnak Choeling Monastery, where she also taught. Eventually, the young Mindröling representative would also establish her own residence near the modern-day village of Gyalshing. This site remains important to Mindröling, and since at least 2016 Mindrolling Monastery in India has been in the process of constructing a new center there, the Mingyur Dechen Leytroling.[78] Not only was the time in Sikkim a respite from the horrors of civil war; it also became the location of Mingyur Peldrön's first large-scale teaching. This marks the moment when she began to engage the Mindröling-style mass dissemination of doctrine and establish her role as a full-fledged purveyor of the monastery's teachings. With the demise of the remaining first generation of religious leaders in the family, practitioners and politicians began to seek her out as a teacher and representative of the tradition.

Return to Tibet

In 1721 the women of Mindröling received word that it was safe to return home.[79] Upon their arrival Mingyur Peldrön's first step was to begin reviving the monastery.[80] Initially, this meant reconstructing the physical edifice of the monastery, which she oversaw for a short but highly productive time. By the time her brother Rinchen Namgyel returned from his own exile, she had done much of the major external reconstruction. However, once he returned, he promptly took the lead in overseeing all such projects, and it became clear that Mingyur Peldrön should turn her attention elsewhere.

At this point the narrative of Mindröling reconstruction projects and relations between the siblings becomes somewhat murky and is represented with what appears to be intentionally vague language in *Dispeller*. According to the text, after her brother's return, Mingyur Peldrön was sent to rural Kongpo, apparently at the behest of unnamed "virtuous ones" who were members of the Mindröling household.[81] At their request the military general Polhané Sönam Tobgyé in Lhasa proclaimed that she should be sent away to Kongpo, arguing that many people there would benefit from her teachings. Urged by the unnamed members of the household, Polhané ordered her to Kongpo, and off she went. This moment in *Dispeller* suggests several things. First, it hints at potential strife between Mingyur Peldrön and other members of the Mindröling leadership, specifically her brother Rinchen Namgyel. It is possible that the people who requested her departure had really thought that her skills would be put to good use in such a remote region. Or they might have sought to remove her from the center of power and authority as her renown grew, adding a sarcastic undertone to the reference to their "virtue." This moment also highlights Polhané's influence and therefore the close alignment of at least one central Tibetan political leader with Mindröling. Mingyur Peldrön's relationships with Polhané and the Seventh Dalai Lama, Kelsang Gyatso (1708–57), who had ascended the throne in 1720, are reinforced in the text. They were instrumental to her role as a sort of emissary for Mindröling. Throughout her adulthood Mingyur Peldrön would form relationships with other religious and political leaders, engaging across denominational lines to share teachings with Nyingma and Geluk practitioners and continuing relationships with multiple generations of the aristocracy in central Tibet and Sikkim. Many of these relationships, including other connections with less famous disciples, were forged through her teaching efforts.

After Rinchen Namgyel's return to Mindröling, Mingyur Peldrön's focus shifted to reinforcing the monastery's teaching tradition. This meant traveling from place to place to give empowerments and initiations, visiting pilgrimage sites with an entourage that often included her mother and sisters, and participating wherever she could in the postwar revival of the Nyingma community. She also wrote multiple works over the course of her adulthood. She is credited with eighteen written pieces, ranging from prayers and lineage lists to liturgies and ritual instruction manuals. Most of these were focused on Dzogchen practice, and more than half centered on her father's revealed treasure texts. She also gave teachings at Mindröling and at its associated nunnery, which is referred to in her hagiography as "Menji,"[82] and at the Samten Tsé retreat center. The extent of her relationship with Menji and Samten Tsé is not fully fleshed out in *Dispeller*, but she visited one or both sites at least once a year and often remained there for months at a time. Her solitary retreats were generally undertaken there, and they were also frequently her sites for hosting teachings.

There is not much discussion of her health in the work, although in 1720 she was afflicted with a tumor that caused her severe pain. In *Dispeller* the incident of her illness is not treated with the same detail as the illnesses of her family members. For example, Terdak Lingpa's own illness and death and her mother's illness in later years both receive much more attention than hers, which is mentioned only briefly. Each of these events received extensive description of her own experience witnessing her parents' illnesses, while her own struggle with a painful tumor is the subject of a few short phrases. The mention of her illness is described in terms of her teaching schedule, explaining that she was able to recover well enough to depart for a large teaching tour a few months later.[83]

> In the intervening period between returning from Sikkim and leaving for Kongpo, she bestowed the gift of the holy doctrine throughout the four regions of Ütsang, Ngari, Lhomon, and Lhodrak. She also went to the three regions of Dakpo, and Upper and Lower Kham, as well as Uru and Yoru. In all these places, the hopes of many faithful men and women were gloriously and completely fulfilled.[84]

This focus on Mingyur Peldrön's teaching activities is a focal point throughout *Dispeller*. There are many accounts throughout the work that echo this one, with overjoyed people to whom her teachings finally brought hope after years of unrest.[85] In *Dispeller* Gyurmé Ösel claims that Mingyur Peldrön taught thousands of people, ranging from monastics and ardent religious practitioners to the general population of laypeople. While the numbers and accounts of miraculous realization are almost certainly a case of devotional hyperbole, it is generally accepted that Mingyur Peldrön followed the inclusive ideology of her father and uncle and offered mass empowerments and made teachings accessible to the general public. Here Gyurmé Ösel is asserting that she had a significant impact on the central Tibetan religious community at large, or at least those who were interested in learning from Nyingmapa teachers. With each year of her adulthood, the story reports where she traveled in Ü, Tsang, and Kham to give teachings and where and when she exchanged teachings with other Nyingmapa leaders. According to Gyurmé Ösel, she met grateful faithful people wherever she went and acted with humor and some fierce compassion in her relationships with her students and tended to argue for the monastic path over others.

As an active teacher with a significant following, Mingyur Peldrön continued the previous generation's project of developing the Mindröling name and spreading the teachings widely. She exchanged teachings with other religious educators as well and had a tumultuous relationship with some of them, including the Fifth Lelung, Jedrung Rinpoche. Throughout all of these engagements she negotiated the shifting atmosphere of the eighteenth-century Nyingma community and that of central Tibet more broadly. She also wrote several works in her adulthood, including Dzogchen instruction manuals, prayers, and a collection of advice in response to questions posed by her disciples.

Mingyur Peldrön was a prolific author whose works were used by her religious community (and related Nyingma institutions) both during and after her lifetime. Her authorial reach was broad both in the material she produced and in the variety of communities in which her work was transmitted. She composed her first instruction manual at age fourteen and continued to write until the year of her death.[86] She wrote eighteen pieces in all, which varied in genre and focus. While centered largely around Mindröling's Dzogchen tradition and her father's terma, they also addressed the monastery's kama tradition. Two-thirds of her corpus are directly related to Terdak Lingpa's treasure revelations and include related prayers, practical advice for how to engage the rituals therein, and guidance for proper meditative praxis. The majority of her works offer some kind of instruction along these lines.

Among her written works is an eighty-page instruction manual for how to properly perform the *sādhanas* (meditative and ritual practices) that are part of the kama text called the *Churner of the Depths of Hell*.[87] The Churner of the Depths of Hell is a Vajrasattva ritual that was taught by Lochen Dharmaśrī and would eventually come to be practiced elsewhere, most prominently at Katok Monastery in Kham.[88] Mingyur Peldrön's commentary describes which implements should be used in the ritual and how the sādhanas should be performed as well as what both master and disciple should be doing throughout the practice. Other instruction manuals give similar guidance on rituals and praxis for Highest Yoga Tantra (Atiyoga) practices of the Great Perfection. In this case they also correspond to Terdak Lingpa's own treasure texts. These works focused on instruction and were intended for anyone who had received the proper empowerments and initiation to participate in the practices. Some of her writing was directed at an elite group of religious practitioners who had received the proper teachings and initiations to engage in advanced Atiyoga praxis.

Mingyur Peldrön also cultivated relationships with prominent political and religious leaders in Lhasa throughout her adulthood. She ultimately molded her approach to institutional development at Mindröling to accord with the Geluk mores of the time. Her relationships with Polhané and to a lesser extent the Seventh Dalai Lama will be of particular interest for understanding her relationship with the Geluk religiopolitical establishment during her lifetime, particularly in the post–civil war era. Her relationship with Polhané is emphasized in *Dispeller* and exemplifies both her position at Mindröling as well as the long-standing relationship between Mindröling and the Ganden Podrang, to say nothing of her individual political savvy.

The details of her adulthood, including her teaching exchanges and methods and her relationships with her students are attended to with more depth in later chapters. Of particular interest are her apparent disapproval of the non-monastic communities of her day, which were conveyed through accounts of her visits to wayward groups; her admonitions against improper behavior; and her recommendations that practitioners strive to become monastics. In spite of a few bouts with bad health in her early adulthood, Mingyur Peldrön lived to the age of seventy. According to her hagiography, she taught right up until the time of her death in 1769. After her long teaching career, she died a recognized leader of Mindröling. Her death, which will be discussed at length in chapter 5, was as imbued with signs and portents as her birth had been, including miraculous apparitions, spontaneous rainbows, and unusual celestial phenomena.

The narrative arc of Mingyur Peldrön's story establishes the basic significant moments of her life and reveals her positionality with regard to her family, her religious community, and the social and political world into which she was born. Both privilege and lack of privilege influenced key moments of her lived experience, springing from the conditions of her birth into an influential family actively committed to her success as a lineage holder and religious educator. By being born into an elite family, she benefited from a high level of class status. As that family was also at the center of a community of religious elites, merely carrying the family name and lineage (*düngyü*) would open doors. Moreover, her actual religious training meant an even higher level of privilege: she received of a corpus of doctrinal knowledge that she was empowered to pass on where and how she saw fit. By carrying the initiations and education of Mindröling, Mingyur Peldrön attracted support from those who might not have otherwise acknowledged her extensive agency. Her relationship with the Sikkimese royal family and her special dispensation to bestow teachings on the monks of Pemayangtsé after her arrival in Sikkim are great examples, especially when compared with her sister Lady Peldzin's plight of being sent by Mingyur Peldrön into an unhappy marriage ostensibly for the sake of maintaining good relations between two families.

Access to privilege was varied among the children of her generation, though. For example, Mingyur Peldrön's position as a girl in her family likely led to a reduced education (especially when compared with her brother Rinchen Namgyel's training). She missed the opportunity that he had had for formal *rikné* scholastic training, for which Mindröling was so well known. Nevertheless, she was able to pursue the life of a celibate woman with full support from her family, an occurrence that speaks volumes to the level of combined privilege that she enjoyed, even in comparison with that of her sisters. The hagiographic tone of *Dispeller* makes it difficult to draw conclusions, but it seems that in many contexts Mingyur Peldrön's brilliance and ability overshadowed her gender in the eyes of her teachers so that she was allowed and encouraged to pursue a celibate religious life. This meant that she had a larger modicum of freedom, especially when compared with Lady Peldzin, who was compelled to marry for the benefit of the family.

For Mingyur Peldrön privilege meant access to education and to high-level political figures as well as birth in a family that for whatever reason was not preoccupied with whether or not she should or would secure an appropriate marriage. She received an unusually extensive religious training in the sense that her father, uncle, and elder brothers passed teachings on to her at an early age. Yet we have little evidence that this level of education was extended to other girls and young women in the family. While her sister Lady Peldzin may have had some religious education, it is not described in any great detail in the histories or namtars of Mindröling. Therefore, it is clear that access was not solely determined based upon birth into the family; there were likely other factors at play. It is possible that personal affect—including charisma, aptitude, and interest in religious study—also influenced who was allowed to take up the role of religious practitioner. Even with the uneven distribution of education in her generation, Mingyur

Peldrön's birth into the family, combined with other factors, clearly paved the way for her education. In turn, this education empowered her with the authority and the means to pass Mindröling teachings along to the next generation of practitioners, acting as a conduit for family tradition. Both the knowledge encompassed in this education and the authorization to act as a religious educator herself were the foundation of a privileged beginning. This made it significantly more likely for Mingyur Peldrön to become a publicly recognized Nyingma representative and a powerful religious practitioner in her adulthood. She was able to build on her privilege to cultivate relationships with Tibetan and Sikkimese political and religious leaders as well as her many disciples. The shifting institutional landscape had a powerful effect on Mingyur Peldrön's experience as a member of a Nyingma family, in that it first put her in grave danger and later acted as a resource for her to develop her role as an influential nun in a largely male-dominated world.

Beginning with her position as a foreign guest and spiritual advisor of the Sikkimese royal family, Mingyur Peldrön cultivated teaching relationships with several elite families in Tibetan society. In many cases these relationships were mutually beneficial. Her adulthood was defined by such relationships as well as by her role as a representative of Mindröling who engaged in dialogue with a variety of political and religious leaders. The markers of privilege that Mingyur Peldrön received as an educated member of the monastery and the daughter of a famous treasure revealer made it possible for her to navigate the challenging historical moment for political and institutional benefit, both for herself and for Mindröling. It also made it easier for her to survive the regional political contestation of the period, and the attendant sectarian and intra-sectarian divisions, while pursuing a soteriological path that she apparently wanted to tread.

Mingyur Peldrön's high privilege allowed her to negotiate a path in spite of—and in some cases because of—the great adversity that she met beyond the walls of Mindröling. She was able to leverage her privilege to rise to a position of authority. The following chapters will continue to explore the question of her gendered positionality and how that influenced the arc of her life story. For her, privilege and gender acted as the foundation that both supported and impeded her progress as a religious practitioner and teacher in a complex web of potent social indicators. Privilege led to her access to authoritative positions, even as her association with Mindröling sometimes resulted in persecution. Her gender contributed to her broad amalgamation of markers of privilege and non-privilege, adding a complexity to her status in a way that was highly context dependent. Her gender was not such a detractor as to keep her from pursuing her spiritual goals or rising in institutional leadership, nor was it necessarily always a negative attribute. Her status as a woman is made more complex in Gyurmé Ösel's representations of her when he seems to elevate her through expressions of positive femininity in a hagiography that we might understand as the creation of her public identity supported by a complex use of the themes of privilege, gender, and authority.

CHAPTER TWO

Authorizing the Saint

> The desired boy was not brought to the Terton's Dargyé Chöding lineage. This unwanted girl was brought instead. Now she will sustain it. The treasury will not be forgotten.
> —LOCHEN DHARMAŚRĪ

> I respectfully bow at the feet of the infallible supreme bliss queen of the ḍākinīs, the essence of refuge for all.
> —GYURMÉ ÖSEL

GYURMÉ Ösel worked within the confines of the namtar genre to establish his argument for Mingyur Peldrön's greatness, engaging the intersectional nature of authority and gender to further his argument. In composing *Dispeller*, he drew on the methods found in most men's namtar, but at turns he also included and elided feminine language and references to Mingyur Peldrön's status as a woman, engaging or erasing her gender in different moments to skillfully present her as authoritative. Her gender status is a continuing site of complexity throughout her hagiography. There are ways in which it seems to have affected her religious positionality and moments in which the importance of gender is superseded by other factors. The treatment of her status as a woman also connects with and diverges from how gender is treated in other Tibetan women's *Lives*.

A frequent theme in Tibetan women's life writing is that being born a woman is less desirable than being born a man. Gendered hardship and its karmic implications have been frequent narrative foci for women practitioners, and this theme revolves around the concept of the "lesser female birth."[1] Generally presented as the karmic result of previous negative actions and a (sometimes contested) hindrance to enlightenment, the topic has also been used more specifically in auto/biographical life writing as an outlet for engaging "self-humbling strategies" that position the author as speaking from a position of humility.² In both hagiographic and auto/biographical subsets of *Life* writing, women are depicted as facing additional trials and tribulations in their lived experience. This is coupled with the implication that life as a woman is an undesirable samsaric state that is a direct result of one's karmic conditioning, which has been generally treated as a foregone conclusion in Buddhist traditions for centuries and across diverse geographic regions. Some women worked to actively reframe their status as embodied women from a negative to a positive, which is reflected in Gyurmé Ösel's approach to Mingyur Peldrön's status as a woman.³

In *Dispeller* the idea of gender becomes more complex as themes of womanhood and femaleness are sometimes elevated and presented as beneficial for religious practitioners and then disparaged in other moments. A multivalent approach to understanding the role of gender in this text is helpful, as considering gender alongside a host of other factors reflects the literary representations of gender as well as the social context in which Mingyur Peldrön lived. These factors were employed in the process of asserting her position as authoritative and relaying that in *Dispeller*. As rhetorical moves, they were directed by the social dynamics at play in any given moment, and the ways that these dynamics influence perceptions of her privilege and authority are highly context dependent.⁴ In different moments her access to authority might be impacted by her gender identity, perceived connections with deities (most importantly, Yeshé Tsogyel), religious institutional affiliation and educational training, wealth, personal relationships with political leaders, and relationships within her family, all of which were used at different points as means for asserting individual authority.

Rather than adhering strictly to the trope of the lesser female birth, Mingyur Peldrön's status as a woman is treated with complexity throughout *Dispeller*, as elevating and positive gendered language is juxtaposed with Mingyur Peldrön's own apparent self-humbling references and expressions of desire to be born a man in the future as well as occasional negative statements uttered by those around her.⁵ If we take a multivalent approach to Mingyur Peldrön's *Life* and depictions of her gender, these rhetorical moves make more sense. Studying the variable dynamics between gender and authority and the ways these dynamics affect social positioning can help us understand her hagiographic presentation (and potentially her lived experience) more clearly. She was able to leverage various aspects of her privilege to support the women who studied and became nuns under her guidance and to act as a leader at a time when institutional leadership from women was unusual. Meanwhile, on at least a few occasions she referred to herself as being of lesser female birth, pointing to the normative gendered representations that would be expected in a namtar and likely reflected broader assumptions about her approach to gender and religious status. For the women of Mindröling, the challenges of being born a woman were often mitigated by other forms of privilege. For example, her sisters were harassed and nearly assaulted by Dzungar army men as the result of being women affiliated with a Nyingma institution. However, Mingyur Peldrön and her sisters and mother were able to draw upon their personal and institutional connections in order to escape that same army. In their moment of escape, their association with a Nyingma monastery meant both their being targeted for attack and also the potential for making connections with the people who would help them escape that violence. Likewise, while one daughter became a religious teacher in exile, the other became the wife of a king, and it is possible there was a discrepancy between the autonomy present in each daughter's path. Therefore, while gender is an active construct in *Dispeller*, it cannot be read in isolation from other aspects of Mingyur Peldrön's identity and must be understood in relation to privilege.

"Authorizing referents"—or the terminology used to elevate historical figures—are evident in depictions of Mingyur Peldrön's position and in Tibetan hagiography more broadly.[6] In hagiography, authorizing referents serve to remind the reader about what legitimates the main subject. They work by helping the audience recall or recognize personal connections between the subject and other people, moments, or institutions that support their authority in one way or another. For example, by likening a woman to a well-known buddha, the woman is able to take on a bit of that buddha's personality. When a reader is reminded of the main character's brilliant education, they hold in their mind that character's intellectual legitimacy and perhaps their institutional connections. Likewise, other modes of authorization can imbue literary and historical figures with cultural cachet as they evoke shared personality traits. These referents take many forms in *Dispeller*, from the discussions of Mingyur Peldrön's connection with important deities to the very organization of the text itself.

The format of *Dispeller*—its very structure and layout—is informative for understanding the ways that Gyurmé Ösel argued for the significance of his master. The text follows an organizational pattern that will be familiar to scholars of the more hagiographic forms of namtar. It begins with an invocation to primordial deities and buddhas who were most closely associated with the Nyingma tradition, before turning to a description of Mingyur Peldrön's previous emanations. Only then does the narrative begin to discuss her life *as* Mingyur Peldrön. Each section details what Gyurmé Ösel considered to be significant aspects of or moments in her life, from birth to death, with an emphasis on the factors that would authorize her as a Mindröling teacher, including her education and family connections. The narrative of her youth is presented in the format of lists of teachings (senyik) and the names of those who bestowed them, while her adulthood is depicted in anecdotal prose narrative. It includes supporting citations sprinkled throughout that come from tantras and other religious texts. Gyurmé Ösel uses them to support his argument by emphasizing the prophetic nature of her existence. Finally, the narrative ends with a lengthy discussion of Mingyur Peldrön's death, funerary rites, and a colophon discussing his creation of the namtar. Most of the text is in prose, with Mingyur Peldrön's own verse and occasional quoted verses from sacred texts emerging at particularly important moments. Another notable component of the hagiography is the literary device of quoting Mingyur Peldrön, her father, uncle, and others from her life. While we cannot be certain about their veracity, Gyurmé Ösel attributes these quotations to historical figures as a means of reiterating his points or to fill in details of the events he is discussing.

Part of what makes namtar texts so dynamic is that they can convey important information about a wide range of literary and social meanings. The religious and cultural references they employ and the events that are featured can give the modern reader hints about what the author found to be important as well as the author's assumptions about the general knowledge of his or her readership. We know almost nothing about Gyurmé Ösel beyond what is found in *Dispeller*, in which he presents himself in a self-deprecating light as a struggling student of the Great Perfection who benefited from Mingyur Peldrön's profound compassion, in spite of his shortcomings. His reasons for writing *Dispeller*, and the subjects that are his focus in the text, echo the usual reasons for writing a namtar. Generally speaking, the literary purposes of namtar were threefold: to authorize the saint *as* a saint, to serve as an exemplary narrative that could guide practitioners, and to offer biographical descriptions of important figures. Gyurmé Ösel adheres to this formula closely, including narratives of the hardships his subject overcame, inspirational quotations he attributes to her, and signs of her important social status and enlightened nature. *Dispeller* served as a place for him to memorialize his beloved teacher, a feat he accomplished by first elevating her in accordance with the strictures of the namtar genre and then recounting her activities in service of the tradition. According to him, Mingyur Peldrön was a highly respected and authoritative figure at Mindröling, but this does not necessarily mean that her lived experience reflects the elevated existence that he claims for her. This is a hagiography, after all, and modern readers might take his exhortation with a grain of salt.

Modes of Authority

Understanding how Gyurmé Ösel constructed a public identity for Mingyur Peldrön is made easier by analyzing the several systems of authority that are also relevant for other namtar, as they mirror common themes found across the genre. They are defined here as emanation authority, institutional authority, and educational authority. This tripartite delineation of authoritative types draws on Max Weber's division of a somewhat similar set of "pure types" of authority, which are organized and differentiated in order to more easily indicate the specific societal structures and concerns that are engaged when each one comes into play in a social system. The division into different authoritative types will be useful here, but it is important to understand that more than one type will almost always be simultaneously active in any given situation. While authority is presented in three discreet ways in *Dispeller*, these types often work simultaneously to lend authority to Mingyur Peldrön. Each one authorizes her in ways that would have been legible in the eighteenth-century context in which Gyurmé Ösel was writing. Briefly, emanation authority is derived from someone's identification as the emanation or incarnation of a deity, buddha, or bodhisattva. Likewise, institutional authority affirms an individual's connection with reputable religious institutions. Finally, educational authority is that which is gleaned from training as a religious practitioner and teacher.

These forms of legitimation are common throughout Tibetan hagiographies, and many *Lives* draw on the same socially reinforced modes of authentication. The fact that Mingyur Peldrön's hagiographer engages in this form of argumentation is not unique. Rather, her *Life* serves as an example of some frequent rhetorical moves that hagiographers employed in the process of legitimation. More specifically, Gyurmé Ösel's use of these modes of authentication exemplify one way these methods could be implemented for the sake of women's legitimacy. Notably, he emphasizes her position as a woman throughout. This suggests that her privilege in other arenas was significant enough that her status as a woman could be represented as negative, positive, or neutral, without fully undermining her authority. Ultimately, this gave her hagiographer the flexibility to present gender at turns as both negative and positive and to speak directly to in its impact on her positionality generally as well as in specific moments. Her status is often related by repeatedly finding ways to connect her to her home institution and reminding the reader of her position as a highly educated woman. Gyurmé Ösel frequently applies gendered language at key moments in the narrative and gives us a sense of how Mingyur Peldrön was situated in her community. In using these prompts, he reinforces the types of religious authority that were present in his lifetime. It is illuminating to examine these types of authority in the sequence in which they appear in *Dispeller*, so as to convey the relative literary emphasis placed upon each form (although after their introduction, they appear throughout *Dispeller* both in concert and individually). Each pertains to Mingyur Peldrön's specific context and also is used by Gyurmé Ösel to express her identity and her social and religious positioning.

Emanation Authority

The first type of authority attributed to Mingyur Peldrön in *Dispeller* is that which comes from being recognized as the emanation of enlightened beings.[7] According to Buddhist tradition, a buddha or bodhisattva—no longer fettered by the bonds of karmic accumulation—can direct one's own rebirth in order to help mundane beings escape suffering and attain enlightenment. Thus, a person might be identified as the incarnation of an enlightened being on Earth and therefore be considered to be imbued with the wisdom, compassion, and potential for engagement with others that befit an awakened one. It is common for Tibetan namtar to begin with a discussion of the subject's previous lives, evoking both their enlightened status and their subsequent ability to emanate wherever they are most needed. This also positions them within a tradition of mythically and historically important personages as a means to contemporary legitimation.[8]

Gyurmé Ösel follows this traditional narrative arc by beginning Mingyur Peldrön's *Life* with descriptions of her previous incarnations. This section starts directly after the opening invocation and occupies approximately 10 percent of the total namtar. As in all namtars, this connection with important Buddhist figures of the past always acts as a mode of legitimation. But for the few women for whom we have namtars, it serves the dual purpose of giving them female-sourced authentication in a male-dominant environment. That is, by engaging the common namtar trope of previous lives but focusing solely on previous female lives, Gyurmé Ösel presents the reader with an all-woman version of a *Life* that offers a woman-centered focus on the literary conventions that are most often used in recounting the lives of men. Gendered identity is centered in this section of *Dispeller* in a way that is wholly positive. By connecting the historical woman Mingyur Peldrön with eminent female figures of the past (ranging from buddhas to semihistorical Tibetan figures), emanation authority also reinforces the idea of positive models for women's religious development. Gyurmé Ösel was not the first (or the last) author to do this with a focus on a woman as his literary subject. The importance of past lives in establishing a woman's authority is well documented in English-language Tibetan scholarship. For example, in the *Life* of Sönam Peldren, previous female lives acted as authorizing referents to offer legitimated feminine imagery to support a woman's religious identity.[9] Likewise, in the few cases of highly privileged women who also have namtars, such as that of Tāre Lhamo, a woman's connection with past female figures is first asserted and reiterated by the men who dominate the world in which she was born.[10] Echoing Tāre Lhamo's case, Gyurmé Ösel acted as a male voice asserting Mingyur Peldrön's legitimacy by connecting her to a long string of previous female incarnations.

Frequently in Tibetan Buddhist communities, important people are associated with the illustrious figures of the community's past through the institution of rebirth, that is, the *tulku* lineage system. Or they might be identified as the emanation of an enlightened deity (a buddha or bodhisattva) or a semihistorical figure. Tibetan studies scholar Hildegard Diemberger points to the important difference between incarnation as a buddha/bodhisattva and rebirth as a mundane human, fettered by the chains of samsara: "The former refers to the manifestation of a spiritual entity in a human being, whereas the latter implies the transmission of a principle of consciousness from one human being to another. The two are normally interlinked in the Tibetan context, as the reincarnating beings carry with them their divine attributes as emanations of the deity."[11] Mingyur Peldrön's previous lives include a mix of references to buddhas and bodhisattvas, well-known historical figures,[12] and legendary heroines. All in all, she is identified as ten different female figures.

MINGYUR PELDRÖN'S PREVIOUS LIVES

Mingyur Peldrön's previous lives	Name as it appears in *Dispeller*
Samantabhadrī	kun tu bzang mo
Tārā	Ar+ya ta re, sgrol ma
Yeshé Tsogyel	ye shes mtsho rgyal (and variations)
Machik Labdrön	ma gcig lab sgron
Nangsa Öbum	snang gsal 'od di 'bum
Gelongma Palmo	dge slong dpal mo [sic]
Machik Jomo	ma gcig jo mo
Machik Zurmo	ma gcig zur mo
Zukyi Nyima	bram ze ma gzugs kyi nyi ma
Sukhasiddhi	su kha si d+hi

Emanation authority bears a strong resemblance to Weber's routinized "charismatic authority," especially in the sense that prophecy and revelation are used to establish the divinity of the individual, after which the subject may come to be recognized as being imbued with the idealized personality of the deity.[13] The significance of this type of authority is borne out in its presence in most extant namtars, with the main subject always identified as the emanation or incarnation of at least one (if not more) figures. This is the case for women's *Lives* as well as those of men, and the pattern recurs even in namtar that are more or less hagiographic in nature. For example, like in Mingyur Peldrön's *Life*, Sera Khandro's auto/biography engages the frame narrative of her status as a reincarnation of Yeshé Tsogyel. In Sera Khandro's case this worked to authorize her presence in a community in which she lacked roots. It supported her claim to authority in a community in which she might not have what Sarah Jacoby describes as the "biological pedigree from her present lifetime to reinforce her identity as a Treasure revealer" but one in which she could claim that "she was none other than Yeshé Tsogyel incarnate."[14] For Mingyur Peldrön her associations with ten different female figures (foremost among them Yeshé Tsogyel) would connect her with a longer institutional history that included widely known popular deities who were more universally recognized and who were respected beyond Mindröling. Reflecting the privilege she enjoyed by being born into a religious family, several of these lineages were ascribed shortly after her birth. Others were applied later, by herself and others. Her association with all of these lineages would ultimately support her social prestige in a way that meant she could be connected with her immediate familial and institutional history as well as with more broadly recognizable religious individuals and their respective soteriological systems.

What is most notable about the section of *Dispeller* dedicated to past lives is the large number of incarnations with which Gyurmé Ösel identifies Mingyur Peldrön. In listing ten important female deities and people, he draws on nearly every female deity or folk heroine available in the Tibetan Buddhist literature of the time. They range from the primordial buddha Samantabhadrī to the somewhat lesser-known Machiks (Jomo and Zurmo) and include figures both native to Tibet and also those who arrived with Buddhism. Some of those mentioned are historical figures, while some are heroines of the mythic Buddhist past. Regardless, all of them would have been familiar to a mid- to late-eighteenth-century readership (that is, Gyurmé Ösel's audience). In considering the past life narrative as a frequently employed method for transmitting important cultural information, it draws social and religious connections that were considered important in different contexts. For example, Sönam Paldren was identified as the "Great Mother," Vajrayogini, and Dorje Pakmo.[15] Chökyi Drönma was likewise identified as Dorje Pakmo, Sera Khandro as Yeshé Tsogyel.[16] In fact, Orgyan Chökyi's *Life* is unusual in that she does not "evoke lineage as a source of authority," even though "she does employ the past to give meaning to her present tale" by relating her narrative to those of Machik Labdrön, Gelongma Palmo, Nangsa Öbum, and Lingza Chokyi.[17] Each of the past figures would have conveyed a certain collection of information based upon their particular personalities, trials and successes, and so forth.

These women's *Lives* engage well-known female figures as incarnates or at the very least as inspirational stories to relate to their own narrative arcs. That said, Tāre Lhamo's namtar—*Spiraling Vine of Faith*—is the most similar to Mingyur Peldrön's for its emphasis on previous lives. Tāre Lhamo is identified as the reincarnation of six female figures, and the story of her previous lives takes up fully half of her namtar. In comparison with the other women mentioned here, her *Life* compares most closely with Mingyur Peldrön's. While *Dispeller* lists more incarnations for Mingyur Peldrön (ten) than Tāre Lhamo's (six), these sections both take up substantial quantities of the text (in the case of Tāre Lhamo's, a full 50 percent, while Mingyur Peldrön's occupies much less but is still notable at 10 percent) and are used to convey the significance of these women through their connection to incarnate authority.[18] There is even overlap between the two women's incarnations. They are both identified as Samantabhadrī, Tārā, and Yeshé Tsogyel. Interestingly, these are also both women for whom we have evidence of birth into religiously privileged families that actively supported their goals. Both were the daughters of famous treasure revealers, and it is possible that their family privilege can be linked with the extensive use of incarnate authority. There was more opportunity for early connections to be drawn with the mytho-historical narratives held in these communities and more opportunity to create community-wide buy-in to recognize their status as incarnations.

Throughout the narrative of Mingyur Peldrön's *Life*, Gyurmé Ösel frequently mentions these past incarnations. His references to them in pivotal moments remind the reader of Mingyur Peldrön's significance, acting as the foundation for her legitimacy. Just as the lengthy section on previous lives imbued Tāre Lhamo with certain attributes through suggestion and connection in *Spiraling Vine of Faith*, Gyurmé Ösel employs the emanation model at first in *Dispeller's* section outlining previous lives and then refers back to particular incarnations throughout *Dispeller* to associate Mingyur Peldrön's actions with the attributes that he claimed she shared with these deities and heroines of the past. By drawing on the specific attributes of each emanation, he uses the personalities of each one to support Mingyur Peldrön's authority in dynamic ways.

The list of Mingyur Peldrön's previous lives and emanations begins with the bodhisattva Samantabhadrī, a female deity who was often paired with her male counterpart Samantabhadra to form the primordial consort couple considered to be the co-progenitors of the Great Perfection teachings and the Nyingma school.[19] At the beginning of *Dispeller*, Gyurmé Ösel writes:

> From the natural state of ultimate pure bliss, the natural state of all phenomena in *saṃsāra* and *nirvāṇa*, profound and peaceful and free from all construction, which is suchness itself, arose the glorious Lord Samantabhadra in the form of the spontaneous wisdom body; she [that is, Mingyur Peldron] appeared as his self-manifested consort, Space Mistress Samantabhadrī, and she requested [him] to create the various greater and lesser vehicles of the dharma, and in particular the essence of the marvelous teaching of the secret instructions of The Great Perfection.[20]

As one and the same with Samantabhadrī, Mingyur Peldrön becomes identified with the co-progenitor of the Great Perfection and in this way is made integral to the creation and dissemination of all instructions associated with it. Starting this section with the focal point of the Great Perfection is unsurprising, given Mingyur Peldrön's relationship to these teachings at Mindröling. As mentioned previously, the Great Perfection was central to the establishment of Mindröling, and Mingyur Peldrön was one of two recipients of the entire corpus who survived the civil war to pass them on. Here her authenticity as a Great Perfection teacher does not come from her own religious education or her affiliation with the monastery but, rather, from her identification with Samantabhadrī, who, according to this telling, actually initiated the study and practice of the Great Perfection by requesting that Samantabhadra bestow the teachings. With this opening Gyurmé Ösel establishes Mingyur Peldrön with primordial female authority before moving on to discuss other pre-lives. The rarified form of female divinity found in Samantabhadrī is most starkly contrasted with her identification as a reincarnation of Nangsa Öbum.

In our second example of emanation authority, Mingyur Peldrön is depicted as the fifteenth-century folk heroine and *delok* Nangsa Öbum.[21] Deloks are people who are believed to have died, traveled to hells, and then come back to life. After reviving, deloks generally have ethical lessons to share with their communities, which are supported by accounts of their experiences in the hells.[22] The socioreligious influences of people who become identified as deloks is related to their social positionality within their communities.[23] In particular, the hardship and subsequent recognition of otherworldly power that attends the shift to identification as a delok supports a parallel shift in social agency. The ability to gain social authority and to wield it based on one's delok identity has additional potential for the social mobility of women.[24]

Living as a delok has been a notably accessible way for women who have little authority to gain power and recognition within their immediate community. While both men and women have become deloks, the potential for it to shift one's agency is arguably most pronounced for women. Convincing revenants are able to become identified as authoritative religious voices through their discussions of what they learned on their journey into and back from the realms of the dead. This of course depends entirely upon the community's response to the narrative of what the delok saw while he or she was dead. Nangsa Öbum is an example of a woman of little privilege who became known as a religious specialist solely based on her transition from a mortal woman to a convincing delok. Other women in Tibetan history (such as Orgyan Chökyi) have also been likened to Nangsa Öbum.²⁵ In most ways Nangsa Öbum has little in common with Mingyur Peldrön's privileged narrative. Instead, she was a woman who suffered abuse at the hands of her in-laws, epitomizing the narrative of the oppressed woman who manages to escape the householder's life only in death. Her return from death imbued her with power in her community, making it possible for her to pursue religious practice and avoid further torment from her family.

While the stories of the two women's lives are quite different, there is one moment in *Dispeller* in which Gyurmé Ösel has occasion to argue for Mingyur Peldrön's previous existence as Nangsa Öbum, drawing on the delok's struggles in order to position Mingyur Peldrön's triumphs over suffering and hardship. He likens his teacher's return from exile in Sikkim and her efforts at post–civil war reconstruction to Nangsa Öbum's death and subsequent rejuvenation. Mingyur Peldrön had waited out the war in Sikkim accompanied by her mother, sisters, and a small entourage, until they were able to safely return home around 1721. Gyurmé Ösel describes the moment when they are joyfully traipsing over the last mountain pass and stop for their first view of home:

> What had formerly been a place equal to the delightful pleasure groves of the gods had (with the exception of the Sangnak Podrang) been ruined. The residences, the *stūpas*, the walls, everything [had been destroyed]. The empty buildings sat like corpses. Remembering the former wealth and prosperity of her father and uncle, she was tormented by woeful suffering. She said that because of that, a flash of memory arose of her suffering in her previous life as Nangsa Öbum.²⁶

This initial view of the destroyed monastery—the embodiment of her family legacy and her natal home—fills her with extreme sorrow. In this moment of mourning she suddenly remembers her previous life as Nangsa Öbum. Her suffering of lost home and extended exile is likened to the treacherous odyssey that constitute the delok's narrative of death and return. Here Gyurmé Ösel is able to name Mingyur Peldrön's trauma in such a way that it is contextualized within female divinity and authority. Her experience of exile and loss link her to a well-known Tibetan woman whose experience of suffering acted like a fire in which her authority was forged. According to *Dispeller*, her memory of this past life is what gives her the strength to go on.

After her realization and subsequent visions, she is newly resolved to get to work rebuilding Mindröling.

The connection with Nangsa Öbum makes Mingyur Peldrön accessible and human. It reminds readers of a famous figure's trauma and, in linking the two women, gives readers a familiar literary context upon which to hang their understanding. Her sorrow at seeing her home destroyed changes the otherwise privileged young woman into one who experiences the suffering of mundane loss just like all other people. There are several moments like this throughout *Dispeller* in which Mingyur Peldrön's suffering is made legible to the reader. But in this moment she is relieved of that suffering by her supernatural ability to remember past lives. Here the reader is presented with her suffering as contextualized within her divinity without detracting from her sainthood. By connecting her with the female delok, Mingyur Peldrön's fallible humanity is also articulated, and her struggles become a source of legitimation. Although her *Life* is for the most part completely different from Nangsa Öbum's, the two figures become unified in this scene in which the author points to a woman whose narrative of hellish experience authenticates her role as a newly emerging religious leader. Reminding the reader of the familiar tale of Nangsa Öbum, the story of exile in Sikkim becomes more potent.

Equating Mingyur Peldrön's traumatic exile with Nangsa Öbum's journey to hell suggests that Mingyur Peldrön's time in Sikkim imbued her with a similar authority. In emphasizing her experience of pain and suffering, Mingyur Peldrön's own privileged status is elided. Here she becomes authenticated through an emphasis on hard-won experience forged through hardship and the realization of suffering. Gyurmé Ösel draws on Nangsa Öbum's charisma-driven legitimacy to argue for Mingyur Peldrön's ability to recover from the trauma of escape and exile in order to revive Mindröling. In this moment in the text there is no mention of the support that Mingyur Peldrön would receive from well-wishers during the monastery's reconstruction. Nor are her years of training in the Mindröling teachings or her support from the Sikkimese royal family and the religious community discussed at this point. Of course, in reality, training and external support would both help her preserve and then revive the Mindröling name. But here the focus is on the dangers she and her community faced during the civil war and the experience she gleaned from it. Also, it is important to note that even at this low point in her lived experience, the author does not lament her female birth nor cite it as the reason for her suffering. The authoritative woman here gained power through her deathlike experience and in doing so strengthened her role as an asset to the community. Beyond the case of Nangsa Öbum, the hardships Mingyur Peldrön faces throughout the *Life* are not otherwise connected with her past emanations. Rather, her connection to female emanations is generally presented as a source of positive authentication, while moments of suffering are connected with the mundane world in which she lived.

Mingyur Peldrön's past lives associate her experiences with those of strong female figures, impressing upon the reader that her status as a woman is synonymous with supramundane power. The case of Yeshé Tsogyel is the most abiding example. Throughout *Dispeller* the semihistorical, semimythical apotheosized figure is mentioned more than any of Mingyur Peldrön's other incarnations. As in the auto/biography of Sera Khandro, the story of Yeshé Tsogyel creates the frame narrative for the rest of Mingyur Peldrön's *Life* by being presented at the beginning and end of the text and at key moments throughout. Yeshé Tsogyel is arguably the best-known female religious practitioner in Tibetan literary and oral tradition. She is most easily recognized as the consort of Padmasambhava (also known as Guru Rinpoche) and is mentioned in the tales of him concealing Buddhist treasure texts, to be revealed in a future time when the world is ready to receive and study them. Additionally, she was a teacher in her own right and had her own solitary practice for at least part of her career. She has come to be recognized as a Buddhist heroine associated with the treasure revelation tradition that cropped up during the Renaissance period (in Tibet the eleventh through fourteenth centuries CE), as a protector of the teachings, and as a manifestation of divine femininity who helped practitioners along the dharma path. Meditation caves throughout the Buddhist Himalaya bear her name; these pilgrimage sites are often marked with imprints of her hands and feet, ostensibly left in rock as a sign of her spiritual accomplishment and power. Her role as Padmasambhava's consort is generally accepted as a core component of her personality, connecting her as it does to non-celibate practice and her association with the predominantly Nyingma tradition of treasure revelation. Padmasambhava and Yeshé Tsogyel are foundational for Nyingma historical identity, and this is reflected in Yeshé Tsogyel's depiction in *Dispeller*. It is noteworthy that she is presented differently in *Dispeller* than in most other women's *Lives*, and these differences are informative in what they tell us about the significance of previous life depictions and how these narratives support the personalities of the women whose namtars are being told.

Yeshé Tsogyel is referenced frequently in women's *Lives*, sometimes as a previous incarnation, as a model of inspiration for the main subject, or some combination thereof. As with other deities or heroines, her presence establishes the main figure as an authoritative and iconic teacher of the tradition, worthy of the same reverence as Yeshé Tsogyel herself.[27] Given her connection to the Nyingma school and the treasure tradition in particular, her presence is especially authorizing for women who were connected to these communities. As with Mingyur Peldrön, Yeshé Tsogyel features in the frame narrative of Sera Khandro's auto/biography; Sera Khandro self-identified as Yeshé Tsogyel and was later recognized as an incarnation of her.[28] Yeshé Tsogyel is also listed as one of Tāre Lhamo's six previous incarnations and plays a key role in authorizing her and Namtrul Rinpoche as treasure co-revealers and practitioners.[29] For both of these women, identification as this famous figure had grounding and authorizing effects for their *Lives* and their public identities. Interestingly, Yeshé Tsogyel's depiction in these other namtars has very different content from her representation in *Dispeller*.

In other women's life stories, the narratives of Yeshé Tsogyel describe her as a female consort of Padmasambhava and as a woman who later took a man as her own consort. Her specific identification as a woman who engaged in consort relationships is central to both Sera Khandro and Tāre Lhamo's narratives, as both women were Nyingma practitioners who engaged in consort relationships as part of their role as treasure revealers.[30] While not strictly necessary, the consort relationship was considered to be beneficial in helping treasure revealers recover hidden treasure texts.[31] The hermeneutical goals of treasure revelation were helped along by a consort who could help a treasure revealer in the process of locating and discovering a text.[32] Sera Khandro became renowned in her lifetime as a legitimate treasure revealer, and a consort was considered a necessity for her successful treasure revelation.[33] She also saw other benefits to taking a consort; in her auto/biography she mentioned that such relationships had soteriological and pragmatic benefits for speeding the path to enlightenment and supporting health and longevity.[34] Sera Khandro also reinforced her public identity as a treasure revealer, calling upon one of the commonly held expectations of how a treasure revealer behaves and practices, by taking on a consort. There are also unspoken benefits for a woman—especially one with few other authorizing referents—to identify herself as an incarnation of Yeshé Tsogyel. She can then reinforce this connection by creating relationship connections (such as taking a consort) that mimic the activities of Yeshé Tsogyel narratives. Performing similar acts would aid in establishing such a woman's public role as a community-recognized treasure revealer.

Tāre Lhamo was likewise recognized as an incarnation of both Yeshé Tsogyel, and also as Sera Khandro.[35] Like Mingyur Peldrön, Tāre Lhamo was born into a treasure-revealing family and the *tertöns* in her community immediately identified her as Yeshé Tsogyel, thus passing on the religious authority of the well-known female figure in their process of formal recognition.[36] This identification would have acted as an authorizing referent for the baby, regardless of what her future plans held.[37] However, when she took the path of a treasure revealer, her role as an incarnation of Yeshé Tsogyel was especially beneficial, as it connected her directly to the origin tale of treasure revelation. Later, when she and her partner, Namtrul Rinpoche, practiced and revealed treasures together, their identification as Yeshé Tsogyel and Padmasambhava reinforced their identities as legitimate tertöns through their connections to the progenitors of the tradition itself.[38] For them the erotic innuendo of some of their epistolary exchanges authorized their agency as a treasure-revealing couple.[39] For both Sera Khandro and Tāre Lhamo, their identities as religious practitioners and treasure revealers were reinforced by their association with Yeshé Tsogyel as a practitioner of sexual rites. Neither woman was celibate, and both eked out successful religious careers in their roles as treasure revealers who engaged in heterosexual sex in order to edify their own practice. Their identification with Yeshé Tsogyel was wrapped up with this practice and supported their careers and spiritual paths as tertöns. While Mingyur Peldrön is also identified as Yeshé Tsogyel, the nature of her identification is very different. In that difference we can see both the ways that the specifics of religious identity are reinforced by connection to well-known figures through echoes of past stories as well as the unique nature of Mingyur Peldrön's role as a celibate female religious teacher and the ways that the figure of Yeshé Tsogyel was likewise altered in *Dispeller*.

Compared with these other *Lives*, *Dispeller* gives a very different backstory for Yeshé Tsogyel. Rather than being described as a consort to Padmasambhava, here she is depicted simply as his student and then later on as a solitary and celibate practitioner. To support this claim, Gyurmé Ösel includes a quotation that he attributes to the *Pema Katang*:

Moreover, in the *Pema Katang*, the woman Yeshé Tsogyel said:

> "Ema Ho! Adorned with many good qualities, the Ornamented Lotus [Padmasambhava] arose."
>
> Also, she said:
> "Thirteen years later, born in Tibet—
> a father called Drakpa Namka Yeshé,
> a mother called Nubmo Gewa Bum—
> in the female wood bird year I, Tsogyel, was born.
> In the female fire bird year I met with the Lord.
> One who has attained unfailing memory
> must be a student of the dharma.
> Serving until the age of eighty-five,
> remaining pure,
> no male or female children whatsoever,
> I am a nun, unblemished by the faults of *saṃsara*."[40]

Gyurmé Ösel repeatedly references Yeshé Tsogyel throughout *Dispeller*, pointing to well-known and important religious texts, Mingyur Peldrön's visions, and his own dreams as evidence of the legitimate connection between the two women. *Dispeller*'s alternative reading of Yeshé Tsogyel reflects how Mingyur Peldrön's unique privilege put her in a position to remain celibate. While invoking the famous figure as an important authorizing presence from Nyingma myth and history, he does so in a way that allows for and even highlights his subject's celibacy, which later becomes a prominent theme in her life story. When Gyurmé Ösel talks specifically about Yeshé Tsogyel, it is as a student of Padmasambhava and a protector of his teachings but also as a celibate woman. Much of the Yeshé Tsogyel story remains familiar. As in other tellings, she escapes an unwanted marriage, studies with Padmasambhava, and engages in twelve years of solitary meditation, during which time she fights off an attack by brigands, meditates in cemeteries, and becomes known as a "wrathful subduer of evil."[41] As in other versions, this telling of her story emphasizes the teacher-disciple relationship with Padmasambhava but takes the additional step of mentioning that he passed all Dzogchen teachings on to her.[42] Considering Mingyur Peldrön's role as a lineage holder at Mindröling, it makes sense that the author would identify her with Yeshé Tsogyel. This connection would have been particularly powerful, since her father, Terdak Lingpa, was considered an emanation of Padmasambhava who had already been credited as a successful tertön by the time she was born.[43] It makes sense that his daughter and disciple would be identified as a close disciple of Padmasambhava in a way that reinforces these aspects of Yeshé Tsogyel's narrative. The depiction of Yeshé Tsogyel as celibate is highly unusual, but it would reinforce her position within both family and institution while adhering to her particular attributes.

By the time Gyurmé Ösel was working on *Dispeller*, Mingyur Peldrön had already embarked on a celibate path. He positioned his narrative of her as an emanation of Yeshé Tsogyel in such a way that it corroborated Mingyur Peldrön's narrative of monasticism. By emphasizing Yeshé Tsogyel's dedication to practice, going so far as to equate her life with that of a nun, he more effectively connects the historical woman with the mytho-historical heroine. However, it also seems he is reaching a bit or perhaps creating his own reading of Yeshé Tsogyel altogether. As far as I am aware, in all of her depictions she appears rarely (if ever) as a completely celibate woman. Compared with Sera Khandro and Tāre Lhamo's associations with Yeshé Tsogyel, which reinforce her association with consorts, we see how in *Dispeller* the same heroine can be invoked but with different emphases that effectively reflect the person whose life story is being told. Gyurmé Ösel's choice of presentation speaks to his particular focus on Mingyur Peldrön's monastic path while reinforcing it with emanation authority. As a well-situated member of Mindröling who was identified with one of the most important heroines in the Nyingma tradition, it seems that Mingyur Peldrön's privileged status is here reinforced in her presentation as a monastic version of Yeshé Tsogyel.

The use of this famous figure throughout *Dispeller*'s frame narrative reinforces Mingyur Peldrön's importance. She was recognized as Yeshé Tsogyel by a large collection of people, not just Gyurmé Ösel. For example, she is described as "an emanation of Yeshe Tshogyel" by Dudjom Rinpoche and Jamyang Khyentse Wangpo.[44] As an emanation, she could embody Yeshé Tsogyel's authority, and through connection with such a heroine her status as a woman became partial evidence of her religious significance, rather than a hindrance to religious authority. By asserting the attributes of Yeshé Tsogyel that resonated most with Mingyur Peldrön, the section also serves to establish the historical woman's attributes with support from a semihistorical and well-known figure. By creating a connection between the two women in the context of rebirth, Gyurmé Ösel references a popular narrative that affiliates Mingyur Peldrön with ideas of enlightened, powerful female buddhahood and a form of authority that is especially potent within the Nyingma imaginary. It is important to note that she was recognized as an incarnation of Yeshé Tsogyel by her larger community, beyond Mindröling.

To return to her many past lives, emanation authority creates a literary space in the text in which gender can be centered in a positive way. By referencing ten well-known Buddhist figures, Gyurmé Ösel reminds the reader that she is not the first important woman in the tradition and that there were in fact many others who came before her. By connecting her to this lineage, he places her in good company with a host of other women and feminine deities. Drawing on the similarities between her and others, he employs these women to begin framing Mingyur Peldrön's own concerns and personality. As Samantabhadrī, Nangsa Öbum, Yeshé Tsogyel, and seven others, she takes on the religious authority of each figure as well as their characteristics. Recognition as an emanation of powerful females could reinforce one's practical religious authority in eighteenth-century Ü through engagement with gendered divinities. For the narrative's audience, it could also serve to position a woman in a broader, well-known literary and historical context.

It is also worth noting that *all* of Mingyur Peldrön's past lives are presented as female. In part Gyurmé Ösel is arguing that authoritative women need not embody culturally masculine traits to be powerful. But he is also participating in and reinforcing the normative gender binary. For him his teacher's authority could—and should—be legitimated solely along female lines. This is a common occurrence, with men's stories often only recounting previous male lives. Incarnation lineages frequently follow a pattern of reincarnation along one or another of the two normative gender lines. That is, women are rarely recognized as incarnations of men. However, there are some cases in which men have been recognized as incarnations of female figures. The modern-day case of the Kagyu lineage's Garchen Rinpoche is a great twentieth-century example. He is widely considered to be an emanation of the bodhisattva Tārā. With that said, there are few (if any) examples of women being identified as reincarnations of male deities. In Mingyur Peldrön's case the legitimating power of female figures is used to authorize the saint, without male representation in the story of her past lives.

Meanwhile, the sheer number of female figures listed in her previous lives suggests that Gyurmé Ösel was worried that one or two incarnations would not be enough. The list of ten female identities gives an overabundance of evidence for her significance, to the point where the author seems to be overstating his case. As a comparison, while her brother Rinchen Namgyel was described in his own namtar as "clearly an incarnation of the teachers of old,"[45] the details of his previous lives are only mentioned briefly. They appear at a similar point early on in his namtar, amid a description of his early years and unusual propensities for learning, and directly prior to a discussion of his early education. But the brevity in this section of Mingyur Peldrön's brother's *Life* makes it seem as though this is merely a nod to the expectation that he would be recognized as reincarnate in some fashion or another and that, according to convention, it should be mentioned at this point in the namtar's proceedings. It is of course possible that this was the result of stylistic differences between the two hagiographers. Rinchen Namgyel's hagiographer might have been less interested in past lives than Mingyur Peldrön's. However, given the weight that an incarnation lineage can lend to the life of the saint and what that weight can signify for the reader, the fact that incarnations is less prominent in Rinchen Namgyel's story than in his sister's likely has a gendered component.

When we consider the comparative rarity of the composition of a woman's *Life*, it is likely that the large number of past-life narratives acted as a grounding force for Gyurmé Ösel's argument, reminding the reader of the many other women in the Tibetan past who also held similar roles. By drawing on Tibetan literature's most important religious women almost to excess, Gyurmé Ösel sought to represent Mingyur Peldrön as the ur-woman, an ideal in her authoritative and conservative leadership and teaching style. Samantabhadrī, Yeshé Tsogyel, and Nangsa Öbum exemplify three very different female emanations who convey a range of legitimacy that Gyurmé Ösel calls upon to reinforce her authority in diverse ways while maintaining her previous existence as having occurred in female form. These lives also reinforce his presentation of Mingyur Peldrön's character and activities. While she became an emanation grounded in an excess of authoritative femininity, in each example her authentication reflected her different personality traits. In this exposition he points to the legitimating potential of female incarnation couched in the socially accepted terms of namtar. He asserts a specifically feminine narrative to the figures involved and, in so doing, reinforces her authority with female identities. There is a contrast with Rinchen Namgyel's narrative, which did not require as much reinforcement to establish his position as legitimate through the literary reminder of great people of his gender who had come before. He was in a privileged position of being one man among many for whom hagiographies had been written in this style. Here *Dispeller* is working in parallel with a model that had most frequently been used for men, but Gyurmé Ösel supports it with solely female evidence and in excess when compared with that of Rinchen Namgyel's namtar. What Rinchen Namgyel's hagiographer could take for granted, Gyurmé Ösel had to work to prove. In doing so, Gyurmé Ösel puts forth an idealized vision of female authority built from a literary tradition dominated by men in a bid to establish his beloved teacher's authority in a mytho-historical context.

INSTITUTIONAL AUTHORITY

Mingyur Peldrön's institutional connections are where privilege most obviously impacts her position as an authoritative religious figure and where gender is least prominent. As someone born into and educated by a powerful religious family, she had a level of privilege only accessible by birth. The term *institutional authority* here refers to the authority derived from this proximity to the leadership at Mindröling and all the benefits that flowed from this proximity. Institutional authority loosely resembles Max Weber's "traditional authority," in that both are transmitted according to a communally held belief in an institution's enduring legitimacy, rather than an individual's charisma. Weber's description of traditional authority can be helpful insofar as it is based "on an established belief in the sanctity of immemorial traditions and the legitimacy of those exercising authority under them."[46] Mingyur Peldrön inherited multigenerational financial and religious privilege, and as a result she had a closer proximity to institutional traditions that instilled in her an inherent authority beyond that of the average person with similar educational training. This institutional access would influence the relationships that she forged with powerful figures throughout her adulthood, opening doors for her that would have otherwise been closed. On the relationship between institutional power and intersectional identity, Brittney Cooper explains that "institutional power arrangements, rooted as they are in relations of domination and subordination, confound and constrict the life possibilities of those who already live at the intersection of certain identity categories, even as they elevate the possibilities of those living at more legible (and privileged) points of intersection."[47] While Mingyur Peldrön's institutional privilege did not necessarily completely override her gender status, it was also not negated by her role as a woman.

By the time Mingyur Peldrön was born, Mindröling Monastery had been functioning for nearly three decades and was well situated as a center of learning for the affluent families in the central Tibetan religious and political world as well as those from farther afield. When Terdak Lingpa and Lochen Dharmaśrī founded the monastery, they enhanced its prestige with support from the Fifth Dalai Lama's Ganden Podrang government. Terdak Lingpa and the Fifth Dalai Lama had a long-standing relationship of religious exchange and mutual influence and also used similar methods to develop their institutions. Their inclusivist approaches to ritual and praxis were quite similar.[48] Mingyur Peldrön's familial connections with a historically prominent Nyingma family and that family's connection to the Ganden Podrang government made her childhood education possible in the first place and certainly influenced her relationships with political and religious leaders in her adulthood. During the civil war, institutional relationships influenced her welcome from the Sikkimese royal family when she sought refuge there during the destruction of Mindröling. These connections also meant financial support from other institutions to reconstruct the monastery after her return. Beginning in her early twenties and continuing throughout her adult life, her connections to leaders such as Polhané and the Seventh Dalai Lama almost certainly began as the result of her institutional affiliation.

Institutional authority is similar to social privilege, but the two are not identical. While Mingyur Peldrön's social privilege informed her institutional authority, it did not guarantee her access to the privilege that she could draw on through family connections. For institutional authority to work, her social standing had to be recognized by the group in which she was exerting her authority. A counterexample is Sera Khandro, a highborn central Tibetan woman who sought inclusion in a non-monastic religious community in Kham. When she arrived at her chosen community of practice, her natal origins did nothing to reinforce her social standing in the new context. On the contrary, she faced ridicule about her high status.[49] There was potential for women to struggle for recognition at the margins of the communities they sought to join, regardless of whether or not they were born into aristocratic families. A highborn woman who was recognized as such in her community of origin would not benefit from this status in another community if it did not recognize that status as worthy of consideration. If a woman's social privilege was not consistent with the expectations of her religious community, it would not generate greater ease of institutional access. In other words, it would not be a source for institutional authority.

Institutional privilege here goes beyond that of simple wealth, familial status, social standing, or religious affiliation. But it can include any of these advantages, and in Mingyur Peldrön's case it included all of them. Her story is different from that of women like Sera Khandro in that, beyond membership in the social elite, she also benefited by being born into a family that sought institutional expansion and valued her influence in that project. That is to say, she did not need to leave home and defy her aristocratic parents in order to pursue a religious vocation. Instead, she was designated as a recipient of the empowerments of the family lineage shortly after her birth and remained within her natal institution throughout her life. She was expected (or at least invited) to participate in the goals of her family's religious projects and was educated accordingly. To be raised in a context in which her religious pursuits (including an interest in celibacy) were considered beneficial for the family seems to have been relatively unusual among the women for whom we have *Lives*. With that said, she does share this unusual combination of institutional support and privilege with Tāre Lhamo and Chökyi Drönma. Like these two women, Mingyur Peldrön's privilege was beyond that of a wealthy girl with a supportive family because she was also born into a religious dynasty, and her religious interests were cultivated to support the family itself. The institutional authority that resulted from this affiliation remained accessible to Mingyur Peldrön throughout her life and was especially beneficial after elder generations had died. At its most basic, this meant that she had external support in key moments of hardship that would have been less accessible for those without family ties to Mindröling. But it also meant that she could draw on institutional authority to expand her teaching base. As a member of the central family at Mindröling, she had unprecedented access to the religious institutional complex and therefore a position of privilege that resulted in a much smoother experience in acquiring authority than that described in the *Lives* of other religious women. Her institutional authority also impacted how her gender was treated in her namtar.

In highlighting Mingyur Peldrön's direct access to institutional authority, Gyurmé Ösel's telling of her *Life* shows how different forms of privilege can shift the ways that life stories are told.[50] As he explains, his teacher's institutional affiliation meant that she did not face several of the traditional obstacles so readily present in other women's *Lives*. In moments in which the challenges of being a woman might otherwise become the focal point, *Dispeller* instead forwards the benefits of her institutional relationships. She and her female family members are taken in by the Sikkimese aristocracy when they flee civil war. She is relieved from languishing in obscurity in Kongpo when Polhané calls her to Lhasa as a Mindröling representative. She and her brother are called upon to assist in settling disputes among political figures in Lhasa, due to their connections with Mindröling. These moments do not make gender any less important in the overall narrative, but they do point to the ways that the relationship between gender and authority was complex in her case. The multifaceted nature of Mingyur Peldrön's identity meant that in different contexts, different aspects of who she was would be emphasized and recognized by those around her. Insofar as intersectionality denotes the complex connections that make power accessible, her privilege frequently overrode her non-privilege in helping her to exercise power in her community.[51] The combined attributes of her identity could become more impactful in combination; the result would be more than the sum of its parts, so to speak. Protected by her institutional authority, Mingyur Peldrön's gender could be less of a burden in certain moments, leaving room for positive renderings of feminine identity to prevail throughout most of *Dispeller*. While there is a narrative of hardship in her *Life*, it is not tied to overcoming institutional exclusion, and only rarely is it connected with her gender identity.

Rather than struggling for recognition within the institution, Mingyur Peldrön was acknowledged as an important potential transmitter of empowerments and therefore a significant conduit for the tradition from the time of her birth. The literary effects of this were such that in *Dispeller* she is not daunted by either her gender or through institutional exclusion but is instead elevated through family connections. However, institutional authority could only propel one so far. For Mingyur Peldrön to establish herself as an authentic teacher and practitioner, she needed more than high birth and family acceptance; she needed an education. Luckily, her institutional privilege gave her an entry point to unprecedented access to the knowledge that would help her establish her role as a religious teacher.

Educational Authority

Mingyur Peldrön's religious education meant that she was also imbued with an authority specific to the details of that education. Here educational authority concerns the authorization of an individual to transmit teachings based upon their religious training. While the term *education* might elicit specific notions of formal scholastic training, here it refers to a wide-ranging idea of Buddhist education that includes religious transmissions as well as empowerments and other forms of instruction beyond book learning, such as contemplative and ritual practices, in addition to scholastic guidance. Regardless of the style, *education* is meant to evoke the processes of passing down normative modes of produced knowledge and methods of intellectual and spiritual practice. *Education* here also implies the systematization of knowledge production and its dissemination. By receiving training in these areas, Mingyur Peldrön would have been recognized as authoritative within and even beyond Mindröling.

Like other modes of authority, this type was hardly unique to Mingyur Peldrön, although its expression in her hagiography is unusual for a woman in that she was educated by her own family at the institution where she was born and raised. It is also tied closely to her status as a nun, insofar as she was able to identify as a religious specialist from a very young age in a way that her sisters were not. In her case her educational authority meant that she was authorized through official channels to pass on teachings held to be important at Mindröling and other Nyingma communities during her lifetime. Lineage systems are important in this process, as teachings are passed down from authorized teachers to their students and the students are then empowered to perform the practices and pass on the teachings themselves. In the Tibetan context this process is often sealed with an empowerment, a ritual formally acknowledging the student's ability to perform the practice. For Mingyur Peldrön this meant that her empowerment was coming directly from people like Terdak Lingpa and other leading figures at Mindröling.

A brief comparison between educational authority and Max Weber's "legal authority" will indicate some of the differentiating components of educational authority in the context of the authoritative types that were functioning in *Dispeller*. According to Weber, legal authority is based upon "a belief in the legality of enacted rules and the right of those elevated to authority under such rules to issue commands."[52] In the same way, educational authority adheres to norms that are passed down institutionally. These are rule bound and authorized by institutions. However, this does not indicate a one-to-one correlation with Weber's pure type of legal authority, in which, as he explains, "obedience is owed to the legally established impersonal order. It extends to the persons exercising the authority of office under it by virtue of the formal legality of their commands and only within the scope of authority of the office."[53] Educational authority, on the other hand, draws on the individual's aptitude for learning and personal charisma in order to transmit teachings as well as their direct relationships to similarly authorized teachers. If one cannot develop a following based upon recognition and trust from the larger community, the individual will not be sought out to pass on the teachings they hold. Like charismatic authority, educational authority requires the confidence of the recipients in order to function. Mingyur Peldrön's educational authority was expressed from her young adulthood and reiterated throughout her life, but it is most firmly established in the education of her youth.

In *Dispeller* Mingyur Peldrön's educational authority is first mentioned with senyik, the aforementioned lists of teachings and empowerments she received in her youth. It is then reinforced with brief vignettes recounting her learning experiences as a child and young adult. According to *Dispeller*, Terdak Lingpa directed his daughter's studies from her early childhood until his death in 1714, at which point Lochen Dharmaśrī became Mingyur Peldrön's primary teacher.[54] By this time she had already become a nun, the only girl in her family's generation to do so. In place of a detailed narrative of her childhood activities, Gyurmé Ösel chose to include the senyiks of teachings she had received from these two men. Rather than a narrative of youthful clashes with family expectations or hardships and suffering overcome or even idyllic depictions of bygone days, the reader is met with an eight-folio list of the teachings received by the young woman that establishes her educational authorization. This follows a similar pattern to the hagiography of Rinchen Namgyel, which also includes a senyik of the teachings he received in his youth. In Mingyur Peldrön's case the most attention is given to the Mindröling-specific teachings, especially the treasure texts of Terdak Lingpa. Just as with her previous female incarnations, by including these lists in the hagiography, the sheer volume of teachings impresses upon the reader the extent of her high level of training.

For a young woman like Mingyur Peldrön to be educated and imbued with empowerments meant that both she and the institution were safeguarded. This would benefit both nun and institution when chaos threatened to overwhelm the community and its knowledge bearers were being dispersed and killed off. With the onset of the civil war in 1717, men from the older generations were murdered, and only one other person with the same level of education escaped. Mingyur Peldrön and Rinchen Namgyel were the only people who lived through the destruction with such an extensive education and therefore the ability to pass on these trainings to others. During their exile her religious training meant that she could launch her teaching career in Sikkim. While it is likely that she and her female family members would have been well cared for by the Sikkimese royal family because of their connections with Mindröling, she was allowed to teach because she held a set of important empowerments. This led to her being granted the permission to establish a mountaintop retreat center and trying her hand at disseminating a Mindröling education to the Sikkimese community. Thus, she was able to forge institutional connections for the monastery while also bestowing an education that would have otherwise been inaccessible for this community so far from Mindröling. Ultimately, her educational authority was employed to be of religious benefit for herself and her community. After the destruction of the earlier generation, her role as one of the few surviving lineage holders meant that she could rise to become an important figure for the community. In exile her education meant that she began to transmit Mindröling teachings—and therefore its legacy—even as the edifice itself burned to the ground.

As with the forms of authority discussed here, Mingyur Peldrön's educational authority intersected with issues of gender and privilege as she navigated the religious environment of her time. It is important to keep in mind that different people—even within the Mindröling family—had access to different types of privilege and therefore different types of authority. While she and her brother were highly educated, there is little evidence that their sisters received similarly robust training. For example, Lady Peldzin is mentioned rarely in the hagiographic and historical records and seems to have had little influence beyond her ability to marry the king of Sikkim at her sister's behest. Likewise, while brief biographies of Mingyur Peldrön, her grandmother, and Rinchen Namgyel all appear in the modern-day record of Mindröling, there are no accounts of her sisters. In *Dispeller* the sisters' roles were relegated to keeping Mingyur Peldrön company (along with their mother) during pilgrimages and other events and playing the important role of making religiopolitically important marriages. In comparison, Rinchen Namgyel is portrayed as an active religious teacher and community figure, leveraging his authority and working alongside his sister and also on his own. The sisters are once described as attending teachings alongside Mingyur Peldrön, although their education is not described beyond that (whereas Rinchen Namgyel's is described in detail in his namtar). Initial research has uncovered little discussion of these sisters outside of *Dispeller*. Whereas Mingyur Peldrön is mentioned frequently in Rinchen Namgyel's namtar, his other sisters are not. They are mentioned as adults going to receive blessings from and make offerings to their brother, but they are not recorded as having taken part in the same level of early education as Rinchen Namgyel and Mingyur Peldrön. When compared with the lengthy discussions of their more educated siblings, this absence suggests that educational authority was not equally bestowed in their generation or among all girls in the family.

Another differentiating factor between Mingyur Peldrön and her sisters was that she alone was a nun. While it would have theoretically been possible for her to pursue religious education without becoming a nun, the distinction bears attention here. Without making assumptions based on my own twenty-first-century Euro-Western context, it is clear that in her case status as a celibate religious woman correlates with her relative freedom to follow religious pursuits and her position as a prominent figure in the ordering of Mindröling at that time. This also led to a higher level of bodily autonomy than that of her sisters. With that said, we also know that in spite of her education, Mingyur Peldrön still did not receive the same extensive training as her brother. Thus, access to educational authority was uneven among this generation at Mindröling. This has significant repercussions for how we think about privilege in their context. While economic privilege may have been balanced between them, the privilege associated with education was doled out unevenly by the community that raised them.

It appears that Mingyur Peldrön was the only woman at Mindröling to adopt a position of religious leadership during her lifetime, and her education would cement this role. Her ability to lead the community was also predicated on the absence of other (male) leaders in her young adulthood. Upon return from Sikkim, Rinchen Namgyel was still in exile, which meant that Mingyur Peldrön was the most qualified to guide Mindröling's reconstruction.[55] The absence of male leadership combined with her education meant that she could step into a leadership role. Her adoption of a more prominent role in leadership after the Dzungar destruction seems to have been unique to her situation. After her brother's return home, she continued in her role as a teacher and maintained the relationships she had begun developing in her time as director of the monastery's reconstruction. She would continue to be a sought-out teacher long after others had taken up official positions as the heads of Mindröling.

In *Dispeller* Mingyur Peldrön's institutional and educational sources of authority are contiguous and mutually reinforcing. The lists of teachings she received and accounts of her education, as well as accounts of meetings with male religious leaders, show that she was entrusted with and expected to disseminate her family's teachings. Gyurmé Ösel's approach suggests that for a woman to become a religious leader in the eighteenth century, she would have to be educated and empowered in religious teachings, and the more the better. Educational authority did for Mingyur Peldrön what the other two types of authority could not. It instilled legitimacy in her own personal religious accomplishments beyond the purview of the familial relationship or past-life connection. Rather than her previous lives or her family's clout, her religious training and her ability to engage with and pass teachings on to large groups of people was what ultimately solidified her authority. It also meant that anyone who received teachings from her (including Gyurmé Ösel) would be directly linked with the likes of Terdak Lingpa and Lochen Dharmaśrī.

Gendered Referents and the Complexities of Privilege

The three authoritative types active throughout *Dispeller* converge at some points and stand alone at others. The referential terms used to refer to Mingyur Peldrön reinforce these three types of authority and highlight the complex ways that different aspects of her identity interact. The use of gendered referents speaks to the complexity of how Gyurmé Ösel portrays both her identity and her positionality. In reading *Dispeller* as a site in which the socially embedded notion of gender is negotiated, we can see the potential benefits and downfalls of living as a woman in an eighteenth-century Nyingma community. In the narrative contrary statements about gender, about best methods for religious practice and so forth, exist alongside one another. These create a sense of multiple extant perspectives on gender and whether it was beneficial to emphasize Mingyur Peldrön's position as a woman in any given moment.

A brief consideration of the semiology of the pronouns and appellations used to refer to Mingyur Peldrön shows how in very important moments Gyurmé Ösel elevated her using gendered terminology, leaving androgynous language to less important but more frequent scenes. His use of overt feminine language suggests a positive perception of her birth in female form, while the routinization of masculine references seems to establish her authoritative role. For example, quotations attributed to different male family members employ different "voices" to reveal Mingyur Peldrön's familial positioning in gendered ways. These include some of the few notable negative appellations, such as calling her an "unwanted girl" and so belittling her female identity. These moments provide a sort of argument for the author to work against, addressing the potential concerns about the fact she was a woman with assertions that her actions helped ensure the survival of Mindröling. In other words, Gyurmé Ösel emphasized or minimized her gender according to specific contexts. By referring to her at turns using feminine or androgynous language in the honorific register or in quotations attributed to family members that simultaneously gender her and assign her roles within the family, he exhibits the complexity with which her status was treated. These gendered and agendered references are used in *Dispeller* to construct a sort of dialogue about her identity that is elevated through feminine language and that reverts to androgynous-masculine language that positions her as an authority within a normative male-dominant framework. In some places he engages femininity as a positive attribute to be forwarded at important junctures in the story. Elsewhere, he uses androgynous language to position Mingyur Peldrön as an insider in a male-dominated context.

Androgynous and masculine language puts Mingyur Peldrön on a par with the men who dominated the religious world into which she and Gyurmé Ösel were born. There were no living examples of institutionally influential women in their community.[56] Gyurmé Ösel's androgynous and masculine references to Mingyur Peldrön act as subtle reminders urging the reader to think of her as one of these leaders—all of whom were men. The most frequent phrase that he uses to refer to Mingyur Peldrön is *jé lama*.[57] *Lama* is a notably challenging term to translate, conveying as it does a complex collection of ideas that include the notion of a highly revered religious teacher. It is sometimes cross-translated into the more familiar *guru*, but this has the potential to also carry the problematic ballast of exoticization that the term *guru* has taken on in English. I tentatively translate *lama* as "master teacher," when I translate it at all, as it conveys the supreme authority held by the teacher as well as the reverence accorded to the religious master. *Lama* could likewise simply be translated as "teacher," although in modern English that might not hold the same powerful connotation that "master" does. Throughout *Dispeller* Gyurmé Ösel also sometimes returns to phrases closely related to *jé lama*, such as "the master themself," "my lama," and "venerable supreme lama."⁵⁸ While these terms are not inherently masculine, historically they were almost exclusively used to reference male religious figures.⁵⁹ More specifically, to my knowledge, Mingyur Peldrön's context is the only one in which the phrase *jé lama* is used to reference a woman. And yet *jé lama*—and derivations of the term—are used in reference to her more than fifty times throughout *Dispeller*. In using this terminology, Gyurmé Ösel centers on Mingyur Peldrön's position as his beloved teacher and as a respected and important teacher more generally while simultaneously presenting her as a figure naturalized and embedded in an otherwise male world. He removes all feminine identity markers in his most frequent references to her, normalizing her role as an androgynized teacher and member of a male-dominated religious educational complex, including Mindröling but also extending beyond its walls.

While the default references to Mingyur Peldrön are androgynous, Gyurmé Ösel uses feminine language to elevate her in key moments in the narrative. This has the dual effect of showing her importance through ornate and feminized language and also reinforcing that her status as a woman is a potential source of positivity. The departure from masculine or androgynous referents at these junctures adds to the complexity of how gendered language reinforces authority in the hagiography. For example, at the most pivotal moments he employs some variant of the lengthened and feminized phrase *Venerable Master, Excellent Queen of the Ḍākinīs*, to refer to her.⁶⁰ Throughout the text this long title is also split into several abbreviated forms, and Gyurmé Ösel uses them thematically according to the significance of that particular anecdote. *Ḍākinīs* can be fierce or friendly, pleasant or terrifying. They are a designation of female dharma protectors and translators of revealed treasure texts, who keep religious texts and practitioners safe from menacing forces. Notably, they act as guides for treasure revealers and other practitioners in need, visiting dreams and visions to help those who are stuck or confused. *Ḍākinīs* are generally referred to as enlightened and are by far the most consistently positive expression of female power in Tibetan Buddhism. Due to their role as guides for serious practitioners, the abstract concept of the ḍākinī holds high status in Buddhist literature and iconography. *Ḍākinī* is also a term that is often used to refer to religious women in a polite or elevating way.

In *Dispeller* several lengthy references to ḍākinīs are used when Mingyur Peldrön is engaged in a life-changing event, especially one in which her status shifts dramatically. Moments important enough to warrant long appellations of her as "*ḍākinī* queen" occur throughout: at the very beginning of

Dispeller, when Gyurmé Ösel first describes Mingyur Peldrön as a protector of Atiyoga teachings;[61] at her birth; when she receives complete Atiyoga instructions and initiations from her father; when, having just arrived in Sikkim, she first bestows Atiyoga instructions on the Dzogchenpa and the Sikkimese king; when a messenger arrives in Sikkim with the good news that she, her mother, sisters, and attendants can safely return home and that the threat to Mindröling had passed;[62] when she rebuffs the advances of the Fifth Lelung, Jedrung Rinpoche;[63] and finally, after her death, at the end of a description of her tomb.[64] There are two unifying themes across these instances. First, they indicate transformative moments in Mingyur Peldrön's existence. From birth to death these episodes pinpoint profound junctures of change in her lived experience and public position. They are also formative moments that establish her public identity in one way or another. She becomes a publicly recognized exiled teacher. She returns home to take the lead in reviving Mindröling. She asserts her celibacy and so forth. Second, at many of these junctures, the Atiyoga teachings of the Dzogchen tradition are the focus of the context. This furthers the prominent role that Atiyoga—and therefore Dzogchen—takes in all of these moments and highlights the importance of these teachings for Mingyur Peldrön's identity. In using this elevated feminine language, Gyurmé Ösel is also reinforcing her relationship to these advanced teachings. He is centering Dzogchen and Atiyoga, and her connection to them, with the use of feminine imagery. Rather than refer to her as androgynous "master teacher," in these moments she becomes a highly powerful and authorized woman, depicted as the Queen of the Ḍākinīs. The importance of these moments called for a departure from the usual androgynous language to the more florid, feminine, and still powerful language.

Whether feminine or androgynous in tone, these honorific references have the cumulative effect of elevating Mingyur Peldrön in a way that correlates to two of the modes of authority that are used to authorize her in *Dispeller*. As the ḍākinī queen, powerful feminine imagery echoes the narratives of her emanation authority, reinforcing her position in an overarching theme of authorized Buddhist femininity. As the *jé lama*, she is depicted as an androgynous-masculine teacher, recalling her educational authority and empowerment to teach and pass on the teachings that are the heart of the institution where she was educated. But what of her institutional authority, that gleaned from simply being born into the right family?

When Gyurmé Ösel quotes Mingyur Peldrön's family members, they refer to her using feminine language that does not obviously elevate her. For example, in interactions with her father, Terdak Lingpa, she is the "girl" or "daughter."[65] Gyurmé Ösel engages these terms frequently in moments when it is important to affirm Mingyur Peldrön's position in a parent-child relationship. In doing so, they established her institutional authority by placing her within her familial context and also in a gendered and generational hierarchy below the first generation of male Mindröling leadership. These terms are used most often to show the relationship between Mingyur Peldrön and Terdak Lingpa but are also applied to her relationship with her mother, Phuntsok Peldzöm, and her uncle Lochen Dharmaśrī. They are effective as "authorizing referents" because they directly connect her to her father, uncle, and other family members. In scenes in which these terms are used, Mingyur Peldrön's position as an accepted and valued member of the family takes primacy over any other aspect of the conversation.

There are a few types of child-parent denotation that are used in the text, and one of these holds specifically religious connotations for the namtar readership. What I have translated here as "daughter" is the term *sremo*, which also identifies Mingyur Peldrön as a spiritual heir to Terdak Lingpa, rather than merely his biological child. In this case *sremo* might be rendered more effectively as "spiritual daughter" or "(female) spiritual heir." Her position as a child within the Mindröling family is reinforced with this type of language, which is utilized at least thirty-two times in *Dispeller*. In every case the term is quoted and attributed to some member of the previous generation of the Mindröling family (usually Terdak Lingpa and Lochen Dharmaśrī but also occasionally Phuntsok Peldzöm). While not obviously elevating in tone, these references support Mingyur Peldrön's institutional authority by reminding the reader of her natal origins. It is worth noting that these are feminized.

While abundantly establishing Mingyur Peldrön's legitimate authority, *Dispeller* also adds complexity to the issue of her gender by including references to her role as an "unwanted daughter." When she was fourteen, there was apparently some discussion about her position in the family. She was struggling with some of her studies and sought help from Lochen Dharmaśrī. Responding to her frustration and doubt, her uncle reminded her that although she might be an "unwanted girl," she was destined to carry on the family's religious tradition. He is quoted in *Dispeller* as having declared: "'The desired boy was not brought to the Terton's Dargyé Chöding lineage. This unwanted girl was brought instead. Now she will sustain it. The treasury will not be forgotten."⁶⁶ Mingyur Peldrön seems to have been buoyed by this reassurance, happily going about her practice. It is an interesting moment, heavy as it is with misogynistic language. In spite of her gender, the gifted girl was considered to be capable of upholding and propitiating family traditions of Terdak Lingpa's lineage and protecting the future of Mindröling. However, these successes are still qualified as having been achieved in spite of her status as a girl. Here even her teacher (who we should remember was also her uncle) felt the need to point to her gender as potentially problematic, harking back to the impediments of the lesser female birth. Succeeding in spite of her gender introduces a different narrative to the text—one that is more familiar in the *Lives* of other Tibetan women. This juxtaposition of her femininity as at turns elevated and detracting shows how gender remains a complex aspect to her identity, even within the context of hagiographic narrative. In spite of all the positive references to her in gendered terms, there are brief hints that her position as a girl, and later a woman, would be detrimental to her status at Mindröling.

In a sense Gyurmé Ösel's linguistic choices gendering Mingyur Peldrön in *Dispeller* exemplify how femaleness can be at turns elided or elevated when the figure has enough privilege cachet. The three most prominent referents used for her are interesting because they position her differently within her family structure, community structure, and Buddhist cosmology and reinforce the three authoritative types that were described earlier. The cumulative effect of frequent honorific references to her is that the overall portrait of Mingyur Peldrön is exemplary and glorified. In the most important places these are lengthy gendered epithets, generally likening her to a ḍākinī. Elevated feminine language deifies her while emphasizing her gender. Elsewhere, the frequent references to *jé lama* establish her as an actor embedded in a normative androgynous-masculine context. The androgynous terminology forwards her status as a prominent Mindröling teacher over and above her gender. Meanwhile, references to her as a female child at Mindröling reinforce her familial position alongside her gender. Diminutive references to her as a "girl" or "child" position her in close proximity to Terdak Lingpa and Lochen Dharmaśrī. Each of these phrases sends a message that positions Mingyur Peldrön differently as an authority in her socioreligious context.

In *Dispeller* social religious authority is at times built upon notions of a specifically feminine identity and relayed in references to Mingyur Peldrön's past-life narratives. In drawing on these, her personal authority is reinforced through positive representations of idealized and enlightened female figures. Meanwhile, in other moments attributes such as education, social status, and family connections are asserted over and above her gender. Throughout, different appellations (whether they be gendered, elevated, both, or neither) also reinforce her positionality in the given moment. All of these factors come together in complex ways to establish her authority by drawing on different aspects of her privilege. The authoritative types used by Gyurmé Ösel are present in other namtars as well, where they reveal similar concerns for other auto/biographers, hagiographers, and their subjects and reiterate different namtar tropes. Mingyur Peldrön's gender is presented in complex ways. It is not always a detractor to be overcome and not always a support that elevates her. Rather, gendered identities authorize her in some moments and in others remind the reader of the "inferior female body" so often found in Tibetan Buddhist *Life* writing, including in *Dispeller*. The complexity of gendered language in the hagiography points to the continued role of gender as part of Mingyur Peldrön's identity. Gender is not completely obscured by her privilege or vice versa; rather, the two social constructs inform one another.

Gyurmé Ösel substantiates Mingyur Peldrön's authority by drawing on literary and cultural references that would have been recognizable to his eighteenth-century readership. By engaging familiar authoritative types, his choices point to the intersectional nature of authority, especially as it relates to gender and privilege. For example, his use of emanation authority signals that the *Life* will adhere to the normative traits of namtar but in a feminine register, presenting her identity as a nearly overwhelming number of female buddhas and heroines. In doing his, he validates her female birth while reminding the reader of the preponderance of female practitioners in the Buddhist canon. Through diverse narrative and literary reference, he connects her personal attributes within a larger program of divine femininity. By refusing to cross the binary gender divide in her pre-lives, he asserts that the forms of emanation authority so prevalent in men's *Lives* can be easily translated to the context of a female teacher. He presents a feminized version of the more frequently male literary *Lives*, replacing what might in other narratives be presented as the downfall of being born a woman with an emphasis on positive female representations. In these and other moments, he uses ornate feminine appellations likening Mingyur Peldrön to a ḍākinī queen.

But how do we make sense of the impact of gender on a person's *Life* story where content is openly gendered in some places and elided or downplayed in others, the manifestations of gender are complex and often nuanced, and they regularly depart from the dominant narratives about being born a woman in a Buddhist world? While frequently present, Mingyur Peldrön's position as a woman was not always the defining aspect of her personality or her authority. But that does not negate its importance in her lived experience and in her literary representations. Her role as an educated and highly trained individual and her position as a privileged daughter of Mindröling are also both signals to the reader about her authority. In Gyurmé Ösel's discussions of her institutional and educational authority, he highlighted privilege and access, particularly that of being born into the inner circle of a prominent religious institution. In describing her as a daughter of the tradition, he emphasized her institutional authority by forwarding her privilege and her gender. It is notable that this was presented within the boundaries of a positive female context that draws on feminine identities to reinforce Mingyur Peldrön's own status as a legitimate lineage holder.

Mingyur Peldrön's *Life* articulates her access to religious education and her role among the highest echelons of the privileged religious elite. For her, to be an authoritative woman meant being a teacher respected by the aristocracy and available to the masses. But it also meant having the ear of governing leaders, receiving the education of an elite religious institution, and becoming an indispensable protector and holder of institutional lineages.[67] Her educational authority is at times gendered female (as when she is labeled a ḍākinī while giving Atiyoga teachings), and elsewhere she is gendered androgynous-masculine (as in most frequent references to her and while giving teachings to Gyurmé Ösel or groups of nuns). During moments in which educational authority is most important, the references to gender switch frequently.

In eighteenth-century Tibet, as in other times and places, women's accessibility to roles in leadership and to education in general were as varied as their markers of social privilege, even as they were bound to societal structures and organization. Mingyur Peldrön had the unique privilege of being born into a position in which she could easily access religious prestige and training. As a result of this privilege, her gender had a less restrictive effect on her experience and could be celebrated and elevated. Gyurmé Ösel could engage her gender in more flexible ways than if she had had less privilege to access. In her case family connections, wealth, and other markers of privilege also helped determine whether or not she would have access to religious education and what kind of education that would be. An intersectional approach to her life narrative reveals that gender was merely one of the factors influencing the scope of her lived experience. As a woman, her proximity to and relationship with a doctrinally and geographically central religious institution was highly unusual, and privilege informed her viability as a leader.

As we continue to investigate gender dynamics at different moments of Tibetan Buddhist history, Gyurmé Ösel's gendered treatment of Mingyur Peldrön reveals how important it is to look at the variety of types of authority available to an individual including—and also always beyond—gender, especially in specific historical and religious contexts. Dividing her authority into the three types and examining each separately reveals how accessibility to authority is largely grounded in the privilege of her family background. This in turn made it easier for her to receive a high-profile training and build her persona as a Buddhist teacher. The elevation of her feminine identity often contradicts much of the narrative of the disadvantages of being reborn in a female body that are regularly found in Buddhist literature, without jettisoning her gender. In Buddhist contexts—as elsewhere—authority is wrapped up with specific cultural signifiers. For Mingyur Peldrön these included positive gendered references, education level, and markers of privilege such as wealth, institutional affiliation, proximity to centers of authority, position within her family, and political connections. Each of these were shot through with context-dependent privilege, in this case a privilege that contained an amalgamation of class-based and educational markers and was not evenly available to all the children of her generation. With all of its complexity, privilege laid the foundation for Mingyur Peldrön's Buddhist education, her rise to prominence, and ultimately her authority.

Chapter Three

Multivocal *Lives*

> Although I only had a brief glimpse of her youthful face, it was wondrous and overwhelmingly beautiful. As soon as I gazed upon her, I shed many tears. I went after her, hoping to ask if I could follow her. Thus my faith involuntarily arose.
>
> —Gyurmé Ösel

> I have become just like the hunted deer
> Before Lord Yama—terror's face of death.
> Back bowed, I drag the weight of endless fear.
>
> —Mingyur Peldrön

At the center of *Dispeller* sits the relationship that is integral to any hagiography: that between author and subject. Rather than the multiauthored *Life* of Sönam Peldren or the auto/biography of Sera Khandro, Mingyur Peldrön's namtar was penned entirely by the monk Gyurmé Ösel, with any suggestions or quotations from Mingyur Peldrön herself remaining wholly managed by the author of the work.[1] Gyurmé Ösel would spend most of his life either in the care of or in service to her, first as her disciple and student, then later transitioning to her amanuensis, before eventually becoming her hagiographer. This trajectory is not unusual; the writing of a hagiography by a spiritual disciple is a commonality that spans Tibetan and non-Tibetan examples of the genre. Literary expressions of the master-disciple relationship are typical in Tibetan namtar, elevating as it does the "master" to the position of enlightened person. While these narratives are often devotional in tone, they can also be multivocal and complex in their representations of the subject and her environment. Hagiography can be a sort of ground for cultural negotiation in which hagiographers posit new ideas, support long established patterns, or argue for the value of either. These texts become sites in which cultural norms and questions are worked out and reinforced. As such, topics that are in question at the time of composition are emphasized in the text, whether they are of concern on a wider social scale or solely in the mind of the author.

In *Dispeller* Gyurmé Ösel depicts Mingyur Peldrön as someone deeply concerned with issues of religious education who approached the topic in a markedly gendered way. Her advice to men and women was notably distinct from each other, underscoring specific concerns along the normative eighteenth-century gender bifurcation. Alongside topics related to religious education, monasticism and a general concern about the future of Mindröling are also prominent points of conversation in *Dispeller*. The variety of opinions presented on these issues result in a sort of dialogue of ideas in the text. While *Dispeller* purportedly had a single author, perspectives on these contemporary social issues are introduced and furthered by the multiple voices in the narrative. These are generally depicted in the form of quotations that Gyurmé Ösel attributed to different people, including Mingyur Peldrön. He presents multivocal renderings of conversations that he claims occurred between Mingyur Peldrön and others and, in doing so, portrays Mingyur Peldrön as a woman with strong opinions on topics as diverse as access to religious education, the importance of monasticism, and the dangers of alcohol. Tracking these dialogues shows how hagiography as a multivocal genre can do the work of revealing a society's cultural tensions. Broadly speaking, Mingyur Peldrön's own written works took the form of instructions directed at anyone who had received the proper empowerments, explanatory texts that revolved around her father's work, and the occasional prayer. These texts show the depth of her immersion in Mindröling's Great Perfection training system, addressing a range of stages of progress, from preliminary to higher-level practices. They also show her wide versatility as a teacher and practitioner (from introductory practice to secret tantric teachings) and are generally focused on the preservation of the Great Perfection. She composed her work at the behest of a variety of people, from her own students, including Gyurmé Ösel and assorted monks and nuns related to Mindröling; to local royalty, including the central Tibetan prince Gyurmé Samten Chogdrup; and other Nyingma teachers, such as Tulku Rinpoche Gyurmé Pema Chogdrup, who was himself a teacher of Jigmé Lingpa, among others.

While Gyurmé Ösel makes no direct references to Mingyur Peldrön acting in a maternal role for him, she had surely witnessed his childhood and his transition through various stages of life. He basically grew up with her as his guardian, beginning at the age of eight. It is easy to imagine a maternal role for her and a mother-son bond between the two. However, no such relationship is ever expressed in *Dispeller*. She is presented as his enlightened, beloved, compassionate religious teacher, but no maternal language is used to reference her. It is important to also keep in mind that there were few women who held positions such as Mingyur Peldrön's during Gyurmé Ösel's lifetime. He likely had few other living models for what a female religious teacher would be like, and yet he did not draw on maternal imagery to speak about his beloved teacher. This was in spite of the fact that at Mindröling a precedent for men writing about women in maternal tones had been established more than a half-century before Mingyur Peldrön's hagiography was produced.

In 1701 Lochen Dharmaśrī had published a *Life* of his mother, Lhadzin Yangchen Drölma.[2] This brief *Life* is different from Mingyur Peldrön's longer hagiography in several ways. First, there are no discussions of Yangchen Drölma's previous lives and no descriptions of her ability as a practitioner. The text focuses on her aristocratic background, her financial management abilities at Dargyé Chöding, and her role as mother to six children.[3] The son's narrative conveys a deep love and respect for his mother and her role and suggests an expectation that women should be included in Mindröling's institutional history, even in the absence of any official religious position or authority. In his case a man is elevating a woman by acting as the author of her *Life* without fully deifying her but while referencing her maternal qualities and her role in the household. Lochen Dharmaśrī's namtar of his mother set a precedent for men to write reverently about Mindröling women and in maternal terms. Gyurmé Ösel would have surely had access to this work, and yet he did not emulate it in the language he used to reference his teacher.

In thinking about the chronological relationships between these two texts, their authors, and subjects, it is worth mentioning a few points. First, Lochen Dharmaśrī wrote his mother's namtar when Mingyur Peldrön—the first daughter of the next generation—was two years old. This marks the year that her younger sister Lady Peldzin was born. Lady Peldzin would later be recognized as a reincarnation of her grandmother.[4] Second, it is noteworthy that we have no namtar at all for Mingyur Peldrön's mother or sisters. It also seems unlikely that any *Lives* were ever written for these women, as the *Festival of Victorious Conquerors* does not include them in its comprehensive list of Mindröling *Lives*. It mentions Mingyur Peldrön's and

Yangchen Drölma's namtars as well as another namtar, which was unfortunately lost, that had been written for a son born a few generations after Mingyur Peldrön. This suggests that if life stories had been written for other women, they would have been mentioned here, even if they were later lost. It seems that after Yangchen Drölma's namtar was written, the next one to be dedicated to a woman's life was *Dispeller*, written some sixty-eight years later. Whatever inspired Lochen Dharmaśrī to write about his mother's life, similar stories were not written by his nieces and nephews about their own mother, nor were namtar recorded for other women in Mingyur Peldrön's generation. With the exception of this one text, Gyurmé Ösel had no other *Lives* of Mindröling women to turn to in composing his work.

In thinking about Gyurmé Ösel's creation of *Dispeller*, it is useful to question how we balance the amplification of women's narratives that these hagiographies provide while mitigating the fact that their stories are being conveyed by male interlocutors. Texts like *Dispeller* give us a sense of how religious women were perceived by their devotees as well as an idea of their lived experience and how they engaged with the world. But when a *Life* is written by someone other than the main subject, it is necessarily influenced by the author's own ideas. How, then, can we understand dialogue, dialogic narrative, or multivocality in this type of hagiography?

Scholars of European medieval *Lives* have considered whether and how we might understand the subject's identity as being effectively conveyed in hagiographic accounts. Drawing on the theory of Hélène Cixous, Luce Irigaray, and Julia Kristeva, the European medievalist Gail Ashton has addressed the challenges of liberating women's voices from a perceived silence in medieval European hagiography.[5] She seeks to locate female saints' voices in hagiographies that she describes as dominated by the voices of their male hagiographers. She uses modern concepts of gender distinction to dissect the author-saint relationship in the creation of medieval hagiography and works to disrupt what she describes as a univocality of male discourse. Treating the life stories of women that were written by men as ground on which culturally embedded concepts of saintliness are presented, contested, and reinforced, it is useful to consider the challenge of actually locating women's voices in these texts. Arguably, the voice of the subject is likely to be obscured by that of the author, even if this is not the author's intention. There is a danger that this could lead to cases of gendered censorship. Thus, one antidote would be to establish the autonomous selfhood of female saints so that their voices and authority are properly acknowledged. In the context of medieval hagiography, Gail Ashton highlights how the *Lives* of female saints can be considered a field in which gendered voices contend for primacy within the genre (in particular, male voices attempting to forcibly unify views about women).[6] This treatment of the authorial agency in the creation of hagiographic works across gender lines offers a useful line of inquiry, as such texts risk valuing men's perspectives on women over and above those of the women themselves.

Taking a different approach in the European medievalist context, John Coakley treats the male-female, author-saint relationship as a potentially collaborative and devotional act.[7] Here the model for interpreting hagiographic life writing is focused on social context, gender dynamics, and issues of authority and divinity. Together, author and saint create a text that reflects important information about social and religious engagement in a specific context. In the same field Catherine Mooney addresses gender as a negotiated dynamic and questions how textual dialogues about gender differentiation act to construct and maintain gendered ideals in women's hagiography reflected in the social-historical moment in which they were written.[8] There is a benefit to considering the work of each of these scholars, insofar as they call on scholars of hagiographic literature to consider the relationship between author and subject in these works and the ways that a hagiography might reflect the social and cultural concerns of the time in which it was written.

The collaborative and multivocal readings of hagiography that these scholars describe are useful for understanding Mingyur Peldrön's *Life*. In particular, thinking about these dynamics can help us understand *Dispeller* as a locus for dialogue about pressing social and soteriological concerns, presented in the mode of multivoiced conversation, while attending to and questioning the social dynamics behind the voices found therein. This multivocality—whether literary artifice or historical refraction—provides the opportunity for the author to present issues as though they are being navigated in lived experience, not solely in the text. That is, it gives the impression of being a more genuine account of what happened in real time, regardless of whether or not the events ever occurred. In some places these moments of contestation are presented as different views placed one after the next, so that they appear side by side, but not in the format of a conversational dialogue. Where these moments of dialogue or disagreement are not necessarily quarrelsome, their presence in the text still allows for a multiplicity of perspectives to be presented for the reader.

Mikhail Bakhtin first asserted multivocality as a useful concept for understanding the multiplicity of voices in the modern novel.[9] Scholars have found this to be useful far beyond the purview of the novel, as in Sarah Jacoby's examination of the auto/biographical works of Sera Khandro. Sera Khandro's many conversations with deities, spirits, and humans are a means for understanding her concerns and, by extension, the vagaries of her twentieth-century sociocultural context. They also reflect a "relational selfhood" in which "the subject was constituted by relationships with others rather than separation from them."[10] Jacoby points to the historically and culturally grounded nature of Tibetan life writing and the creativity involved in these texts. She explains: "Auto/biographers like Sera Khandro did not construct a life narrative *ex nihilo*, nor did they simply apply available narrative scripts to formulate their life stories. They creatively engaged, adapted, and resisted elements of their culture repertoire."[11] Both relational selfhood and multivocality are employed by Gyurmé Ösel in his construction of Mingyur Peldrön's hagiography. Whether through depictions of his subject as an incarnation of female deities and semihistorical women or in her conversations with her community, her individual identity is always wrapped up in her relationships to her religious world.

As an author, Gyurmé Ösel engaged the social world around him to create a literary depiction of Mingyur Peldrön, and the dialogic narrative found in Mingyur Peldrön's *Life* navigates contentious conversations about femaleness, monasticism, and the possible futures of Mindröling. While he took full responsibility for composing the text, he also claimed that Mingyur Peldrön had acted as an interlocutor in this process, further expanding the breadth of the creative process and relying on her involvement to further reinforce the validity of his assertions about monasticism, celibacy, abstention from alcohol, and the importance of religious education for men and women. In so doing, *Dispeller* makes an argument for a set of social concerns of its day that, while perhaps not widely shared, are presented as though they were being discussed widely among Nyingmapas.

The collaboration between Mingyur Peldrön and Gyurmé Ösel began when he was only seven years old (eight, according to the Tibetan reckoning) and she was in her twenties. This is attested in *Dispeller* when he recounts their first meeting. The young woman was on a pilgrimage and teaching tour, and her retinue passed by the boy's home. Although she was only in her twenties, she was already known for her institutional and educational authority:

> At that time, they passed by and my grandmother meant to make prostrations to the master teacher, so went out to meet her. This was the first time that I—an eight-year-old—had seen the face of the great master teacher, the Bliss Queen of the *Ḍākinīs* herself, and I thought myself very lucky indeed. Although I only had a brief glimpse of her youthful face, it was wondrous and overwhelmingly beautiful. As soon as I gazed upon her, I shed many tears. I went after her, hoping to ask if I could follow her. Thus, my faith involuntarily arose.[12]

So moved, the little boy reportedly asked to join her group and never looked back, remaining her devoted disciple until her death. Throughout *Dispeller* Gyurmé Ösel presents himself in self-deprecating terms, as a slow student who always sought to live up to his teacher's expectations. Likewise, Mingyur Peldrön is described as a compassionate teacher to the clumsy student, admonishing him gently for his mistakes and instructing him on his meditative practice. Their relationship is depicted as positive, and in his anecdotes about their interactions, Mingyur Peldrön is described as an engaged teacher with a sense of humor. The nature of her instructions will be discussed later on, but for now a brief anecdote will serve to show how she is presented as a teacher whose concern for her students and their learning surpasses any preoccupation about conventional etiquette.

In perhaps the most awkward account in the text, Gyurmé Ösel goes so far as to describe a time when he sought guidance from Mingyur Peldrön to discuss a particularly difficult aspect of his practice. While he does not go into detail about the nature of his questions or her guidance, it seems that during their meeting he accidentally passed gas while they were sitting next to one another. He reports, "She chuckled a little and said 'when I go near you, I smell sweet farts! The boy has given me a gift!' 'Precious Lama,' I said, 'I am so sorry. I ate some of the nomad's yogurt and it has made me ill. I didn't think it would happen.'"[13] He reports that she responded with good humor and that the interaction was followed by a very productive fortnight of instruction and practice. This is all to say that in spite of her notably strict approach to religious practice, she is clearly skilled at putting nervous—and gassy—interlocutors at ease. Gyurmé Ösel's frankness suggests an honesty in his depictions of himself and that the tenor of their collaboration was generally relaxed and friendly.

Gyurmé Ösel also claimed that Mingyur Peldrön was actively involved in determining what would be included in her namtar. In addition to his occasional mention of how he received doctrinal instruction particularly focused on the Great Perfection, he reports that he frequently sought out her advice about what to include in *Dispeller* and what to omit. He first asked permission to write about her life in 1742, and she consented.[14] After that his composition of her *Life* occasionally came up as a topic of conversation between them. Mingyur Peldrön offered suggestions and in some cases commands about what Gyurmé Ösel should write. He recounts conversing with her about the writing of the hagiography itself and mentions that she directly commanded him to "include this in the *namtar*!"[15] For example, she considered the account of the miraculous occurrences surrounding her refuge ceremony to be particularly important and made sure to command him to include the story in *Dispeller*, with all of its prophetic underpinnings. However, while she advised him in creating the text, it does not seem that this constituted a direct authorial voice. In these cases, if her voice comes through, it does so only after being filtered through Gyurmé Ösel's literary decisions. With that said, collaboration is not a necessary factor in Tibetan hagiography, and so it is notable the extent to which he highlights her involvement in the process of creating the text while still identifying himself as the sole author. Mingyur Peldrön's position with regard to the work is clearly established as subject. But the frequent reminder of the subject's consent—and sometimes creative input—works in concert with direct dialogue to give the sense of Mingyur Peldrön's permissive voice in the narrative. The hagiography serves as the ground on which the contested categories of gender and authority are defined and negotiated.

Where Mingyur Peldrön's statements are quoted in the text, filtered through Gyurmé Ösel, can they be taken at face value as her own words? There is a challenge in interpreting the attributions found in any hagiography, and the reliability of the quotations found in *Dispeller* often cannot be corroborated outside the namtar itself. What is perhaps more interesting for our purposes is that it is clear that he attributes phrases to his teacher in ways that contribute to an overall sense of her personality—as he saw it—and an argument he forms about her social and soteriological concerns. The text makes distinctive linguistic and grammatical shifts that denote when she is speaking. These tonal shifts in the narratorial voice reinforce the possibility of a genuinely multivoiced narrative but could also be a surprisingly expert use of linguistic conventions on Gyurmé Ösel's part. For now it will remain an open question whether these words were actually spoken by her, and we will be content with knowing that Gyurmé Ösel saw it as important to attribute them to Mingyur Peldrön. Reading *Dispeller*, we can inquire about his goals in narrating his beloved teacher's life story and the ways that he filters her voice according to his own concerns.

Mingyur Peldrön's shift to adulthood came during the postwar reconstruction of Nyingma institutions that followed the destruction of non-Geluk sites by Geluk-backed Dzungar forces. Her hagiography presents her as actively concerned with monasticism, suggesting that she advocated for a conservative turn toward monasticism at Mindröling. It also points to her teachings for women, and nuns in particular, and her focus on their religious education and praxis. Likewise, in her writing she perpetuated her father's treasure revelations as well as Great Perfection practice. It is important to distinguish between her own works and the depictions of her voice in *Dispeller*, as one represents her direct concerns, while the other shows her through the eyes (and pen) of Gyurmé Ösel.

In her own writing Great Perfection praxis takes center stage. Mingyur Peldrön's educational authority is emphasized insofar as her focus was to propagate those teachings as extensively as possible. But in *Dispeller* she is also portrayed as someone profoundly concerned about the mundane and soteriological welfare of her students and her community. In many sections Mingyur Peldrön is depicted as a fully realized, semidivine being. However, in the same text in which she is depicted as a miraculous person from birth, she is also shown to be capable of experiencing the gamut of human emotions and reacting to them in human ways. This wide array of presentations about her personality remains well within the realm of hagiography while presenting tensions that reinforce the dialogic nature of the text. In effect these give the reader a variety of representations of who she was.

A Song of Loss and Fear

Mingyur Peldrön is rarely portrayed as an effusive emotional being in *Dispeller*. However, Gyurmé Ösel attributes quotations to her that reveal her susceptibility to human emotion. This is most apparent in her poetic verse, which Gyurmé Ösel connects with a pivotal moment in her transition to a leadership role for Mindröling. The song appears in *Dispeller*, and he attributes it to her, claiming that she spontaneously composed it in a moment of deep suffering. This piece is written in a Tibetan poetic style of metered verse called *gur* that was made famous by the songs of Milarepa and has been translated variously as "songs of realization," "poetical songs," "meditative songs," "enigmatic spiritual songs," and "songs of experience."[16] In Tibet gur developed over the earlier and later diffusions of Buddhism as part of a larger movement toward poetic form influenced by classical Indian poetry such as *dohā* and *caryāgīti*, which Buddhist studies scholar Janet Gyatso describes as "coded metaphorical songs about esoteric yogic experience from late Indian tantric Buddhism."[17] Caryāgīti were spiritual songs meant to convey spiritual truths in a commonly intelligible manner.[18] By the Renaissance period,[19] these verses came to refer to specifically religious experience and included accounts of realization as well as instructions for the hearer. In general gur are known for providing accessibility to spiritual truths through song and came to be associated with an "experience" of spiritual realization that was often highly personal in nature.[20]

The gur that Gyurmé Ösel attributes to Mingyur Peldrön consists of thirty-two lines of seven-syllable metered verse, which was a popular format in the seventeenth century.[21] The presentation of gur as a spontaneous production that was often the result of an emotional upheaval (either positive or negative) adds to the mystique and veracity of the author's role as realized spiritual practitioner. While traditional narratives will argue that one requires no training to produce spontaneous gur and while it is also possible that Gyurmé Ösel composed the gur and attributed it to Mingyur Peldrön, there are several indicators that suggest that she was in fact the author of this song. Born into a period of literary efflorescence in Ü, she was trained and raised by those who participated in the flourishing literary aesthetic movement of the time. Alongside the Fifth Dalai Lama and the Desi Sangyé Gyatso, Lochen Dharmaśrī wrote a treatise on traditional Indian poetic meter.[22] Terdak Lingpa wrote in gur verse, even composing letters to the Fifth Dalai Lama in this style.[23] While many people around Mingyur Peldrön were writing gur, it is almost certain that she knew of the genre, even though she was not trained in it herself.[24] Taken together with the fact that Mingyur Peldrön was an author of multiple works and that the literary style of the gur matches her work more closely than that of Gyurmé Ösel's, it is quite likely that she actually did compose this song. Its style and composition is notably different from the rest of *Dispeller*. The tone and use of emotive words go above and beyond the rest of Gyurmé Ösel's writing, and the poetic style differs completely from his somewhat terse grammatical tendencies. While we have no other evidence of his work (*Dispeller* is the only text for which he is attributed authorship), we do have Mingyur Peldrön's own writing, and her style mirrors the song in its literary sophistication.

As described earlier, Mingyur Peldrön's journey to exile in Sikkim was precipitated by the arrival of Dzungar soldiers at Mindröling in the winter of 1717–18 and the harassment of her sisters. It became clear that the family's lives were in danger, and the decision was made that she should flee. Thus, the harrowing task of traveling was overlaid with the fear of being caught by this army and concern for the lives of her community. As a brief reminder, during this period the inmates of Mindröling were scattered to different regions, for their protection and to preserve for posterity the teachings they carried. Many people were killed or otherwise harmed, and fear was all around. Gyurmé Ösel describes her departure and journey as filled with hardship. She nearly becomes lost in the wilderness at one point, and she has a close shave in which the army nearly discovers her and her entourage hiding among a collection of boulders. This traumatic experience is compounded by the fact that she and the rest of her family are in mortal danger. One can imagine the combination of fear and unknowing and concern for those closest to her as she made this journey. At the nadir of the story she receives word that Mindröling has been destroyed and her uncle and brother have been executed in Lhasa. In learning this, she is overcome by grief and breaks into a song of woeful prayer. She directs her lament to her most important teacher and root guru, who also happens to be her deceased father:

Je Namo Guru!
To you—my only steadfast refuge vast—
With heart so kind atop your Lotus Throne,
My only father—Dharma King so high—
To you Terdak Lingpa, I pray alone!
Supposedly compassionate supreme
(And yet compassion without action's but a thought),
I wander here alone and pray you look
To Mingyur Peldrön, lost and overwrought!
The King of Oddiyana's Treasure fine,
Your Secret Great Instructions reigned most high,
Shone brilliant like the sun and moon above,
But now dark clouds obstruct them in the sky.
The living line of masters once grew strong.
Instructions wise, to these they once gave life.
Spring flowers bloomed, and likewise teachings grew
But now they're choked as autumn's frost spreads rife.

> Delightful home! Celestial garden sweet,
> I gave it up—cast off like oozing rag—
> To wander fearsome forest all alone,
> Through canyon of despair and dreadful crag.
> This worldly form is nothing but a lie!
> No "youthful flower"—naught but fantasy.
> I've run from army and samsara's hold
> And yet from terror I could not break free.
> True mind—I can't embrace it on my own.
> I have become just like the hunted deer
> Before Lord Yama—terror's face of death.
> Back bowed, I drag the weight of endless fear.
> Oh Terdak Lingpa, you I beg alone:
> My foes approach! Please tame them—don't you see?
> Without your refuge how will I escape?
> Look there as now the army comes for me![25]

Rather than a beatific practitioner effortlessly transcending pain, in this moment Mingyur Peldrön is consumed by human emotions, her experience likened to wandering in a frightening wilderness. Her song conveys the experience of mere mortals when we witness the destruction of the people and places we love best, the loss of home and family. It sends the message that at her core she was just as human as everyone else and that all beings—even privileged and educated women—face suffering and adversity. Even as she escapes, she remains imprisoned in her fear, akin to the hunted deer. The song points out her combined religious and familial connections; for her, religious and biological family were one and the same. In Mingyur Peldrön's own words, we see her here at her most vulnerable, her least assured. In this moment she does what any ideal practitioner would do: she calls upon her root guru for guidance and protection. She also does what any child would do: she calls upon her parent for help. At the end of her lamentation, her anguish is dispelled by reassuring visions of her father (here simultaneously presented as Padmasambhava) and Yeshé Tsogyel, who appear before her in the sky:

> Thus, by singing this sad song she called from afar. As a result, she saw clearly in the sky before her an image of the mother and father of Oddiyana and the excellent highest lama in an expanse of rainbow light. As a result, her torment was cleared away.[26]

This vision is said to lighten her heart, and she is able to bravely continue her journey. The inspirational message is simple and clear: praying to her apotheosized father results in a vision of supportive deities. In this moment the reader is reminded of Mingyur Peldrön's combined familial and religious connections, which are well ensconced in gendered assumptions of the contemporary Nyingma world. Here they take the emblematic forms of Padmasambhava and Yeshé Tsogel. The human experience of a young woman fleeing danger and worrying for her family is the at the center of the song, rather than more positive experiences of enlightenment that one might expect from verses of spiritual realization. If the reader imagines Mingyur Peldrön's situation, the spiritual realization found here might be a realization of the suffering of human experience as acutely portrayed in her own moment of abject terror. The despairing tone of her song need not be viewed as contradictory to Gyurmé Ösel's emphatic representation of his master as fully enlightened. While it does not convey the elated experience of realization found in other "songs of experience," it imparts a sudden recognition of being hunted, pursued by murderous soldiers. Here the concept of realization becomes something akin to but different from the soteriological experience of nirvana. She has an experience of complete awareness of her situation, and in doing so she becomes aware of the nature of suffering in samsara. In a simultaneously conventional way, she is also describing the high alert of being chased by an army set to destroy her.

Mingyur Peldrön's song can be read as a description of the human experience of traumatic separation or as a model for the path to enlightenment. It does the double work of conveying mundane and spiritual concerns of the fear of bodily harm and a longing for release from the suffering of cyclic existence. Speaking simultaneously of escape from physical danger and release from the suffering of samsara, both escapes are equally necessary for her. The poem alludes to the painful human experiences of a woman on the Buddhist path, pursuing a way to high spiritual realization. The terrifying wilderness represents the world of suffering, the guidance she seeks that of liberation. As the story goes, from the moment of this vision, Mingyur Peldrön cultivated disgust for worldly things. With her gur the message is clear: strive to work for the teachings; do not be daunted by terrible destruction; and if you call upon them for help, powerful deities will guide you. The song also holds an important position in her hagiography as a literary work. It acts as a pivot in her narrative. At the outset she is a student of the great teachers of Mindröling, training to assume a role in religious leadership. At the end of her lamentation, she carries on, having been elevated to a fully participating member of the institution. In one profound moment of intense sadness and fear, she goes from disciple to teacher, from child to adult.

Exemplary lives and gur have been closely connected since at least the twelfth century CE.[27] Over time in Tibet this poetic style became associated with the wisdom of yogins, who were in turn associated with the tantric practitioners of India.[28] However, gur were also composed by monastics and laypeople, and these compositions symbolized much more than literary prowess.[29] The ability to spontaneously produce versified song was considered a sign of soteriological achievement and drew an implicit connection between spontaneous gur and advanced realization.[30] Frequently, gur show up in literary works when a protagonist experiences a sudden insight and breaks into song. It is hard not to think of these narratives in terms of the Broadway musical or the European operatic tradition, wherein actors express the greatest emotion (and the more mundane story progression) through song. Gur are meant to reflect the spiritual insights of the singer and can be thematic or temporal, abstract or narrative, but generally convey their personal experience. To write gur was to exemplify enlightenment. The topic of realization is often present in analogical form in gur, which frequently connect contemplative practice, imagery, and understanding with mundane activities.[31] The mood of gur can vary widely: some are celebratory, others melancholy or mournful, but they are generally considered to represent a moment of soteriological insight or realization. In some cases— including that of Mingyur Peldrön's gur—the song conveys an experience of sadness or dejection that is relieved by calling to the guru or a deity for help. In this moment in *Dispeller*, the reader is drawn closer to Mingyur Peldrön through her own voice. She is portrayed as one who experienced suffering herself. By illustrating her humanity, Gyurmé Ösel's choice to include this gur also contributes to the sense of multivocality in the text.

Mingyur Peldrön the Author

A brief look at the reception of Mingyur Peldrön's texts and their inclusion in larger Nyingma collections reveals the importance of her work in the continuation of Dzogchen praxis into the nineteenth and twentieth centuries and her combined roles as an educational and institutional authority. Her instruction manuals are included in collections found at Katok and Lelung and in the collected works of scholars such as Jamgön Kongtrul. The writing of several well-known Nyingma practitioners from the eighteenth, nineteenth, and twentieth centuries reveals that Mingyur Peldrön was an important transmitter of the lineages associated with Terdak Lingpa's treasures, especially those related to the Great Perfection. Dudjom Rinpoche describes her as "a brilliant teacher" who "authored several important meditation manuals."[32] The inclusion of her instruction manuals in these collections, such as Jamgön Kongtrul Lodrö Thayé's (1813–99) well-known collection the *Great Collection of Precious Treasure (Rinchen Terdzö)*,[33] suggests that they were considered to be of abiding importance, while their proliferation across multiple Nyingma communities indicates that they were in use to at least some extent. It is clear that her writing was considered important by and transmitted to people beyond Mindröling.

Mingyur Peldrön's corpus reflects particular doctrinal and educational concerns, most notably a strong focus on Dzogchen and Terdak Lingpa's own treasure revelations. Soteriologically, they portray her as a strong proponent of Dzogchen practice over other systems. Interestingly, they tell us little about her focus on monasticism or women's education, both of which are prominent as Gyurmé Ösel's focus in *Dispeller*. There is almost no discussion of abstention from alcohol, prioritizing monastic life over non-monastic practice, or the importance of women's learning. Rather, the focus is on proper meditative approach, exposition on Terdak Lingpa's treasure texts, and other guides for initiated disciples. This creates a sense of disjuncture from *Dispeller*, in which Gyurmé Ösel forwards these concerns, portraying her as a teacher predominantly interested in monastic life, offering highly gendered themes in her lectures to students. However, there is one place in which she does address such things.

The informal *Ambrosial Feast of Questions and Answers* is a document written in question-and-answer format in which Mingyur Peldrön responds to assorted questions on a variety of topics directed at a general, uninitiated audience. A few quotations from *The Ambrosial Feast* give a sense of some of the advice she offered. These include direction on proper meditation technique, the correct use of mantras, methods for optimal visualization practice, and introductions to preliminary practices for the Great Perfection. But the *Ambrosial Feast* also includes some life advice. For example, Mingyur Peldrön was asked whether a layman who has committed an egregious action should be allowed to become a monastic. This is one of the few unusual places where Mingyur Peldrön gives direct moral advice in her own writing and discusses the liberatory potential of the monastic life. She writes:

At the time when a layman commits a grave moral wrongdoing, and so feeling remorse shaves his head and turns to [monastic] life, having conceived the urge to escape, [he'll do this] just as [money] is quickly earned and then [quickly] spent. During that time, something like a weak awareness will have arisen and he'll have [gained] some capacity. In the future, either he'll [continue to act] like a householder, or if he has really taken profound caution [and] deeply focuses on his wrongdoing, he will be completely different from before and condemn [his earlier actions.] And what of [one who maintains] a bad disposition? He will taste that bad karma.[34]

Here we get a sense of Mingyur Peldrön's perspective on the ethical and karmic implications of bad actions and the role of monasticism in the rehabilitation of character. She pragmatically points out that the layman's feelings of remorse may very well subside as quickly as they arose. But if remorse and desire for change does take root, then he will be able to successfully change his behavior. The implication is that he should not be hasty in taking monastic vows as an escape from his own actions, since he will not have changed himself enough at that point and the impulse to renounce may quickly fade. The desire to take up the monk's life is perhaps a momentary response and not something to be too quickly chosen, although it does have the potential to be of benefit. She then responds to the question of how one should react if a man has already left his household and taken vows under suspicious circumstances, such as to avoid unwanted responsibilities at home. For this she advises:

To determine whether or not he is casting off obligations:
    He should again honestly state his activities before his good wife, and then later if he gives over all his wages [to her] he can [go forth]. Moreover, there's no need to protect [him] in any negotiations that arise. I [assess] how he speaks to me, and whether or not the good wife [says] "give me an income." If [the exchange] appears bitter, discipline should be exacted [on him]. But again, if the request for aid comes from the gentleman [himself], he will not be disgraced, [and] the vows will come forth from him wondrously. In the advice of Siddha Yolmowa on liberation in a single life he says: "In a bowl of beer, there are many muck experts."[35] As this quote indeed indicates, to have the experience of taking vows, your dedication should be fully born. Firmly reaching

sublime non-existence, we will long remain, thinking of the present and the future. Or, if [one's dedication] is incomplete, one will enter the endless knot of the mind.[36]

In order to assess the earnestness and motives behind a wayward layman's intention to suddenly take vows and become a monk, Mingyur Peldrön suggests going to his wife and observing their interactions with one another. She cautions against shielding him in the course of the exchange but instead indicates that the observer should rely on the wife's response to the situation to determine whether or not he is genuinely ready to take up the monastic life. This is an interesting moment, as it calls for the reader to rely on the wife to determine what is best for her husband and the household. Rather than trusting the "muck expert" swimming in his bowl of beer,[37] she suggests looking to his wife to assess whether the layman is ready for monastic life. It also points to the reality that some chose the monastic life to evade the unwanted responsibilities in the householder realm. In turn this would have a significant impact on the rest of the family, should one member leave to become a monk. Her caution here is interesting given that she was generally a strong proponent of monastic life. It is clear that her pro-monasticism also contains nuance, a concern for the families of monastics, and a suggestion that wives should be looked to in determining the futures of their husbands. Prospective monks should first be vetted before they are accepted, for their own sake and that of their families, and each individual case should be considered in its own context. Significantly, that vetting process should include a careful observation of the female head of the house, to determine how his renunciation would impact her and the family. Likewise, this was considered ultimately beneficial for the husband as well. No one wants to end up stuck in the "endless knot of the mind,"[38] apparently a distinct possibility should he take up vows of renunciation before he is ready. Mingyur Peldrön's stance here is in keeping with her more general concerns about men, women, monasticism, and life well lived, all of which were conveyed by Gyurmé Ösel in *Dispeller*.

Admonitions and Advice

Mingyur Peldrön's identity as a religious master and teacher is reiterated throughout *Dispeller* in lengthy and brief references to her engagement with students, in which Gyurmé Ösel quotes her directly or relates the topics on which she lectured. He mentions a variety of students, including members of the aristocracy, laypeople, and former disciples of her father. For example, the entirety of *Dispeller*'s account for the year 1732 is focused on a discussion of Mingyur Peldrön's teaching activities, particularly those dedicated to former disciples of Terdak Lingpa and their families. Here Gyurmé Ösel highlights her relationship with these old students, who requested that she continue her educational activities in a variety of ways:

> At that time the wife and daughter of her father's student Serzang Drupchen Gyurmé Longdröl went together from Tö to the monastery to meet [Mingyur Peldrön]. She bestowed on them the profound instructions of [Terdak Lingpa's] *New Treasures*. In the Male Water Bird year (1732)—her thirty-fourth—her father's disciples came from Latö. The renunciate practitioner Wangchuk Gyurmé Nangdrol, Gyurmé Tharchin, and many renunciates from Latö offered many worthy things, and had an audience [with her]. At that time, she taught about [Terdak Lingpa's] *Shauk Treasures*. Her father's disciple Depa Gyurmé Samten Chogdrup of Yangdrong requested the *Secret Wisdom Ḍākinī* instruction manual. With respect to that, she drafted an illuminating lamp of instruction, and accordingly granted instruction to the renunciates in Tö. Later she bestowed abundant advice on them. And so for three years she kept the three doors engaged, without growing weary.[39]

A few significant things are combined in this passage. Here the central Tibetan prince Gyurmé Samten Chogdrup asks Mingyur Peldrön to write what is here referred to as the *Secret Wisdom Ḍākinī Instruction Manual*.[40] This brief historical account gave basic information even as it reminded the reader that Mingyur Peldrön was both a teacher who was sought out by local aristocracy and an author besides. It is noteworthy that she also took time to meet with and teach a variety of people, including the women of Serzang Drupchen Gyurmé's family. Their presence here shows that Mingyur Peldrön's educational role was not solely focused on one particular group. She taught nuns, monks, laywomen, and laymen.

Mingyur Peldrön's role as a teacher of important Nyingma practitioners can also be traced in texts beyond *Dispeller*. Katok Rigdzin Tsewang Norbu (1698–1755) visited Mindröling in 1737 while on pilgrimage in central Tibet. The famous Katok master and emissary apparently stopped at Mindröling before heading to Lhasa. While there, he made offerings and received empowerments and instruction on multiple aspects of Dzogchen training from both

Rinchen Namgyel and Mingyur Peldrön. He also visited the statues and other sites at the monastery, relating that he found the architecture to be quite beautiful.⁴¹ Signs of Mingyur Peldrön's importance are found elsewhere, as her name is included in lineage lists and supplication prayers found in collections by scholars such as Jamyang Kheyntse Wangpo,⁴² Jamgön Kongtrul, Tsewang Norbu, Dudjom Lingpa (b. 1835), and Chökyi Wangchuk (1775–1837). She is named in two of Jamgön Kongtrul's treasuries. In his monumental *Great Collection of Precious Treasure*—a collection of terma and related materials—she is mentioned in no fewer than nine transmission lineages or lineage prayers, all of which include other Mindröling or Sikkimese Dzogchen lineage holders. One of her instruction manuals for Terdak Lingpa's treasures is also referenced, while two of her own texts are included in the collection.⁴³ These mentions suggest a continued importance in the transmission of Mingyur Peldrön's teachings and an abiding perception of her historical and institutional significance. She is usually listed alongside other Mindröling figures, most often Terdak Lingpa and Rinchen Namgyel. Notably, she is frequently the only woman in each list, with the exception that sometimes Trinlé Chödrön (born a few generations later at Mindröling) is also included. However, the most interesting references to Mingyur Peldrön's teaching are found within *Dispeller*, in which Gyurmé Ösel paints a very specific picture of her pedagogical concerns. Compared to her instruction manuals, the accounts of her teachings in *Dispeller* are more anecdotal, with individually attuned advice directed at the specific needs of her interlocutors.

Mingyur Peldrön began teaching in earnest after she arrived in Sikkim in 1718.⁴⁴ Histories of Sikkim corroborate her role as a teacher during her time there, explaining that while she and her mother and sisters spent five years there as the guests of the king and the abbot of Pemayangtsé, the young woman gave extensive teachings.⁴⁵ In addition to written instructions and prayers, she influenced Mindröling through the teachings that she gave to individual disciples and to large crowds. At events she gave strings of initiations. Gyurmé Ösel claims that at various points in her life she regularly gave teachings to groups of religious practitioners (often monks and nuns but also non-monastics), frequently ranging from two hundred to four hundred people.⁴⁶ These claims are supported by a narrative currently circulating at Pemayangtsé Monastery in Sikkim, where she is remembered as someone who taught large groups. Her throne there was reportedly erected for her to give mass teachings during the few years when she was living in the area.⁴⁷

In *Dispeller* Gyurmé Ösel quotes Mingyur Peldrön's instruction to him and others that suggest she was predominantly concerned with the role of monasticism in spiritual development and directing her students according to their gendered positionality. Her advice to women differed from her advice to men. This kind of gendered bifurcation in advice to men and women is common in Tibetan literary historical contexts and was often wrapped up with the trope of the lesser female birth. For example, in Nyangral Nyima Ozer's hagiography of Padmasambhava, the saint is depicted as advising nuns in spite of the fact that "because of your low rebirth due to bad actions, it is inconceivable that you will become learned."[48] In these cases women were considered unable to achieve the same heights of scholastic or soteriological development as men but should still practice insofar as they are able. However, in the case of Mingyur Peldrön, the implications and goals of her advice were quite different.

Mingyur Peldrön's advice in *Dispeller* not only focused on monasticism; it was segregated by gender in the way that she—or at least Gyurmé Ösel— spoke directly to perceived social challenges within the community. They suggest that one or both of them thought that women in general were underutilized and not well enough respected as teachers of the dharma and that men were not upholding their vows effectively. Both of them were highly aware of the impact of gender on practitioners' experiences with religious life. Gyurmé Ösel mentions her statements about how monks, nuns, nonmonastic male practitioners, and laypeople should work toward enlightenment. The gendered dimension in Mingyur Peldrön's advice to these groups presents her position as a revolutionary proponent of women's education and leadership while also asserting the primacy of the monastic life over non-monastic paths.

One particular quotation will serve as the most robust example in the hagiography. In 1766, after lecturing on one of Terdak Lingpa's revealed treasure cycles to an assembly of about two hundred people,[49] a small group of fifteen monks and nuns stayed on to meet with Mingyur Peldrön afterward. She first advised the monks in the group to practice diligently and cultivate faith in their lama. She reminded them of the danger of rebirth in the lower realms (especially the hells), calling upon them to examine their past deeds and attend to their karmic loads. She likened the illusory nature of the world to that of drunkenness, explaining to her disciples that "one who has drunk much beer thinks their innate realization is elevated and their speech impressive, when in reality their speech is slurred, their brain faltering and sluggish."⁵⁰ Even worse, if one fails to practice with diligence, they will swiftly receive punishment from the ḍākinīs and end up in a bad rebirth.⁵¹ The suggestion here is that the monks, although ordained, are in danger of falling off the path. Threats of punishing ḍākinīs and hellish rebirths are the order of the day. Mingyur Peldrön then turns to the nuns and addresses them in a completely different tone:

> You nuns! Taking care of oneself independently, acting in definite accordance with the dharma: working beyond these things to teach and propagate the dharma is difficult. However, you are great and powerful nuns! Your self-interest having fallen away, you must perform your ability to teach and propagate [it]. Previously there are some who said "I am a niece of so-and-so." There are several [nuns] like this, we all know. But now if you are wondering whether practicing the righteous dharma will leave you materially poor, do nothing to contradict the vows and precepts, and be devoted to your lama. If you cultivate unceasing confidence in these instructions and endeavor [to work hard] at them, then the obscurations of previous actions will be purified, and subsequently the karma that arises in the beguiling desire realm [will also be purified]. In particular, the Great Tertön himself has said, "If one exerts effort in my revealed teachings, there will be no need to worry about the concerns of livelihood. And so, keeping in mind that each person's livelihood is attuned to the result of their capacities, one should offer jewels and endeavor to donate to the poor." All of you should keep death in mind. Being certain in the truth of the explanation about the worldly suffering of the three lower realms, which are found in the Kangyur, Tengyur, and the oral teachings, you have to bear this in mind diligently.⁵²

Here Mingyur Peldrön is urging the nuns to expand their influence by going out and teaching. She points to their strength and independence, their ability to care for themselves and to reliably act in accordance with the dharma. Citing their advanced capacity, she calls on them to think of the soteriological concerns of others. She argues that they should turn their worries away from whether or not they will have enough to eat. She seems to be suggesting that if they practice and teach, they will always have enough to survive, even if they forgo the comforts to which they are accustomed. This even includes those privileged women from highborn families who, she argues, should not fret over their social status as nuns. They should care for themselves minimally, focusing their attention instead on the education of others. The implication here is the importance of sacrificing one's own comfort for the sake of the more challenging role of helping sentient beings toward enlightenment. This moment forwards the material concerns that women face when they become nuns. This perennial problem of whether and how women could attain material support in monastic life was also an issue for the nuns she taught. Here she attempts to assuage their worries, although she falls short of promising that they will be cared for by the larger institution of Mindröling. Rather, she points to their ability to act as model practitioners and as teachers as a means for exhorting them to take up the role of educating others.

This exhortation speaks to the concerns of her immediate audience and also the concerns of other women at different moments throughout history and the barriers that they faced. Economic and physical security and status were clearly issues for nuns in Mingyur Peldrön's world, and preaching seems to have been considered an unlikely path. She was aware of these challenges, in spite of her generally privileged status. Her statement here suggests that at least some of the women she spoke with came from well-to-do homes and were concerned about the hardships that a life of teaching might entail. It is assumed that they have already taken a monastic path and that now is the time for them to turn their attention toward active teaching in the community. As a woman who lived this life herself, Mingyur Peldrön acts as a model for the nuns. In speaking about women's engaged religious practice while simultaneously modeling this life, her own legitimated experience as a female practitioner serves as an unspoken aspect of her argument in favor of female monastics becoming teachers of religion. Here she is also engaging her role as an educational and institutional authority, urging these women to follow in her footsteps.

In this moment Mingyur Peldrön expresses concern about women's roles in the religious world. She argues that women rather than men should be relied on more to preach the dharma and gives her female disciples compassionate encouragement along these lines. In doing so, Mingyur Peldrön is counteracting gendered marginality in this advice to nuns. Her instructions are calls to action, exhorting nuns to use their training and education to become dharma teachers themselves. She urges these women to move past any fear or reservations and rise up and become leaders in the tradition. By calling on these women to teach, she is drawing them in from the margins of the monastic community, inciting them to take on a new role even as she asserts their centrality in the tradition. This encouragement is not the only form of socially significant and gendered advice that she gives. There are a few accounts in *Dispeller* that emphasize her concerns about the monastic community's ability to maintain celibacy and her worries about male practitioners using their practice space to get drunk and carouse.

There are many other places in *Dispeller* in which Mingyur Peldrön is portrayed as concerned about nuns' welfare. For example, Gyurmé Ösel includes an account of her meeting with a nun named Kunzang Drönma, who was doing practice at Shauk Taggo (the site of one of Terdak Lingpa's treasure revelations). Upon their meeting, Mingyur Peldrön is most concerned with whether or not Kunzang Drönma has enough resources to stay fed and housed and whether she needs additional financial support. Kunzang Drönma reports that all of her needs are being met. When she writes Mingyur Peldrön again, using a local dialect and neglecting the honorific register ("She made the request in the Mon dialect, without using any honorific language"),[53] Mingyur Peldrön merely chuckles at the nuns' lack of etiquette and agrees to meet with her. When they meet, she gives the nun support, making sure to write her instructions in a form that she can read, without mentioning that the earlier letter was not up to the usual standards. In choosing this account, Gyurmé Ösel portrays Mingyur Peldrön as an approachable teacher who is not concerned with formality so much as she is compassionately worried about her disciples' practice and dedication. When a practitioner is doing her best, Mingyur Peldrön does not worry about proper social etiquette.

There are several times in *Dispeller* when Mingyur Peldrön chastises male practitioners for ill behavior. These accounts are often connected to a critique of the Fifth Lelung, Jedrung Losang Trinlé, who acts as a foil throughout the namtar, representing an approach that is at odds with her monastic conservatism and moralistic approach to praxis. This dynamic is established early on in the story when, in 1726, she is invited to visit his community while traveling on pilgrimage with her mother and sisters:

> Then, a few days from the Olkha hot springs, they received an invitation from Lelung Jedrung Rinpoche, Losang Trinlé—he who at that time was becoming so well-known for actually understanding Padmasambhava's famous Mother-Father Union [practice], and had raised hope among the Tibetan people and all sentient beings without remainder—that same Lelung invited them to visit for a few days. [When they arrived], he said

"Today is the time when wisdom ḍākinīs gather, you must have some 'ambrosia'!" So saying, he pressed beer upon them. From an excess of "offering nectar," his group had all become violently drunk. Then Jedrung led the singing. Monks and nuns, laymen and laywomen, all of them sang incomprehensibly and danced indiscriminately together, creating a wondrous spectacle. The great lama herself took not one mouthful of the "nectar," saying "I'll have a beer substitute." She insisted on a great ladleful of tea, dispensed with a copper dipper.[54]

Among accounts of Mingyur Peldrön's visits to wayward practice communities, her report of the visit to the Fifth Lelung's place is the most scathing. The inebriation of the group is depicted as both humorous and horrifying, while Lelung's attempts to get the new arrivals drunk is shameful yet funny. After briefly observing the community members drinking, singing, dancing, and carrying on, Mingyur Peldrön suggests a nonalcoholic option—tea instead of beer—which she offers to a few monks. Unable to refuse her, they accept and, according to Gyurmé Ösel, all their bad karma is cleared away as a result.[55] Seeing this, some of the drunkards come before her, seeking help. She declares "What's the use of leading [them] from this place of promiscuity?"[56] To which the monks respond with "We were too intent on the great Jedrung Rinpoche. Also, today do we not celebrate the gathering of a cloud of wisdom ḍākinīs? If we didn't drink the 'nectar,' we would go to a bad rebirth." In response to their excuse, she curtly replies, "Oh well, I guess you had to drink it then." With the exception of her companions and a few others who had been convinced, everyone else gets drunk. The next day she leaves with her entourage.[57]

It seems that Mingyur Peldrön departed abruptly after recognizing that Lelung's followers would not be swayed by her conservative approach to alcohol. It is clear that she thought the dialogue closed at that point. Attempting to convince his disciples that their teacher was wrong might also have been considered bad form. And so, rather than arguing with them or working to convince them, she simply left. Gyurmé Ösel claims that Mingyur Peldrön reported the story to him herself and laughed while she was recalling it. In hindsight she found the episode to be amusing, and it acts as the somewhat humorous introduction to her teetotalist approach to consort practice that is revisited again later in *Dispeller*. The moment represents the fall of Lelung in her estimation. She had thought it a good idea to go to his center, but what she and her companions found there is presented as a shocking abomination, far from what they had expected. We might also read the opening phrases indicating Lelung's great reputation as potentially sarcastic. Regardless, she clearly decided that the pilgrims should visit the well-known teacher and were dismayed by what they found. After learning the truth about his behavior, she had no interest in sticking around, but tried to "save" as many people as possible before departing.

In Lelung's literary role as a foil, he represents a non-monastic practice community gone wrong, sullied by excessive drinking and carousing. The one who the community perceived as accomplished in tantric practice is in the best case one who has been led astray by the demon of drink. In the worst case he is a charlatan. Lelung was in fact a controversial figure, and people other than Mingyur Peldrön have noted his love of alcohol and women.[58] It is quite possible that this representation of Lelung stands for nothing more than a simple recollection of the man, not some grand symbol of all that is wrong in strayed non-monastic communities. From another perspective this could also be understood as an incident of one teacher poaching students from another, of whose methods she disapproves. Interpreted differently, the narrative could easily read as her having descended upon a lively religious community engaged in practice, disrupted them, and either scared and/or threatened the practitioners into dispersing. Beer was and is used in some rituals and in literary contexts as a symbol of divine nectar (Skt. *amṛta*; Tib. *bdud rtsi*) that represents profound teachings and soteriological experience.[59] However, here it becomes a means of depicting her position as staunchly anti-booze and immune to pressure from the famous man, who in her hagiography serves as an absurd foil and representative of all that could go wrong in religious communities.

Other accounts of wayward male disciples dot the narrative landscape of the namtar. In 1751 she is called in to redirect the activities of the men at the Drepu retreat center. The head of the community had died in 1749, and without direction the community had abandoned their practice for more worldly activities.[60]

> In the iron sheep year [1751] many harlots and men were singing together throughout the day and night—more than they ever had before. Sometimes they would fight, which created a great clamor. At this point, some earnest people requested [Mingyur Peldrön's help]. She said: "The 'elders,' have not manifested realization of the wonderful *dharmatā*. Their knowledge—which is *not* imbued with renunciation—is overcome with doubt."

Then, she told the great practitioner Tobgyé to go to the Terchen's [Terdak Lingpa's] holy spot at Shauk [Taggo], and meditate earnestly. Because they [the drunkards] were very learned, they returned to [work as] the heads of school [meaning unclear].[61] After that, anyone with a connection to the laywomen no longer acted in conflict with the lama's command.[62]

Mingyur Peldrön suggests that the men have not attained a higher level of practice because they have not sought renunciation. She recommends earnest meditation, and they listen to her, cutting their ties with a group of women who are alternately referred to as "harlots" (*bud med smad tshong ma*) and "laywomen" (*nag mo*). The conflation of one with the other is telling here; consorting with non-monastic women is dangerous as it can lead directly to sex. The quotation says nothing about monastic women, so we cannot extend assumptions in that direction. Here the onus is specifically placed on the men to attend to their behavior; the women are not to blame. In fact, it is a woman who corrects their path and leads them in the right direction. In the end the men are able to pull it together and, abandoning their relations with unseemly women, return to their spiritual responsibilities. Due to their previous high education, they are able to become leaders of the retreat center.

The implication is that serious practice is possible for anyone, but for these men it would be easier with renunciation. Bad habits can always be abandoned. In addition to questioning the sincerity of their dedication to practice, she is recommending that they become monks if they really want to refocus their efforts. Moreover, teaching or leading an institution is a sign of success that Mingyur Peldrön holds in high esteem. It is especially notable that this account takes place at the site of Shauk Taggo, where Terdak Lingpa revealed one of his terma. Geographically positioning a withering critique of non-monastic practice at a place where non-celibate consort practice would have been crucial, such as the very site of terma revelation, signals a strong argument for celibacy even in the face of her family's past acceptance of consort practice. At the same time, Mingyur Peldrön herself passed on terma through her own teachings and benefited directly from this tradition by dint of her own education and doctrinal and familial connections to her father, who was himself a non-celibate practitioner who engaged in consort relationships.

In other moments the focus on teetotalism manifests as genuine concern about her students' alcohol consumption. Another notable case occurs when, nearing her death, Mingyur Peldrön takes the time to chastise Gyurmé

Ösel about drinking. At one point they are discussing his alcohol consumption, and in his defense he claims that he only drank alcohol because he was parched and beer was all that was available. He reports:

> When I was making the water offerings I was parched with thirst, and so drank some beer.... I was later scolded by Her Holiness, who said, "Today when you made water offerings you drank beer, you didn't use good reasoning. If you do this in the future, your students will go the way of bad behavior. So from this time forward, do not do it again!"[63]

Gyurmé Ösel's decision to drink beer during a water offering is ritually problematic, as the consumption of meat, alcohol, and even strong-tasting foods such as garlic are thought to offend the water *nāga* spirits to whom the offerings are made.[64] Mingyur Peldrön questions his reasoning, suggesting that because he was not thinking clearly, nothing terrible will come of the mistake this time. However, now that he knows better, if he does it again, he will experience severe repercussions. Another time she asserts:

> I may be of inferior form [that is, a woman], but nowadays there are those who pretend to be realized. They drink a lot of beer, and their innate realization seems elevated, and they seem happy, but these [perceptions] are only lies. Drinking a lot of beer makes one unable to reason, and one becomes as lazy and slothful as a Mongol. One also naturally gives way to loose speech.[65]

Continuing the theme of the downfalls of alcohol consumption, here the charlatan is likened to the drinker of beer, as self-deluded as one who, having become drunk, experiences false elation. The implication is that just as alcohol makes one lazy and incapable of reason, likewise the practitioner who falsifies their realization is similarly devoid of truth. There are several layers of meaning here. First, to be a woman is not nearly as bad as being a male practitioner who falsifies his enlightenment. Likewise, even "lowly" women can identify such pretenders and see them for what they are: empty husks of practitioners. Also, drinking is bad because it leads to self-delusion and a false sense of happiness. Most important, charlatans are no better than drunks in this regard and should be viewed as such. There is also subtext here that Mingyur Peldrön understands her position as a woman to be considered inferior to men. However, she is more interested in whether one is a legitimate and serious practitioner, rather than whether the person is a woman or a man. Her phrasing borders on the sarcastic in this moment. She might be "inferior" in form (*dman gzugs pa*), but even she can understand how foolish a charlatan looks. This word choice subtly suggests that at least some of her audience was concerned about her role as a woman.

Gyurmé Ösel goes on to claim that in this moment she continued her teaching without thought of fatigue, explaining:

> If one does not meditate, and instead relaxes freely, having previously entered into the religious life, after a short time this will result in punishment from the ḍākinīs, and one risks falling into the three infernal hells.... Moreover, evil and impure deeds will be decreased through unswerving faith and a good lama.... Practice with great diligence![66]

Here she is particularly concerned about those who have taken monastic vows. Monks and nuns seem to have been her primary audience during these speeches. She also gives them positive advice, directing their behavior in terms of what they *should* do, rather than just what they should avoid:

> Thoroughly examine your deeds. Supplicate the lama with unshakable devotion and in the end, one's own heart will be as one with the lama's.[67]

These quotations speak to a concern about the role and nature of non-monastic practice communities and their association with Mindröling. In Mingyur Peldrön's instructions to her disciples, she is falling back on teachings about basic karmic causation, Buddhist cosmology, and reminders about socially embedded morality. She uses them to urge a monastic lifestyle for all of her devotees and finds non-celibate communities abhorrent in spite of their acceptance in the greater Mindröling institutional structure. For Mingyur Peldrön any alcohol consumption would likely lead directly to carousing, wasting one's life, and a rebirth in one of the hells.

Looking at the difference between Mingyur Peldrön's advice to men and women, it seems that her concerns for each group are a response to their relative positions of privilege. The monks, living comfortably in their monastic life, risk falling off the path and into alcohol-fueled debauchery. The nuns, living at the margins, continue to worry about having enough sustenance, although they are educated enough to be teachers themselves. In the exchanges that *Dispeller* presents between Mingyur Peldrön and her disciples, she is speaking from a position of authority that is tinted with her own positional awareness, that of being a female teacher in a male-dominated world. There is a notable gender binary between Mingyur Peldrön's advice to women and to men, regardless of their monastic status. Like the nuns, her male disciples are made aware that they should cultivate devotion in the lama and heed reminders that they could easily be reborn in one of the three lower realms. But her concern for her male disciples is different from her advice for women in the very foundations of theme and tone, regardless of whether they are celibate monks or non-celibate nakpas. In comparing the ways she addresses men and women, her advice and admonitions suggest an eighteenth-century religious institution struggling to keep its monastics on the right path.

Gyurmé Ösel is intent on presenting her as furthering women's education and men's restraint. There is a gendered dimension to her advice to these different groups, which suggests that she was a proponent of educating women to be religious leaders. Her views on gender and monasticism echo the inclusive tenor of the previous generation's goals for Mindröling, even as they suggest significant sociopolitical challenges to the wider Nyingma community of the time. Through Gyurmé Ösel's hagiography, Mingyur Peldrön speaks to her disciples in terms of their positional relationship to their practice, the institution, and herself. The disciples' positionality is furthered by the nature of the instructions they receive, while Mingyur Peldrön's is reflected in her concerns for them. With the men Mingyur Peldrön is concerned about them losing their way with sex and alcohol. They require a more severe reminder of what awaits them in the hells. It is assumed that if they avoid drinking and dallying with harlots and laywomen, they can easily retain leadership roles within the institution. The non-celibate practitioners are a disgrace, while the monks lack focus. In effect, the men need more in the way of reprimand. Meanwhile, the nuns have the very basic challenges of overcoming stigma and dealing with worries about getting enough to eat. With them she is concerned that they are not asserting their authority as they might be, that they are perhaps unsure of themselves and their capabilities and are preoccupied with status. They require less severe reminders of the influence of karma and need no reining in. Rather, the nuns need to be reminded that it is possible for women to be institutional leaders, as was Mingyur Peldrön herself.

Mingyur Peldrön claimed that she would be born a man in her next life, although she had been a woman in many previous lives. When she was nearing the end of her life, she explained to Gyurmé Ösel and a few other disciples that although she had had female lives in the past, the pattern would be interrupted in her next birth, when she would be born in a male body and adopt a monastic life:

> She remained silent for a moment, then said: "From the Dargyé Chöding lineage, none has lived longer than me. I am the oldest, a very old nun. Previously, in India and Tibet, it was necessary that I take up female births. For a short while, this will be interrupted; and so in the next life I will be born as a monk. Moreover, because in a previous life I had the benefit of meeting a spiritual guide, I have the imprint that will allow me to keep working for the lineage of the most essential and secret teachings."[68]

In this statement Mingyur Peldrön's incarnation lineage is simultaneously designated as primarily female, even as it is asserted that her next birth will be male. Both the designation of the line as female and the insistence upon a future male interruption are interesting. The statement suggests a gender continuity across births, at least in Mingyur Peldrön's estimation, as well as some level of flexibility within the system. In the statement she also aligns herself with Mindröling's more protected traditions, which intimates a high level of importance, simultaneously wrapped up with the female form. It seems it was not necessary, at least from Mingyur Peldrön's perspective, for one's future lives to be single gendered.

Taken alone, this claim might reflect the frequent declaration said to have been made by women on the path to enlightenment, bemoaning their birth as a woman and yearning for a future birth as a man. It is possible that Mingyur Peldrön is adhering here to the common Buddhist literary trope of the inferior female birth, wherein a woman laments her form and expresses a desire to be reborn in the "better" body of a man. However, given that these laments are often very overt, it is more likely that Gyurmé Ösel is making an argument for her future birth as a boy at Mindröling. Indeed, in the eighteenth century, at the time when he finally finished *Dispeller*, Mingyur Peldrön's grand-nephew Gyurmé Pema Wangyel had recently been born, and Gyurmé Ösel cites the baby's birth as a reason for finishing the work.[69] It might be that he hoped that this new baby was in fact his teacher incarnate. Ultimately, the boy would be identified as the reincarnation of Terdak Lingpa, not Mingyur Peldrön. It is notable that in her remark Mingyur Peldrön presents her future male birth as a mere interruption in a primarily female incarnation lineage and explains that future births will once more be female. She suggests that for her next birth, the male body would be more expedient, although she does not describe the reasons behind this belief. The dedication to a future female lineage reduces the implication that a male life would be generally preferable, but she still adheres to a normative gender bifurcation in which women are generally reborn as women, men as men, with only occasional exceptions to this rule. There is also the possibility that Mingyur Peldrön wished to take rebirth as a man in the future and that this desire is being glossed over by Gyurmé Ösel, who is concerned with emphasizing his teacher's authority in her present embodiment as a woman.

Elsewhere in the narrative, Mingyur Peldrön addresses her female disciples and expresses an understanding of their position as women and as nuns. While she engages the common trope of the lesser female birth, Gyurmé Ösel downplays this in favor of an emphasis on her role as teacher and enlightened being, drawing on the contemporary literary cachet of female identity to support his presentation of a charismatic leader. His focus on her previous lives in the early sections of *Dispeller* suggests that he viewed gender as a delimiting factor of reincarnation. This brings up the larger questions of who (or what) reincarnates when rebirth occurs, and the male- or femaleness of karmic proclivities. Gyurmé Ösel portrays Mingyur Peldrön as the ur-woman, the embodiment of all those enlightened women known in his context. Between his female-positive and androgynous references, on one hand, and her suggestions of a future male birth and discussion of women's hardships, on the other, a contemporaneous discussion emerges about what it means to be born a woman.

Mingyur Peldrön's status as a woman and the complexities associated with this position are fundamental aspects of her identity in *Dispeller* but are not the focal point of most of her own written works. The hagiography addresses the complications associated with her position and how this affects her public identity. Her position as a Nyingma teacher and author takes on a particular tenor when we consider both her own writing as well as the representations of her in her hagiography. Her own work prioritized instruction in Dzogchen practice and a continued engagement with her father's treasure corpus. Considering her role in the revival and continued existence of Mindröling into the postwar era, it is unsurprising that her work would center the teachings that were unique to Mindröling. The reach of several of her texts suggests her significant influence, appearing as they do in the annals of Nyingma institutions in other regions of the Tibetan cultural world. While these works are geared toward a general audience—albeit an audience with all the proper initiations and empowerments—in *Dispeller* she is presented as a teacher concerned with her disciples' personal welfare.

Dispeller attributes quotations to Mingyur Peldrön that create for her a humane and deeply concerned personality. In contradistinction to her divine identities, her gur expresses the depth of despair felt when one woman loses her home and family. Through this expression she is made more relatable to the average human reader (or hearer) of the song, and she simultaneously exemplifies proper conduct during such a moment of distress. The subtext is that if one prays to one's root and lineage lamas for guidance, moments of deepest despair will be mitigated and one can always find a way through. The song brings out a more human side of Mingyur Peldrön while retaining her divine status through the vision she experiences once she has finished singing. More broadly, the reader is presented with Mingyur Peldrön's own struggles regarding monastic education in her time.

Whether a community-wide shift or a personal propensity, according to her hagiography Mingyur Peldrön recommended a monastic turn within the broader Nyingma community during the postwar reconstruction. This reflects her position as a Nyingma teacher in a period marked by Geluk dominance, which for her meant an emphasis on a monasticism that resonated with the dominant group of this time. The focus on monasticism becomes apparent when we examine the moments in *Dispeller* in which she is quoted. Representations of her encounter with Lelung depict her as far from a meek or acquiescing woman. Rather, she disagreed openly with other Nyingma teachers regarding their methods and refused to deviate from her ideal of celibacy and abstention from intoxicants. It is unclear whether Ü was, in the mid-eighteenth century, rife with drunken and debauched monks. However, Mingyur Peldrön apparently had her share of run-ins with monks behaving badly and wayward nonmonastic laymen. Through accounts of these interactions, we get a sense of what she was like as a teacher and also as a human being. These moments strongly suggest that Mingyur Peldrön was herself aligned with the Geluk culture that was dominant at the time.

Examining both Mingyur Peldrön's corpus and her hagiographic representation, it is easy to understand how she would be depicted as an authoritative woman in her time. Her apparent concern for both proper conduct and sincere practice and her dedication to teachings unique to Mindröling further reinforce her significant contribution to the institution's survival. Gyurmé Ösel's decision to include direct quotations attributed to her and to mention her occasional insistence upon their inclusion gives the narrative qualities of multivocality. However, her voice continues to be mediated by his literary decisions throughout *Dispeller*. He reinforces these decisions with accounts of their interactions. Whether historical fact or imagined exchange, he uses these voices to establish a narrative of dialogic engagement between himself and Mingyur Peldrön that drives underlying arguments in the text. He uses multivocality to suggest that there were discussions happening in the late eighteenth century at Mindröling about issues of monasticism and women's involvement in religious education. Whether or not these were happening beyond Gyurmé Ösel's own mind is unclear.

The dialogic maneuver of multivocality here raises questions about whether and how privilege and status can overcome the trials of being a woman, and also if feminine-gendered identity can in fact be a boon itself. Hagiography is a ground upon which writer, text, and audience all participate in religious actions that define and reinforce culturally embedded concepts of saintliness. As such, it acts as a context where multiple interlocutors present contemporaneous notions of individual identity and religious authority. Mingyur Peldrön's *Life* becomes a space for the discussion of gender and religious authority in eighteenth-century Tibet, and in doing so, it also exemplifies the dialogic nature of hagiography as it is found across multiple religious communities. If we can understand the dialogue taking place within a hagiography, the text will yield information far beyond the (often miraculous and supramundane) details of a saintly *Life*. It makes sense to read *Dispeller* as a work authored by Gyurmé Ösel but created in cooperative dialogue with his beloved master, including her influence (and her words) as a means for further elevating her.

Dialogic hagiography offers space for complexity and nuance without necessarily disagreeing directly with the status quo. As with any record, it is certainly possible that Gyurmé Ösel was using Mingyur Peldrön as a mouthpiece for his own agenda. Whether or not he was aware of this himself or was merely emphasizing the aspects of her story that were significant to him remains unclear. What is clear is the resonance between her own written works, which were focused on Dzogchen practice, with a few occasional discussions of monasticism, and his reflections on her life, which were focused on practice, monasticism, and her advice to women and men, with frequent mentions of Dzogchen interspersed throughout. However, there is also a multiplicity of approaches taken to challenges faced by the community. In composing the *Life*, he also sought to memorialize his beloved teacher. In claiming to draw her in to participate in the creation of *Dispeller*, he encouraged others to read the hagiography as containing a record that accorded with her own views about the life she had lived while simultaneously elevating her. The emphases on monasticism and women's education suggest concerns that were likely shared by both author and subject, supported as they are with direct quotations attributed to her. Her identity is presented in a multiplicity of perspectives as a result of their dialogic collaboration. Through the diverse images of her that we find in the hagiography—as enlightened feminine divinity, as revered teacher, and as outspoken proponent of monasticism—the dialogical interactions between her and others create a rich tapestry of who she was and the challenges her community faced.

In considering the relationship between Gyurmé Ösel and Mingyur Peldrön as negotiated on the page, there are multiple assertions regarding her relationship with her gender. Is this merely a case of self-effacement on the part of the subject and elevation on the part of the starry-eyed disciple? The relationship is complicated by their gender difference, age difference, and the fact that, regardless of when the hagiography was started, it was finished long after she died. Regardless of her input, he had the last say—more than a decade after her death—about how she and her life would be presented.

Gail Ashton argues that when a male hagiographer presents an idealized female saint, whether intentionally or not, he inherently imposes his own, male-centered representation of *woman* and divine femininity. In so doing, his writing acts to silence the saint's own voice (at least in part). Gendered censorship interrupts the autonomous selfhood of female saints so that their voices and authority are not properly acknowledged. The medieval hagiography of female saints is thus a field in which gendered voices contend for primacy within the genre (in particular, male voices attempting to forcibly unify views about women).[70] Gyurmé Ösel did not necessarily intentionally seek to speak over Mingyur Peldrön. However, the idea of contending perspectives existing within one hagiography calls upon the reader to question whether and how female voice might be superseded by the goals of male authors, the result being a female voice that is difficult to perceive through the interference of authorial intent. Arguably, this concern would be relevant regardless of the genders of the author and subject, but in the particular context of a social and literary situation in which men's voices are dominant, it raises the potential for a more problematic erasure. The question then arises as to how Gyurmé Ösel's editorial decisions impacted Mingyur Peldrön in the Tibetan context, and the nature of the texts' contesting multivocalities complicates it further. Even the most positive of representations cannot substitute for the authentic voice of the woman in question.

There are many more of Gyurmé Ösel's words in the hagiography than Mingyur Peldrön's. Here the previous point is salient: his views have supremacy over hers, no matter how assertively her quotations are highlighted. According to him, she was a compassionate and caring teacher, and he clearly adored her. The nature of their relationship resembles a beloved teacher and beloved disciple. She treated him with kindness, compassion, and humor. He in turn followed her advice and showed his dedication through his persistent elevation of her. Regardless, he and his words are still the gatekeeper for hers. Hagiography creation—whether collaborative or univocal or somewhere in between—is always an act of the creation of a public persona. In this case that public persona is engaging the sociohistorical moment and grappling with issues of gender valuation and the various soteriological tracks available in the Nyingma community. With that said, it is clear that Gyurmé Ösel sought to present his teacher's views and opinions, as well as her voice itself, in *Dispeller*.

The complexities of the author-saint relationship are not just important in terms of understanding some very specific gendered dimensions but also in terms of the development of different types of authority, issues of reverence and control, and the literary process. Various cultural issues are at play in the author-saint relationship and can interpret those through what we read in the hagiography itself. In the context of *Dispeller*, Mingyur Peldrön's voice is presented as focusing on the problems she perceives among her students and other practitioners. On the other hand, his purported focus is on Mingyur Peldrön as a divine being and an excellent teacher. While hagiographers act as intermediaries for female saints, there is an important collaborative aspect to be considered alongside other questions of power dynamics and devotional acts.

Most notably, Mingyur Peldrön's highly privileged position made space for her gender to sometimes be leveraged as a benefit, rather than presenting womanhood as the mere result of bad karma. The subject of her gender—and how to value it as a good or a bad thing—becomes especially complex when considering her heightened position as a trained practitioner and teacher at Mindröling. It is possible that Gyurmé Ösel was responding to suspicion about her status as a prominent teacher who was also a woman. The different perspectives on her gender make up part of the dialogic narrative found in the text, presented as they are in contradistinction to one another. There are several voices that can be parsed in the dialogue about her gender, including direct quotations attributed to Mingyur Peldrön, Terdak Lingpa, Lochen Dharmaśrī, Phuntsok Peldzöm, and others. Gyurmé Ösel recollects details of her life that he claims she and others relayed to him and presents opposing views on issues that are not necessarily attached to specific voices. It remains unclear how her gender and authority were bound together in these moments and whether or not this reflected wider concerns about the future of Mindröling. Multiple socioreligious tensions are written into the narrative landscape of the hagiography as words placed in the mouths of author, subject, and others. In the cases depicted here, Mingyur Peldrön herself did not acknowledge any difficulty on her own part with regard to accessing authority as a woman. However, her admonitions to men and women suggest that she perceived gender-specific problems within the community. For men the trouble was staying on the path, and for women it was attaining the ability to dedicate themselves to teaching the dharma.

Chapter Four

Mingyur Peldrön the Diplomat

> [Mingyur Peldrön] prostrated at the feet of the Supreme [Seventh Dalai Lama] Losang Kalsang Gyatso and made offerings. He bestowed on her the name Jetsün Sherab Drönma, flowers fell from the heavens, and then they went to visit several places, including the Fifth Dalai Lama's tomb.
>
> —Gyurmé Ösel

Being born a woman meant that Mingyur Peldrön did not have an official role in the succession of Mindröling, as this inheritance was passed on intergenerationally only through the men in the community. The roles of trichen and khenchen had been established by Terdak Lingpa and Lochen Dharmaśrī and were bestowed on the men of her generation, a tradition that has continued up to the present day. Having not been considered for an official position as a result of her female birth, she was situated differently from her brothers along gender lines. While she retained a cachet of some types of privilege and authority, her role within the community was not as formally established as those of her brothers. The only title she carried was that of jetsünma, a general term used for all the women in the family. Jetsünma is not an official title like trichen or khenchen but, rather, an honorific title that designates a woman as important through her high birth or as a recognition of her involvement in religious life. For Mindröling it is applied to all female family members, regardless of their responsibilities within the community. *Jetsünma* indicates someone's position and responsibility only insofar as she is a female member of the elite religious family. Any expectations that the term might carry with it are highly varied. A successful jetsünma might be a wife and mother (like Mingyur Peldrön's mother, Phuntsok Peldzöm), a director of the household (as her grandmother Yangchen Drölma had been), or she might be a religious teacher and dedicated celibate practitioner, as

Mingyur Peldrön was. Without a more specific title, there was more ambiguity surrounding long-term expectations for her role in the family. However, this lack of official position did not stop her from being deeply involved in the workings of the monastery, nor did it keep her from achieving public recognition as a powerful woman. Her lack of official status meant that the possibilities for her involvement at Mindröling were less clearly defined than the expectations for her brothers. The terms for her role as a teacher and lineage holder were not predetermined in the same ways. Arguably, this meant there was space for her position within the institutional structure to change without notice. It may have left room for Mingyur Peldrön to potentially make her own decisions about her activities at Mindröling. Although such individual agency was never a foregone conclusion, in her case multiple types of privileged status, including her education and her position as a nun of well-known family, allowed her significant autonomy.

In light of this positioning, it is useful to consider how she is represented in *Dispeller* with regard to her monastic institution and the political and religious worlds beyond. Mingyur Peldrön's depiction in the namtar is of a woman who regularly met with religious and political figures, forging relationships for Mindröling—and herself—through these meetings. Her interactions with leadership beyond the purview of Mindröling offer us another way of assessing her role within her family and religious community and the wider political concerns of the period. Gyurmé Ösel writes Mingyur Peldrön as engaging with an array of important actors across sectarian boundaries. When considered in conjunction with her focus on monasticism, an image begins to emerge of her as something of a diplomatic actor working against the religious and political tensions of the period.

The Nun at Mindröling

There was no hard-and-fast rule requiring Tibetan women to become nuns if they wanted to practice Buddhism seriously in the eighteenth century. It is true that in other times and contexts celibacy and the monastic life were considered the most expedient means to attaining enlightenment.[1] These modes of engagement have had different implications for Buddhist practitioners based on the time and place in which they lived. Taking into account the regional and doctrinal variations of Tibetan Buddhism, a person of means could theoretically seek out monastic or non-monastic instruction. And in some places (like Mindröling) multiple paths were available. What is more, there is evidence that in the preceding and following centuries, women were engaging in serious religious practice without taking monastic ordination. Especially in Nyingma communities, both women and men could become non-celibate practitioners. In eighteenth-century Tibet the ability to access religious practice and the promise of soteriological gains were not necessarily precluded by one's monastic status (although this depended in part on the denominations that one could engage with). More simply put, it was not necessary to be a monk or a nun if you wanted to pursue enlightenment or participate in religious community in some form. Mindröling embraced the non-celibate praxis that included pairing up with a sexual consort as an expedient to faster enlightenment and other religious benefits (such as aiding in the revelation of treasure texts). The most obvious example of this is Mingyur Peldrön's own father, Terdak Lingpa, the cofounder of Mindröling. Likewise, non-monastic women have made their mark as practitioners and teachers in Tibetan history. Celibacy and non-celibacy, monasticism and lay practice, were all viable paths.

There were certainly men who were non-celibate religious specialists and prominent teachers at Mindröling, including Mingyur Peldrön's father and some of her brothers. They engaged and excelled in religious life without taking monastic vows. In seventeenth- and eighteenth-century Nyingma communities, non-monastic religious specialists were accepted as legitimate contributors to the larger religious culture of the time; indeed, their contributions were significant. While there were non-celibate women who studied the dharma and women in the family whose roles were imperative to its functioning, we have no examples of non-celibate women in the role of teaching or engaging in public leadership. One might imagine that non-celibate women could become religious specialists at Mindröling. While this very well may have been the case, we have no evidence of this in Mingyur Peldrön's lifetime. Instead, we have evidence of three generations of women who were centrally important for the functioning of the households of Mindröling. These include her grandmother Yangchen Drölma; her mother, Phuntsok Peldzöm; and her sisters. While gendered difficulties continued to be mitigated by privilege for the women of Mindröling, their experiences with this mitigation were still varied.

Given Mingyur Peldrön's focus on religious practice and her adamant stance on remaining a celibate nun, it is possible that for her the life of the nun held promise for pursuing her particular goals. Celibacy is profoundly significant for understanding her positionality within Mindröling and in the world at large. Her outright rejection of Lelung Jedrung Rinpoche, and her reasoning that Terdak Lingpa himself had directed her away from such liaisons if she wanted to practice dharma seriously, suggests that she saw intimate partnership and soteriological pursuits as mutually exclusive, at least in her specific case and in her advice to disciples. As discussed in earlier chapters, *Dispeller* mentions nuns who had anxieties about how they would be supported in their practice, and she advised her fellow nuns to stick to their path in spite of these additional challenges. Mingyur Peldrön considered it the swiftest and clearest path to enlightenment. Beyond the soteriological benefits she argued for, celibacy gave her a certain level of bodily autonomy while benefiting the intersectarian relationship with Gelukpa political leadership in Lhasa.

It is clear that Mingyur Peldrön benefited personally from pursuing a celibate existence. It meant she could follow her own religious path and still rise to a position of importance within the family. This possibility was certainly reinforced by the set of privileges she held. But there are wider implications for her decision. It also situated her in a uniquely beneficial position to act as a sort of diplomat on behalf of her community. Here I refer specifically to her position as a celibate Nyingmapa in a period of Geluk ascendency and the intersectarian diplomacy that she was able to affect. She was well situated to work on behalf of the Nyingma community in conversation with the Gelukpa leadership of the time.

Political and Religious Tensions in the Mid- to Late Eighteenth Century

It would be impossible to sum up the political atmosphere of eighteenth-century central Tibet in one chapter and still do justice to the shifts in government stability and the political intrigue of the period.[2] With that said, some discussion of the political dynamics of this time and the impact that these dynamics had on religious institutions—especially for a Nyingma center such as Mindröling—can help make sense of how Gyurmé Ösel presented Mingyur Peldrön's involvement in political and religious leadership in *Dispeller*. Instability and infighting continued intermittently after the 1717–18 civil war came to an end and lasted for the next several decades, with some periods of relative peace interspersed throughout. The Dzungars were quelled in 1721, and the young Seventh Dalai Lama was enthroned in Lhasa. However, it would be decades before he took control of the government, and there were splits within Geluk leadership in the meantime. At this point a cabinet of five advisors was established to run the Ganden Podrang. The cabinet was first occupied by two men from Tsang, Khangchenné Sönam Gyelpo and Polhané, and three men from Ü, Pesé Ngapö, Gung Lumpawa, and Jara Taiji.[3] The council quickly split into regional factions, eventually leading to the bloody assassination of Khangchenné in 1727.[4] After the death of his compatriot, Polhané understood that his life was in danger and went into hiding. He then regrouped with a more substantial army, and the two sides went to war in Gyantse. Polhané prevailed, and there was a cease-fire in 1728, at which time he began to establish his authority as the political leader of central Tibet. Although he was close with the Panchen Lama,[5] Polhané had a strained relationship with the Seventh Dalai Lama, whose father was suspected of supporting the losing faction from Ü.[6] The Seventh Dalai Lama's family were exiled to Kham from 1730 to 1735.[7] As Polhané amassed his power, he gained the support of the Qing emperor Yongzheng. This ushered in more than a decade of relative stability, until Polhané's death in 1747.

In the wake of Polhané's demise, there was further unrest. Gyurmé Namgyel,[8] Polhané's son, took over his position and attempted to revive relations with the Dzungars. He was quickly assassinated, and his death gave way to a situation in which his supporters and the Qing representatives in Lhasa began killing one another.[9] The Ambans (Qing representatives) subsequently tightened their control of the region, imprisoning Gyurmé Namgyel's coconspirators and reestablishing a political role for the Seventh Dalai Lama. The moment marked the beginning of strengthened Qing authority in Lhasa. Since the beginning of Polhané's rule, the Dalai Lama had maintained a religious role but continued to be excluded from political engagement. In 1751 he finally adopted a role of political leadership.[10]

This period of unrest was driven by tensions that existed largely within the Geluk community and members of the aristocratic ruling class who supported them. The focal point of unrest during this time was not between Gelukpas and Nyingmapas; rather, it occurred between different Geluk factions. While their points of disagreement did not fall along specifically Geluk-Nyingma lines, the different factions had more and less friendly views of non-Geluk organizations. Polhané (who had been educated at Mindröling) and his faction fell on the more Nyingma-friendly side of the divide. Which is to say, members of this group either supported or at least did not actively destroy religious communities that were not Geluk. Gyurmé Namgyel's attempted revival of Dzungar connections seems to have also revived sectarian hostilities that had been suppressed a mere two decades earlier and certainly raised alarm among those who had so recently been harmed by their armies. The continued destabilization of political leadership in the region likely affected sectarian relations between Geluk and Nyingma religious communities, sparking tensions that would remain intact well into the next century.

These political and religious tensions bear some resemblance to the ways that Nyingma religious practitioners responded to and engaged the texts and practices associated with Gelukpas in this period. In particular, Nyingma approaches to monasticism suggest a range of intersectarian engagements. Monasticism was not extensively developed in Nyingma communities until the nineteenth century. Prior to this period, the wider community focused more on contemplative practice and ritual centered around tantric texts.[11] The eighteenth-century masters of Mindröling foregrounded the non-sectarian developments of nineteenth-century Kham.[12] And indeed, Rinchen Namgyel's namtar speaks extensively to his role as an early proponent of a non-sectarian approach.[13] In 1697 Terdak Lingpa had composed a monastic code of conduct, or *chayik*, a constitutional document that outlined the monastic curriculum for Mindröling's monastic community.[14] Attention to Mindröling's general approach to monasticism has involved analysis of the monastic curriculum found in Terdak Lingpa's chayik. According to Buddhist studies scholar Dominique Townsend, his chayik "harmoniously balances potentially contradictory Buddhist values and pursuits, some of which were being contested sharply among the Tibetan Buddhist schools of the time. These include celibacy and lay practice, renunciation and worldly learning, religion and politics, and scholasticism and esoteric meditation."[15] It seems that Terdak Lingpa wrote the monastery's code with an eye toward flexibility, allowing space for individuals to excel in the areas they found most compelling. The result was an enduring document that could work for monastic and non-monastic adherents alike. While supplemented with additional documents addressing modern questions and concerns, Terdak Lingpa's chayik remains important for the governance at Mindrolling Monastery in India today.[16]

Meanwhile, Lochen Dharmaśrī and other eighteenth-century Nyingma practitioners were dedicated to proliferating monastic ordination. According to Dudjom Rinpoche, Lochen Dharmaśrī fully ordained some 447 monks in his lifetime and gave novice vows to 1,298 people.[17] He also composed a forty-three-folio monastic ordination manual outlining rules for monks and a brief two-page set of instructions. Similar ordination efforts are attributed to a contemporary polymath, the eighth Tai Situ Rinpoche, Situ Penchen (1700–1774) as an early development of a more substantial monastic engagement on the part of the Nyingma community in the eastern Tibetan region of Kham. During Mingyur Peldrön's lifetime, Situ Penchen was rapidly ordaining hundreds of Nyingma monastics in the region of Kham. This ordination fervor seems to have created something of a cascade effect among Khampa Nyingma institutions. Once he had ordained the lamas of Katok and Pelyül, they were then able to begin ordaining in their own right.[18] While not directly related to Mingyur Peldrön's activities in central Tibet, there are important connections between the two monastics. In particular, Situ Penchen received training from Mingyur Peldrön's brothers Rinchen Namgyel and Pema Gyurmé Gyatso.[19] There is also evidence suggesting tensions between monastic and non-monastic communities during this period. Rigdzin Pelden Tashi was an ordained monk who studied in Geluk and Nyingma institutions and visited Mindröling and other Nyingma monasteries in central Tibet.[20] In a 1732 text Rigdzin Pelden Tashi calls for peace between nakpas and monastics in the wider Nyingma community. The suggestion here is that disagreement—and potentially even violence—was in danger of erupting between the two.[21]

Study of the nineteenth-century thinker Mipam (1846–1912) has revealed the spectrum of ways that Nyingma scholars negotiated tensions between their doctrinal interpretations and that of contemporary Geluk exegetes in the nineteenth century. In this slightly later historical context, Nyingma scholars responded to the Geluk hegemony of the time by formulating a variety of responses to their interlocutors. The Tibetan Buddhism scholar Douglas Duckworth outlines some of the different Nyingma exegetical responses, which ranged from "a more submissive attitude . . . such as found in the Dodrup tradition" to "a more hostile attitude . . . such as found in the works of Gorampa."[22] These are illustrative of the range of Nyingma modes for responding to Geluk dominance in the doctrinal context in the subsequent century, and the range of responses is valuable for understanding Mingyur Peldrön's responses to that same dominance (or at least Gyurmé Ösel's presentation of her response). According to Duckworth, Mipam "forged an alternative response to Geluk dominance by selectively appropriating certain features of the Geluk tradition while contesting others. It is this response that has become the formula for the enduring legacy of non-Geluk monastic colleges."[23] Although recorded in the century after Mingyur

Peldrön's life, this depiction has resonance with Mingyur Peldrön's promonastic stance found in her arguments for the superiority of celibate monasticism. It also speaks to an abiding tension between the sects and the diversity of approaches that Nyingmapa practitioners took in responding to Geluk dominance. While these exegetical discussions do not necessarily map on to historical actions, they suggest room for different modes of engagement on the part of individual scholars vis-à-vis Nyingma-Geluk relations. In *Dispeller* the representation of Mingyur Peldrön arguing for the superiority of celibacy can be read as her engaging in a wise political move.

In *Dispeller* Mingyur Peldrön is presented as a proponent of monasticism who also spent time working closely with politicians and their aristocratic family members. There was an important distinction between how the Nyingma and Geluk communities treated ordination. Monasticism was important at Mindröling from its inception, and Terdak Lingpa and Lochen Dharmaśrī sought to establish clear but flexible guidelines for the monastery. However, it was far from necessary for those seeking to engage in religious practice. Later, during Mingyur Peldrön's adulthood in postwar Ü, the difference in Nyingma and Geluk approaches to monasticism was likely highlighted by their political differences as well. The dynamics of Geluk ascendency—and their de rigueur monasticism—meant that her focus could be politically beneficial. Institutional and individual relationships could have informed and been informed by her stance toward her own monastic institution. The monasticism found in *Dispeller* is in line with a trend that developed transregionally beginning in the eighteenth century and continuing into the nineteenth.

Thinking in terms of interdenominational relations in the postwar period, it makes sense that monasticism would also be a concern for Mingyur Peldrön, although the tenor of her approach is different from that of her forebears. In particular, she eschewed the non-monastic nakpa path that made religious praxis available to her in the first place (as the daughter of a nakpa), arguing instead that monasticism was superior to other forms of religious engagement. Gyurmé Ösel's representation of Mingyur Peldrön certainly suggests that she was actively engaged in conversations about the centrality of monasticism and that these issues remained salient into the later eighteenth century, when he was writing. Mingyur Peldrön's concern for monastic discipline and wholehearted engagement was preceded by her father and uncle's considerations for how to engage both monastic and non-monastic paths and their inclusive approach to the two options. Her approach was decidedly less flexible. In her arguments highlighting the benefits of monastic life, she engaged in a project dedicated to celibacy while existing within the context of an institution that allowed for a variety of approaches to religious pursuit. Aligning herself with the Geluk norms of celibacy was likely to improve relations with them at a time when the Nyingma were emerging from a period of persecution. While most dominant in *Dispeller*, the vision of her as preoccupied with monasticism has endured among twenty-first-century residents of Pemayangtsé Monastery in Sikkim, who understand her concern for celibacy and monastic etiquette to have been a significant focus for her. This emphasis on monasticism over and above non-monasticism may well have reflected her own historically bound anxieties, which developed as the result of being part of a community that had been violently attacked in her early years. Her fervent focus on monasticism seems to be connected to perceptions of monastic life as acceptable to the dominant religious group of the period.

Being a nun was a key component of Mingyur Peldrön's personality and positionality. It seems that Gyurmé Ösel emphasized her status as a nun for both soteriological and political reasons. Likewise, her stance on monasticism and other matters as well as her position at Mindröling during her lifetime offer a new perspective of an authoritative nun. While she likely could have pursued a similar path as a non-celibate practitioner, her choice had lasting implications for herself and her community. It is possible—if not likely—that her monastic inclinations would have had an ameliorating effect on her relationships with non-Nyingma figures. And whether or not representations of her in *Dispeller* are an accurate portrayal of her actual doctrinal focus, it is clear that *someone* behind the writing of *Dispeller* was focused on monasticism (that is, her or Gyurmé Ösel). Taken in tandem with mentions of political leaders, this may have been informed by a more general concern that one might refer to as "getting along nicely with Gelukpas." By aligning herself with Geluk norms, Mingyur Peldrön raised the likelihood of being perceived in a positive light by Gelukpa practitioners with whom she had contact. In turn, this alliance could potentially benefit relations between Mindröling and Geluk institutions in central Tibet. It could have had a range of practical benefits for a Nyingmapa woman whose organization had been destroyed by anti-Nyingma violence. As with the later Nyingma responses to the Geluk doctrinal deliberations mentioned earlier, it seems as though either Mingyur Peldrön or her hagiographer (or both) were responding to the intersectarian and political tensions of the eighteenth century. This is one example of how religious concerns beyond the purview of Mindröling impacted the nun and literary representations of her. To more effectively assess these relationships and their significance, some examples of her interactions with politically prominent figures and their families will be illustrative. These involve the royal house of Sikkim, the Ganden Podrang government, and Lelung.

Engagements with Political and Religious Leaders beyond Mindröling

Gyurmé Ösel chose to represent Mingyur Peldrön as being actively involved in conversations with regional political leaders, many of them aligned with Geluk interests. In *Dispeller* he discusses her interactions with politicians and members of the aristocracy. These accounts are positioned alongside mentions of the teachings she gave to monastics. An image emerges of her as a teacher of the political aristocracy whose influence extended beyond Mindröling. In the modern day we talk of the "soft power" of cultural exchange, by which international communities can influence one another. Beyond sharing ideas and cultivating learning, education can serve to communicate cultural norms between groups and act as a mode of soft power. Keeping in mind that Mingyur Peldrön was an avid educator, the bulk of her impact likely came from the teachings and empowerments she bestowed.

Mingyur Peldrön also met and engaged with important religious and political leaders in ways that suggest that she played a diplomatic role for the community. It is unclear whether this role was in spite of her lack of an official title (such as trichen or khenchen) or, in fact, because she did not hold such a position. Regardless, her engagements took numerous forms. Mingyur Peldrön cultivated important connections between Mindröling and the Sikkimese aristocracy during her time as an exiled refugee in Sikkim. She visited with and bestowed teachings on the royal family, met with religious leaders at Pemayangtsé Monastery and Sangnak Choeling Monastery, and established her own retreat center nearby. These connections are an example of how she participated in overt institutional diplomacy. She acted as religious advisor to the royal family, remained closely engaged with them during her years there, and also brokered her sister's marriage to the prince, forming a matrimonial alliance between her house and the royal house of

Sikkim. While they were geographically distant from Mindröling, the royal family and the community of Pemayangtsé Monastery nearby had all been significantly influenced by Mindröling's particular approach to Nyingma organization and teachings. Although there is not much detail about these interactions beyond *Dispeller*, Mingyur Peldrön's beneficial presence in Sikkim is also discussed in Samten Gyatso's *History of Sikkimese Monasteries*.[24] In particular, he cites the exchange of teachings with the third Lhatsun Chenpo Dzogchen Jigmé Pawo (referenced in *Dispeller* as an expert in the Great Perfection), visits to the royal palace, and the fact that the Sikkimese people were largely considered to be blessed by her presence. While her gender does not seem to have been a deterrent in these relations, it was apparently worth noting. In Jigmé Pawo's brief account of Mingyur Peldrön's time in Sikkim, he refers to her as a "*jetsün* of high family" and then goes on to explain that "although she has the body of a woman, her way of giving commentaries, explanations and so forth are identical to the Great Tertön [Terdak Lingpa] himself, [they] similarly [instill] complete faith."[25] Thus, Jigmé Pawo overrides any concern about Mingyur Peldrön's gender with the reminder that she was close to her father in behavior and teaching ability. He reports that "she gave a rainbow of teachings, including empowerments and instruction . . . and accordingly scattered scriptural instructions hither and thither."[26] Mingyur Peldrön's relationship with Jigmé Pawo's lineage continued after she returned home; in 1748 his reincarnation traveled to Ü to receive teachings from her.

Of all of Mingyur Peldrön's interactions with political officials and their families, her relationship with the leader Polhané is mentioned most extensively throughout *Dispeller*. He also shows up frequently in Rinchen Namgyel's namtar as a similarly important figure for Mindröling in the eighteenth century. As a boy, Polhané had studied with Lochen Dharmaśrī at Mindröling and remained a great friend of the monastery throughout his tenure as de facto ruler of Tibet. His reign lasted from 1728 until his death in 1747. Prior to that, he had been actively involved in the military and political events of the early eighteenth century, aligning himself with Lhazang Khan in 1714 and working together with the military leader Khangchenné and the Qing army to put down the Dzungar invasion and subsequent civil war.[27] He was one of five members of the governing cabinet of the Ganden Podrang from 1721 to 1726.[28] As a result of these efforts, he became known as an effective military officer and anti-Dzungar political actor. It is notable that he frequently came down on the side opposed to suppression of non-Geluk organizations, and acted against sectarian interests. For example, the Qing Imperial Edict issued in 1726 reinforced the pro-Geluk sentiment of the early eighteenth century. Although it was unpopular among most of the Ganden Podrang government leadership, few were willing to speak out against it, but Polhané was one such person.[29] He is mentioned in *Dispeller* as a financier of Mindröling's postwar reconstruction, as an intermediary between Mingyur Peldrön and the Seventh Dalai Lama, and as one who repeatedly sought out both Mingyur Peldrön and Rinchen Namgyel for their ritual and instructional prowess. Unlike the similar discussions found in Rinchen Namgyel's namtar, Mingyur Peldrön's relationship with Polhané is presented as particularly important in *Dispeller*. For example, immediately upon her return from Sikkim, she oversaw the initial extensive repairs to the monastery, before Rinchen Namgyel had returned from his own exile in Kham. This much is generally accepted.[30] However, *Dispeller* goes one step further and cites Polhané as the source of financial support for her reconstruction efforts. The claim is that he also made offerings to Mingyur Peldrön, including a crown and a white stallion with ornamented saddle.[31] By financing the reconstruction of Mindröling and other non-Geluk monasteries that had been destroyed in the civil war, Polhané was in a sense making a public declaration of the legitimacy of Mindröling in the postwar period. *Dispeller* connects these activities directly to Mingyur Peldrön herself. He remained involved in the workings of Mindröling throughout his lifetime. One particular episode in her *Life* portrays the extent of his influence at the monastery and the real-world effects that it had on her lived experience.

As Gyurmé Ösel tells the story, Polhané sent Mingyur Peldrön and her attendants to Kongpo at the urging of unnamed members of the Mindröling family, shortly after Rinchen Namgyel returned from his exile in Kham:

> In this way, some "virtuous ones" of the labrang approached the Taiji [Polhané] and made a request. Then, [they heard] from the Taiji that [Mingyur Peldrön] must briefly go to Kongpo Dechen Teng to teach. And so she went, and more than a year passed. The teacher [and] monk Orgyan Rabten, and the monk Tashi Wangchuk, went as messengers to the Taiji's place at Doring. There, the Taiji asked them if the *jetsün*—the knowledge bearer—was doing great dharmic activities to benefit beings. Gelong Rabten said, "Except for students who come from Tö and those regions, [she] is not benefitting anyone with the dharma. Gyurmé Chödron is her attendant. As for Gyurmé

Yangzom and the monk Drakpa and the others, they're out working in the fields." To that the Taiji said, "What a terrible pity![32] I have been meaninglessly deceived by these people! A lama such as this, who only abides by the essential truth, shouldn't reside there in that weary way. This malevolence must be remedied immediately!" And so she traveled from Kongpo to Lhasa.[33]

According to this account, after more than a year had passed, Polhané learned from a few monks that Mingyur Peldrön's work in Kongpo was proving to be of little benefit, that she was reaching few students, and that her attendants had been put to work in the fields. His discovery that she was languishing in obscurity was received as unwelcome news indeed. It is never made clear why she was sent to Kongpo. As the story goes, when Rinchen Namgyel returned, he was very pleased with the renovations and the state in which he found the monastery.[34] There is no prior suggestion of tension between the siblings, and they continued to teach together during their adult years. It might be that Mingyur Peldrön's brother—or someone else at Mindröling—genuinely believed that she would do good work in Kongpo. She had also been dangerously ill just before this, and it might be that a period of convalescence was in order. There is the possibility that she sought a rest in the wake of her illness. However, this is not mentioned in conjunction with her trip. In *Dispeller* Polhané responds to the discovery of Mingyur Peldrön's situation as though he had been tricked into sending her away and that she had somehow been wronged in this decision and was suffering as a result of it. It is possible that the "virtuous ones" of Mindröling had sought to remove the young woman so that her brother could take up his position of leadership after his late return from Kham back to a monastery that she had already begun reviving to great effect.[35] Or it might be that they sought to expand their network in Kongpo. Regardless, Polhané's tenor suggests deceit and tension within the Mindröling community. It is no wonder that she and her compatriots were worried as they were summoned to Lhasa.

Having been called back from Kongpo, Mingyur Peldrön proceeded directly to Lhasa to meet with Polhané. On the way she and her attendants disguised themselves as Gelukpas before entering the city. According to *Dispeller*, she was worried about traveling to Lhasa, which had until recently been controlled by Gelukpas who were not terribly friendly toward Nyingmapas. It is likely that she and her attendants were terrified of the violence that had previously been directed at their fellows. It seems she was the first

Mindröling community member to enter Lhasa since the murder of her uncle and brother there in 1717:

> At that time, Dajin Badur only supported the Yellow Hats [i.e., Gelukpas], the Nyingmapas had been destroyed. As a result, any others moving about were really worried, because even though they were virtuous they might be stopped. They were terrified that their *terma* tradition would be destroyed, so they disguised themselves as Yellow Hats in order to enter [the city safely]. The Taiji [Polhané] said, "Don't worry about that—your own ways are fine." And so they changed into their own clothes. [Mingyur Peldrön] prostrated at the feet of the Supreme [Seventh Dalai Lama] Losang Kalsang Gyatso and made offerings. He bestowed on her the name Jetsün Sherab Drönma, flowers fell from the heavens, and then they went to visit several places, including the Fifth Dalai Lama's tomb.[36]

The group's concern about walking openly as Nyingma practitioners in the city where her uncle and brother had been executed some years earlier illustrates just how unsettled Geluk-Nyingma relations remained at this time. While it is unclear what clothing choices or other social cues would have made the group identifiable as Nyingmapas, in Polhané's reassurances that she need not go about in disguise, we see a political actor trying to assuage the very real fear of a recently ostracized religious practitioner. He successfully urged the visitors to change back into their regular clothes and arranged for Mingyur Peldrön to have an audience with the Seventh Dalai Lama, who bestowed on her the name Jetsün Sherab Drönma. They exchanged teachings, after which she visited Polhané's home in the city and saw important pilgrimage sites. The monks of the Dalai Lama's monastery also requested that she compose a long-life prayer that they could recite. In spite of the factionalist environment, it seems that her well-founded worries were not ultimately borne out in any ill treatment. However, the situation they feared was indeed experienced by others. Shakabpa explains that during this time, anyone who was not aligned with one of the two cabinet factions was considered to be unprotected in a politically unstable moment: "They were afflicted with terrible difficulties in terms of taxation and transportation obligations. There are many stories that monks from Namdra Pendé Leksheling Monastery moved to Tsetang, pretending to be monks from Sera, Drepung, or the tantric colleges."[37] It seems it was not uncommon for people to "disguise" themselves in some way or another while in

Lhasa in order to appear in alignment with one or another faction and so avoid dangerous confrontation.

Beyond suggesting some strife within the household and postwar tensions regarding the monastery's reconstruction, this event led to Mingyur Peldrön developing closer ties with Polhané. While uneasy in the presence of both him and the Dalai Lama, it is notable that Mingyur Peldrön was able to forge an alliance with them. It is likely that she and many other non-Gelukpa practitioners in the region were concerned about continued negative sentiment against non-Gelukpas. Cultivating a positive relationship with leaders outside the Nyingma community was important for individual and institutional self-preservation. When we take into consideration the potential tension within the newly established second generation of Mindröling leadership, Mingyur Peldrön's relations with Polhané and the Seventh Dalai Lama were especially important if she was to survive in the post–civil war era. It is noteworthy that it is these relationships, and not others within Mindröling or even within the Nyingma community, that are highlighted in *Dispeller*. Their inclusion in the text, and the detail with which they are addressed, suggests that Gyurmé Ösel found these moments to be especially important for his readership. The idea of a strong friendship between Dalai Lamas and members of Mindröling might be one reason that the Dalai Lama is mentioned in *Dispeller*. In addition to his importance as eventual head of state, the incident reminds the reader of the relationship between the Fifth Dalai Lama and the founders of Mindröling.

The unrest of 1726–27 is also mentioned in *Dispeller* and is related to Mingyur Peldrön's personal experience. After the assassination of Khangchenné, Polhané went into hiding and likewise sent his wife and daughter into hiding for protection.[38] Both his wife and their daughter were ill during this period. At the beginning of *Dispeller*'s account of this episode, Mingyur Peldrön had been in retreat for a year at Luding but emerged to help with the situation. In summarizing events, Gyurmé Ösel takes care to mention that Rinchen Namgyel went to support Polhané in the midst of the upheaval and that Mingyur Peldrön herself related what happened next. She reported that her brother had been important for Polhané's survival during this time and explained that Polhané had prevailed upon Mingyur Peldrön, Rinchen Namgyel, and others to perform rituals for his ailing family members. The Mindröling representatives even traveled to Polhané's home, which was especially dangerous at that time, given the circumstances. There they spent six weeks performing rituals alongside Gelukpa monks for the recovery of his wife and daughter.[39] Directly after this mention of saying prayers for his family in a time of great danger, *Dispeller* mentions a new round of repairs that were completed at Mindröling, with an influx of offerings. As a result of these activities, Polhané made donations that went to the further reconstruction of the monastery, with the result that everything that had been destroyed by the Dzungars—with the exception of a couple of *stūpas* (reliquary shrines)—was finally repaired.[40] This construction included a separate abode for Mingyur Peldrön herself. After the construction was completed, Mingyur Peldrön, Rinchen Namgyel, and learned monks from Geluk monasteries all performed pacification rituals together:

> The throne-holder Ratna Biza [Rinchen Namgyel] and the Great Precious Lama [Mingyur Peldrön] performed pacification liturgies from the *New Treasures* with some *geshes* from Ü monasteries. At that time flowers fell from the clear sky, there was a rainbow halo around the sun, and likewise other marks of virtue appeared. Then, due to the actions of the monastic assembly, along with the relatives, warring serfs and devoted patrons made extensive offerings. Then, for the next three years [Mingyur Peldrön] stayed in immovable retreat, performing the actions of the three buddha bodies.[41]

This passage brings together several important threads that run throughout *Dispeller* in terms of its presentation of Mingyur Peldrön as friendly toward the Gelukpa community and the material, political, and religious concerns that may have been driving these relationships. Here Gyurmé Ösel is claiming that they are engaging in intra-sectarian ritual practice for the purpose of pacifying the larger population. As with the prayers and rituals for the good health and safety of Polhané's family, the practical result of these efforts was the receipt of further donations from him. These went to the reconstruction of Mindröling as the other donations had, but it is noteworthy that they also included a house for Mingyur Peldrön. In fact, the most concrete result of her interactions with central Tibetan political leaders (and Polhané in particular) was financial support for the reconstruction of Mindröling after its decimation by the Dzungars. The moment is also marked with miraculous events, as shortly thereafter we see the use of the name "Great Ḍākinī Queen" used for Mingyur Peldrön. Statements about miraculous events and the use of the sobriquet Great Ḍākinī Queen are regularly applied in *Dispeller* to refer to Mingyur Peldrön in important moments. While receiving offerings from devoted patrons and quelling social unrest through liturgical prayer, this moment also represents an attempt at unity with Geluk religious leadership. If we think of her fraught encounters with the Fifth Lelung Jedrung Rinpoche, and compare those events with this brief mention, it seems that her interests are aligned with the Geluk. Most concretely, after every interaction with Polhané, repairs were completed for the monastery. Whether friend to Gelukpas or no, this connection with Polhané drove the monastery's most basic foundation for revival: its physical structure.

One account in the namtar exemplifies how Gyurmé Ösel used historical events as backdrops to narrate Mingyur Peldrön's life. He takes the documented event of Lelung Jedrung Rinpoche brokering peace between feuding Geluk factions as the starting point for a discussion about Mingyur Peldrön's relationship with Lelung. In this context Lelung's role adjudicating political tensions for the Ganden Podrang becomes a discussion about whether or not he and Mingyur Peldrön would begin a consort relationship:

> In the fire dragon year [1736], while receiving teachings from [her] brother Ratna Biza [Rinchen Namgyel], Miwang Gyurmé Sönam Tobgyé [Polhané] said, "This Olkha Jedrung is helpful, and although he's a Gelukpa, why not invite him?" To this, the brother said, "Fears have arisen that the monastery will be spoiled. But okay, I'll invite him." Just as soon as [Jedrung] went to the monastery, they began preparations; in the intervening three months he and the Heart Son met with a procession of respected invited lamas. In the Chökhor Lhünpo apartment of the Samantabhadra Palace, on marvelous thrones that had been arranged, Jedrung was invited to sit with his consort. The Precious Brother Ratna Biza led a procession with ceremonial scarves of reparation, together with benefactors from smaller subsidiaries in Ü and all the lamas and monastics, and reverently venerated [him] and offered ambrosial nectar. Then, [Jedrung] and his disciples, lay and monastic, women and men all together—all told about sixty people or so—threw a party. Their singing filled the monastery. At that time, Her Holiness the Master Queen of the *Ḍākinīs* [Mingyur Peldrön] came out of retreat in order to meet with Gegen Rabten Gyau, the Gelong Trewang, the Gelong Drakpa, the Zimpön Gyurmé Chödron, and Gyurmé Yangzom, to dispel their misconceptions. Then Jedrung Rinpoche said, "I must make a spiritual connection with Her Holiness the Sublime Master [Mingyur Peldrön]," with the goal of also bestowing the oral transmission of Guru Yoga in detail. Jedrung said, "Minling Jetsün Rinpoche, in this lifetime we two should

make a connection and unify our wisdom and method. If that were all right, then for five hundred years all foreign invaders would be deterred. This has certainly been prophesied." Then Her Holiness, the Highest Lama, Queen of the Ḍākinīs, said, "I cannot do that! The Great Tertön [Terdak Lingpa] himself said, 'You will not join with another. In order to be able to perform sacred incantations, bear in your heart the Great Perfection practice. By meditating, lead faithful sentient beings—men and women—to the sublime dharma.' And so this correct aspiration arose [in me]." Saying this, she held her body erect. Jedrung said, "Okay, well, I have to go to Decheng Ling." Likewise, the Great Lama [Mingyur Peldrön] left in another direction.[42]

It is generally understood that Mingyur Peldrön and Lelung Jedrung Rinpoche exchanged teachings with one another and that Lelung maintained a connection with Mindröling that he had begun as a young man studying with Pema Gyurmé Gyatso. But in this segment of the text Gyurmé Ösel takes the relationship between Lelung and Mingyur Peldrön a step further, suggesting that Lelung propositioned her by requesting a consort relationship between the two of them. The language is only thinly veiled here, suggesting that a "union" (*zung 'jug*) of their "method and wisdom" (*thabs shes*) would be a good thing. In his proposition he points to the spiritual goals of sexual consort relationships and the elements of enlightenment that are joined through such pairings. As far as spiritual pickup lines go, it is a pretty good one. And here we might read Lelung as earnest in his goals for their relationship. However, Mingyur Peldrön was determined to stick to her monastic practice, citing her father's instructions as reason enough to reject the proposal. In order for her to be a successful Dzogchen teacher, Terdak Lingpa instructed his daughter to remain celibate.

It is important to keep in mind that right around this time, Lelung had been working to bring peace to warring factions within the Ganden Podrang government. Given the precarity of Nyingma institutions during this moment in central Tibetan history as well as Mindröling's relationship with the Ganden Podrang, it is likely that a relationship with Lelung would have been helpful for the monastery's survival and that agreeing to a sexual relationship might have improved relations for the institution. Thinking back to the unhappy marriage between Lady Peldzin and the young Sikkimese king Gyurmé Namgyel, we have precedent for the women of Mindröling engaging in such relationships and, in so doing, benefiting the family. Gyurmé Ösel depicts Mingyur Peldrön and Lelung's relationship as a difficult one, centered on diverging views of acceptable religious engagement. Depictions of him as a besotted suitor and her as a woman fending off unwanted attention creates a narrative that presents Lelung as a foil for Mingyur Peldrön to assert her focus on celibacy and the monastic path. After all, she only came out of retreat to attend to her disciples, not to engage with Lelung and his entourage. Her rejection of him here suggests that she had more authority in this moment than Lady Peldzin did later on in Sikkim (which makes sense, given the differences in their positions in the family) and that she felt able to maintain her monastic dedication. But this exchange also shows us that, according to Gyurmé Ösel, the concerns of the Geluk community had affected Mindröling in this period and that the sectarian divisions that had developed in the eighteenth century were considered problematic, at least by him.

In addition to these relationships and interactions with prominent political actors, *Dispeller* emphasizes Mingyur Peldrön's ability to perform magic for practical purposes and suggests that she was called upon to engage these abilities to benefit political leaders. Her use of sorcery, including turning back enemies of the tradition, began in earnest during their flight to Sikkim. Shortly after arriving there, she and her entourage learned that they had been followed by the Dzungar troops. She conjured a snowstorm to stop them and so was able to remain safely in Sikkim.[43] Later, in 1751, she reportedly performed pacification rituals to heal the bad feelings between the political successors of Lhazang Khan and the political enemies they had made during the civil war.[44] This use of sorcery was not unusual among political actors of the day,[45] and a perception that she could use it to beneficial effect to turn back opposition armies would likely have been considered an important skill.

Mingyur Peldrön's involvement in political events has been corroborated outside of *Dispeller*, but only in a few places. Rather than taking her participation as historical fact, it bears considering *why* Gyurmé Ösel would see fit to emphasize her political connections in these moments. This suggests he is fashioning a heroine who was actively involved in supporting the political leaders of the day by asserting mutual concern between herself and Polhané, stimulating Polhané's involvement in the Mindröling project, and reinforcing her support of his family in moments of crisis. In all of her engagements with Polhané, Gyurmé Ösel presents a woman who overcame the traumas of sectarian violence and sought reconciliation with the ruling leadership. It is clear that *Dispeller* is asserting Polhané's involvement in the revival project at Mindröling. But this goes beyond his support of Mindröling to also suggest a mutual support between the two of them in the midst of persistent tension within the Geluk political leadership and between the sects.

Mingyur Peldrön continued to interact with Polhané's family after his death. In 1747 Polhané's son Gyurmé Namgyel received empowerments from her and instruction in some of Terdak Lingpa's treasure texts, alongside a Sikkimese monk named Gyurmé Zangpo. Gyurmé Namgyel took on his father's position the same year. He was apparently concerned with Qing interference, and according to Shakabpa, "in 1748, he pushed through reforms that shifted to Beijing the burden of paying for the upkeep of Manchu representatives in Tibet."[46] He is also known for attempting to rekindle the relationship between the Ganden Podrang and the Dzungars. This led to his assassination in 1750 and subsequently the widespread murder of Han Chinese people living in Lhasa.[47] He was at least somewhat concerned with continuing the family connection with Mingyur Peldrön and likely also concerned with maintaining relations with Mindröling.[48] In 1751, the year after Gyurmé Namgyel's assassination, Polhané's daughter Deden Drölma (d. 1773) visited Mingyur Peldrön with her husband and children, in order to make donations for empowerments and teachings.[49] Given the continued family connection and the fact that Petech refers to her as "a pious patron of the clergy and of the monasteries,"[50] it is likely that a relationship existed between the two women. She and others in Polhané's family continued to cultivate a relationship with Mingyur Peldrön until the end of her life, participating in and supporting the rituals and observances surrounding her death.

Gyurmé Samten Chogdrup, the central Tibetan prince who requested that Mingyur Peldrön write the *Secret Wisdom Ḍākinī Instruction Manual* in 1732, represents a larger pattern of local and regional political leaders arriving throughout the narrative to receive empowerments and teachings from her.[51] A few other examples include the members of the aristocracy who traveled to meet Mingyur Peldrön in 1748. These included a royal prince of Gungthang in Ngari and his wife, who visited to receive a Red Wrathful Longevity empowerment and an explanation of the six-syllable Chenrezi mantra.[52] In the same year she also bestowed detailed instructions in wrathful empowerments from both kama and terma streams to one Ngödrup Namgyel, the son of an army general in Yuthok. These brief encounters are not expounded on, but they serve to remind the reader of Mingyur Peldrön as a figure who was supposedly sought out by military families and the aristocracy.

Sources beyond *Dispeller* make it clear that Mingyur Peldrön was generally considered a prolific and respected teacher. Gyurmé Ösel also presents her as actively engaged with the political and religious developments of the period, primarily through the relationships she had with prominent figures in Geluk and Nyingma communities. He goes so far as to cast her as an unofficial diplomat for Mindröling. While this was secondary to her role as a teacher, it also did the work of spreading awareness about Mindröling by extending her relationships to important political and religious actors beyond the monastery. Her ritual engagements had reverberations beyond her role as a pedagogue. In spite of (or perhaps because of) not having an official title, combined with her position as a celibate monastic, she was able to have relationships with political and religious leaders who were external to Mindröling yet potentially very important for its survival. Her continued relationships with political figures and their families throughout her adulthood reinforce this image of her as something of a diplomatic figure. Moreover, these relationships have interesting implications for her gendered positionality at Mindröling, as overt diplomatic work was not being done by other women then or earlier in the monastery's history. It seems that her unique position as a trained teacher, lineage holder, and celibate nun supported the possibility for these diplomatic engagements.

These relationships would have been beneficial for Mindröling's revival, for both the financial support they could offer and also in relegitimizing a previously ostracized group after a period of persecution. In the recovery after the civil war, to have someone like Polhané closely involved in the monastery's affairs was financially, socially, and politically beneficial for the successful reconstruction of the monastery. The narrative of these relationships also offers a rare perspective of how the political machinations of the time and continued regional strife influenced personal experience and livelihood. Polhané in particular would continue to impact Mingyur Peldrön's social and religious position significantly. He was an important connection to powerful political and religious leadership outside of her own institution, making it potentially easier for her to act as an independent agent of change. These introductions in turn made it more likely for her status to be less dictated by the Mindröling leadership (now in the hands of her brother), giving her the space to be viewed as an important and powerful teacher *in her own right*. The importance of this legitimation from a non-Mindröling entity cannot be overstated. The historical religious context includes active connections between the monastery and the Gelukpas in Lhasa during Mingyur Peldrön's lifetime. It seems there was extensive communication between these groups, with continued mutual influence across multiple generations. Gyurmé Ösel presented his master as someone who had relationships with important political figures, indicating that she engaged with them directly while maintaining her monasticism and her dedication to teaching and retreat. The question arises of what literary work these representations might be doing for Gyurmé Ösel. How did presenting Mingyur Peldrön as connected to political leaders outside of Mindröling and the Nyingma community reinforce his presentation—and his readers' views—of her as a saint and as a character in her own life story?

Chapter Five

The Death of Mingyur Peldrön and the Making of a Saint

> The Precious Lama, Bliss Queen of the *Ḍākinīs*, regained her majestic youthful form. She held her right hand up by her ear as though she were snapping her fingers, and her left in the *mudra* of meditative equipoise. Her eyes had rolled upwards and she had a radiant smile on her face, with the yogic gaze of the *dharmakaya*.
>
> —Gyurmé Ösel

THE year 1769 began poorly for Gyurmé Ösel. According to *Dispeller*, from the very first month of the new year he witnessed numerous bad omens. These included a strange sound in the heavens like the loud lowing of a bull, comets falling from the sky in a web of light, musk deer taking shelter in the stables, and a white-winged raven hanging about.[1] What's more, he was beset by prophetic nightmares:

> I dreamed I sat in the kitchen of Kachö Dechen Ling near a secret door, happily and completely ready to serve the master's [Mingyur Peldrön's] departure. She was preparing to set off right away [when] just below [the building], a river like the Tsangpo overflowed, [and] I thought to myself, "The lama is of an advanced age, and she has but one attendant. She shouldn't go! I myself will go in service to her." Just at that moment the master herself went up into the sky, [and] from Drakpoché to Samdentsé, a five-colored rainbow could be seen stretched like a cloth across the sky. The master's face looked like it had when she was in the prime of life. Her naked body was handsome and bright, adorned with red cloth and bone ornaments, her black hair hanging loose. She sat astride a white lion with

her right index finger pointing at the sky in a threatening manner, and her left hand reaching down to me as though gesturing to help me. She turned her face away and I sensed that she said in a clear voice:

"The free mind, uncontrived
Vajrasattva's face made real[2]
Truly seeing one's own face
Seeing these worldly affairs,
Clear them all away."

Saying this, she flew off at great speed into the westerly sky. I burst into tears of grief and awoke crying. Later, I realized that the most excellent lama is indeed Karchen Yeshé Tsogyel, and she was demonstrating her ability to perform a magical display. Delightfully, this meant that she dwelt [as Mingyur Peldrön] in her ordinary form body. If her nature is one of wisdom, would she then go to the Blissful Pure Lands [when she died]? Another night I dreamt that the noon sun was falling below the horizon and not in the middle of the sky as it should be. Sinking, it dissolved into darkness. I had this and other similar nightmares.[3]

So begins the final section of the *Life* of Mingyur Peldrön. Across a range of religious and historical spaces, including but also far beyond the Tibetan Buddhist context, it was in the death of the individual that the saint was created. In death a saint could still interact with the living through commemoration, visions, and relics.[4] The moment of death was thus definitive in establishing Mingyur Peldrön's sainthood. Descriptions of her decline and eventual demise—including the treatment of her body, the arrival of mourners, and discussion of her funeral services—all contribute to her depiction as a fully realized enlightened woman. Here *Dispeller* takes its most hagiographic tone and becomes driven by reports of signs and portents as well as miracles, all of which were attached to the birth and death of prominent Tibetan religious teachers as a matter of course. Just as in the *Life* of Shakyamuni Buddha and others, miracles communicated that the natural world was itself responding to the arrival or departure of an enlightened being. Various "signs of saintly death," according to the *Blazing Remains Tantra*, point to six classifications for signs of saintly death: images, relics, lights, sounds, earth tremors, and atmospheric phenomena.[5]

The signs in Mingyur Peldrön's death narrative generally line up with these classifications; all six types crop up, with the exception of earthquakes. Miracles play a role throughout the course of *Dispeller*, not just at the time of her death. Extensive miraculous descriptions also mark the other liminal moments in her life, including her birth, first refuge ceremony, and the first time she gives a teaching. These incidents generally contain multiple miracles listed together. An example is when she first arrived in Sikkim and supposedly gave a teaching to a large crowd:

> More than four thousand faithful men and women went to make offerings to her. She bestowed [on them] the Long-Life Empowerment of the *Deathless Essence Compendium* from [Terdak Lingpa's] *New Treasures*. At this time, a five-colored rainbow appeared over where the master was, and infused her body. Having completed the long-life empowerment, before they left, in the sky above the master's head thunder sounded and a vulture circled her head, keeping her on its right side as if in circumambulation. Thus, the seed of faith was planted [in the crowd]. They shouted her name in joy, and prostrated before her. Furthermore, she distributed sacred substances which, in accordance with the teachings, satisfied the desires of each person. The happy crowd broke into dance.[6]

This moment in the narrative marks the beginning of Mingyur Peldrön's teaching career and so includes rainbows, unexplained thunder, and unusual animal behavior. In similar scenes throughout the namtar, flowers fall from the empty sky and rainbows materialize. In this way moments of liminality are set apart and marked with signs that reinforce her divinity. In this case the importance of her teaching career and the strong connection that was formed with the Sikkimese people is highlighted with the narrative tools that define this text as hagiography, and similar descriptions attend the closing section of her *Life*.

Mingyur Peldrön spent the first three months of the year 1769 in retreat, and the remaining months and days leading up to her death were entirely consumed with passing on teachings to her disciples. At the end of her last retreat, a large group of monastics from Drachi, Mön, and Dagpo arrived to pay reverence to her and receive final teachings. The entire group made offerings and aspiration prayers to her, in response to which she expressed her pleasure in having successfully helped so many beings. She urged them to rely only on the teachings of the Great Perfection, in particular the

Definitive Secret Vajragarbha.⁷ At Namdröl Yangtsé she spent three days explaining her last will and testament to the head monastics, before continuing on to Dechen Ling.⁸ These last days of instruction are presented as a testament to her dedication to passing on teachings to her disciples and her concern about the continuity of Dzogchen in particular.

According to Gyurmé Ösel, in the fourth month her winds reversed and she began to show signs of illness and then impending death. A group of 160 people had gathered,⁹ and a new statue and *thangka* painting were created in her image. The group included nuns from Samten Tsé, Samten Chöling, and Ardok Gönsar as well as monastics from other regions. There are no nonmonastic people mentioned in this particular group, suggesting that Mingyur Peldrön's next words were directed solely to the community of monks and nuns. In spite of her disciples urging her to rest, she fought back pain, fatigue, and her continually deteriorating condition in order to give them one last teaching. Arguing with pleas that she forgo teaching, she explained:

> I have grown old, it is quite difficult to practice, but in [my fatigue], I think about the stream of the doctrine, and in particular, awakening. Now, shall I offer what instruction I have left? Now the body grows weary and my eyesight weak, and soon I will depart to the next life, but it's possible for me to wait a little while. In this way, I will now teach, and not depart.¹⁰

Gyurmé Ösel claims that Mingyur Peldrön taught until the very day of her death. Continuing with his penchant for reporting lists of teachings received (senyik), he recalls the teachings she bestowed in these last days and to whom. The texts that he includes in her death narrative reflect her last efforts to pass on the teachings of the Great Perfection before she died. In doing so, he connects Mingyur Peldrön to the next generation of Mindröling religious leadership through the transmissions that she gave to her disciples and an assortment of other people.¹¹ These include people as varied as the monastery storekeeper, her sister Lady Peldzin, and her nephews the Fourth Trichen Pema Tenzin Rinpoche, and the Third Khenchen Orgyen Tenzin Dorjé. Multiple teachings are mentioned, all of which were closely associated with Mindröling and with Terdak Lingpa's treasure tradition. For example, the Adon (A-syllable) instructions that she was first authorized to teach as a teenager, the Khandro Nyingtik, the entirety of Terdak Lingpa's treasure cycles, the Zaplam Deshek Kündü, wrathful empowerments associated with Terdak Lingpa such as the Nyangter Drakmar, and others, were all bestowed in her final days.[12] Gyurmé Ösel claims that right before her death she gave teachings to a large group of laity and monastics, in addition to her close disciples, who together formed an audience of about four hundred people.[13]

Gyurmé Ösel includes a statement that Mingyur Peldrön reportedly made to her attendants while talking with them about how important it is to continue the monastery's teachings. In explaining her concern to her attendants and her reasoning for giving so many teachings while she was so ill, she said:

> As for this Dzogchen teaching, I am an old woman. After I die, how might it be weakened? Like a lamp-flame in a great wind.[14]

From the beginning of that fateful year, Gyurmé Ösel realized that he would soon be separated from the teacher he had been faithfully attending since he was a child. Ruminating on her death, wondering whether she would make a postmortem journey to a Pure Land, it was as though his sun were falling from the sky. Here we witness the disciple's grief as he prepares to say goodbye to the woman who had been his teacher since he was eight years old. In final homage to her, he details her funerary rites and the unusual occurrences surrounding them.

Funerary Rites

In reporting Mingyur Peldrön's death and the funeral services held for her, Gyurmé Ösel is building an argument about her sanctification. He reports that she died in the seventh Tibetan month of the year 1769. Her body was not moved or touched for nine days.

> At that time, on the tenth day just as the sun was rising, the precious lama, Bliss Queen of the *Ḍākinīs*, regained her majestic youthful form. She held her right hand up by her ear as though she were snapping her fingers, and her left in the mudra of meditative equipoise. Her eyes had rolled upwards and she had a radiant smile on her face, with the yogic gaze of the *Dharmakaya*. From the top of her head rushed more and more clear drops, along with her life force and phlegm and so forth, and other demonstrations of her high attainment of wisdom and successful transmigration. I and the other students were completely amazed.[15]

Observing this miraculous physical transformation, Gyurmé Ösel claims that he and the nineteen other disciples who were present in the room immediately experienced realization of the true nature of reality and recognized that their master had attained nirvana. A group of blood relatives and close members of the monastic community performed funeral rituals for her remains.[16] Her body was treated with all the reverence due to a great teacher.

> First a couple of monastics and a doctor together washed her corpse then anointed it with camphor, saffron, and other sweet-smelling herbs. Then the family brought some long white ceremonial scarves, red mourning clothes, and perfumed Benares muslin, which they wrapped tightly around her. They offered tea and incense, the scent of which pervaded the air. On the outside they adorned her upper and lower body in fine red garments. They adorned her with precious ornaments, placing these over her clothes, and seated her body on the throne. Then they made mandala offerings.[17]

Gyurmé Ösel's account of funeral preparations gives us a sense of the reverence exhibited by Mingyur Peldrön's family and disciples and speaks to her high standing in the community. During the cremation itself, Gyurmé Ösel claims that the smoke rising from the site took the shape of conch shells, dharma wheels, lotuses, horses, and jewels.[18] After the cremation, a completely intact crown was found among Mingyur Peldrön's cremains. Likewise, they discovered that her bones were covered in tracings of divine images and syllables.[19] Monastics made *tsa-tsas* (small devotional sculptures of relics mixed with clay) from the ash and interred them in a reliquary stupa.[20] The story of her death is filled with rainbows. Rainbow-colored clouds come into view, lights emerge from her residence, and multiple funeral attendants report unusual rainbows witnessed throughout the region during the time of her death.[21] During her cremation, ravens followed the rainbow-colored smoke, and two weasels were observed circumambulating the area.[22] Gyurmé Ösel reports that all of these miraculous signs and portents instilled deep faith in all those gathered.[23]

In Tibetan narrative accounts of the death of a saint (as in many other contexts of Buddhist death narratives), it is usual for different types of miraculous signs to play a prominent role. Images of deities or of the saint herself might appear in the sky or elsewhere as a means for relating to observers that she has achieved a high level of realization.[24] Gyurmé Ösel's dream vision of Mingyur Peldrön in the sky before him fits into this category, as does her body regaining its youthful form in the week after her decease and a lack of odor emanating from her corpse. Among the other miraculous sights that reportedly induced faith in all of her mourners were the relics found in her cremains and the animals that exhibited strange and devotional behavior at her funeral.[25] The category of "lights," including rainbows and other lights that might emanate from the corpse or near where it lies,[26] abound at the nun's death. The account is somewhat thin on the subject of mysterious sounds and earth tremors, although Gyurmé Ösel does report having heard strange sounds earlier in the year, sounds he likened to a roaring bull and later attributed to her impending death.[27] There are a few examples of atmospheric phenomena, such as fog and a rain of comets on the day that Gyurmé Ösel's nightmares began.[28]

In discussing the death of Mingyur Peldrön, Gyurmé Ösel also describes who attended her funeral and in what capacity. People from all over central Tibet came, including representatives from every single monastery in the region of Ü, regardless of denomination. He claims that all members of Mindröling's branch monasteries, all blood relatives (and their servants), were in attendance as well as a collection of other faithful people from Drachi. He takes care to note that among the throngs were religious leaders, government officials, and ordinary laypeople. Regional governors were there, including an army general from Yuthok and other political figures such as Polhané's daughter Deden Drölma and her husband.[29] The large number of mourners—many of whom held high social status—suggests the life of a woman at the center of the religious elite, respected by religious and political institutional leaders as well as the aristocracy more generally. In *Dispeller* the references to important political figures and their relatives reinforce her connection with these families. Appearing as they do at the end of the story, these details work to establish Mingyur Peldrön's position of prestige both within and beyond the Mindröling community one last time.

Mingyur Peldrön's saintliness was later cemented in the annual memorials for her. These commemorations established her as a figure both significant and worthy of remembrance. A brief description of Mingyur Peldrön's annual commemoration rites is mentioned in the Mindröling catalog (*karchak*) and stands as a testament to her continued importance in the official memory of the institution.[30] For five years after Mingyur Peldrön's death, annual memorials were held in her honor on Guru Rinpoche commemoration days of the summer rains retreat.[31] After that, less extravagant commemoration rites were held annually, beginning on the seventh day of the seventh month and lasting for seven days. During this time offerings were laid out in the great hall, culminating in a large feast on the last evening.[32]

Mingyur Peldrön was also memorialized beyond the Mindröling community in the years and centuries following her death. Two references to her appear in Chökyi Gyatso's (1880–1923/25) early-twentieth-century *Pilgrimage Guide to Ütsang*,[33] which mentions her jewel-encrusted tomb among the architectural wonders of Mindröling. He also reports that Mingyur Peldrön's seal can be found at the Pelchen temple in Rulugang, a temple affiliated with Mindröling.[34] Today Mingyur Peldrön's image memorializes her in modern-day Nyingma communities, including at Mindrolling Monastery in Dehradun, India. At Mindröling in central Tibet, she is represented as a nun, with red robes and a shaved head. There a bronze statue also depicts her sitting in lotus posture, with her hands in *dhyana mudra*, dressed in monastic robes and donning a "paṇḍita" hat. But very different images can be found at Pemayangtsé Monastery and Sangnak Choeling Monastery in Pelling, West Sikkim. At Pemayangtsé she appears in a mural painted by master craftsman Khandu Wangchuk in the late twentieth century. Mingyur Peldrön is depicted in the style of lay practitioner, with long hair and golden earrings, but also wearing the red robes and fanned hat of a religious specialist. At Sangnak Choeling a statue depicts her as a female tantric deity, with her right hand in *vitarka mudra* and her left holding a skullcup. Her breasts are bare, but she is bedecked in the scarves and jewels of a goddess.

In each of these images, a different aspect of Mingyur Peldrön's identity is emphasized. In one she is a tantric goddess, with flowing hair and bared breasts. In another she fully represents the monastic world, with shaved head and red robes. And in the third she sits somewhere between the two—as a respected religious practitioner and laywoman.[35] The image of her that appears on the second page of the Chinese printing of her collected works reputedly comes from the original site of Mindröling Monastery, outside Lhasa, but I have not been able to verify its existence there. In this image Mingyur Peldrön is depicted as a nun, with shaved head and red robes and her hands posed in *dhyana mudra*. What is most interesting about this image is its true-to-life quality. Her left eye crosses inward, as though in life she suffered from amblyopia. Since the provenance of this image has not yet been verified, we cannot be sure of its age or relation to her actual likeness, but rather than a perfected depiction, the image seems to be representing her as realistically as possible. The presence of these and other images at Nyingma institutions across the Tibetan Buddhist world show that Mingyur

Peldrön continues to be important to at least some degree in the modern Buddhist community. The variety of depictions attest to her connection to different aspects of Nyingma life, including monastic and non-monastic representations, and her relevance for religious communities.

The potential for sainthood was established in the events surrounding an individual's death across a range of religious historical and temporal contexts. In Tibetan namtar the death narrative was likewise a moment to reiterate the saint's high religious status while placing them in a larger historical moment. The miracles surrounding Mingyur Peldrön's funeral convey her divine nature, while the host of mourners in attendance establish her as an enlightened religious teacher, a recognized Mindröling representative, and a friend to many powerful political and religious leaders. While the significance of relics has been interpreted in a variety of ways,[36] it is clear that Gyurmé Ösel considered relics to be an important means for reinforcing the legitimacy of his master's sainthood and the hagiography itself. His points of evidence for her high status included all of the elements discussed earlier, including signs and portents, the relics found in her cremains, and lists of the people who came to witness the relics alongside him.

Gyurmé Ösel's dream accounts surrounding the death narrative of his beloved teacher are also a potent example of how hagiography can be used to solidify the sanctity of the saint and show how he bookends the narrative with reminders of Mingyur Peldrön's connection to Yeshé Tsogyel. In interpreting his nightmares, he becomes convinced that it is evidence that she is enlightened, that she has realized the true nature of her mind (as conveyed in the song she sings to him). Accompanied by the strange signs that he witnessed in the same month, these dreams become evidence that she was an emanation of Yeshé Tsogyel. Her death narrative acts as a bookend with the introductory section of *Dispeller* to assert her status as an emanation of Yeshé Tsogyel and therefore a female divinity. However, whereas in the opening section a great number of female buddhas and historical women are mentioned, in the closing she is likened to Yeshé Tsogyel alone. Yeshé Tsogyel is a common presence throughout *Dispeller*, and she is the deified figure most prominent in Mingyur Peldrön's death. Gyurmé Ösel points out that all mourners took refuge in Mingyur Peldrön as a recognized and true activity emanation of Yeshé Tsogyel and explains that he became fully convinced of her accomplished yogini status upon awakening from his prophetic dream.[37] At the very end of the text, he describes Mingyur Peldrön as the "unmistaken reincarnation of Padma's Wife Karchen [that is, Yeshé Tsogyel], the most high Great Bliss *Ḍākinī* Queen herself."³⁸ In working to establish her veracity as an emanation of Yeshé Tsogyel, he presents her as worthy of the same reverence as the iconic figure. In the context of her death narrative, this reiteration establishes Mingyur Peldrön as Yeshé Tsogyel and acts as an apotheosis of sorts. Her identification as Yeshé Tsogyel acts as the frame narrative for *Dispeller*, offering a final argument about the historical woman through her connection with the divine.

A Dispeller of Distress for the Faithful as Legacy

After framing *Dispeller* as a story of Mingyur Peldrön–as–Yeshé Tsogyel, Gyurmé Ösel turns to a brief explanation about why he wrote the hagiography in the first place. He closes with a colophon explaining the circumstances surrounding his completion of the work in 1782:

> Thus goes the *namtar* of Mingyur Peldrön, lord of the hundred buddha families and all-pervasive sovereign, called *A Dispeller of Distress for the Faithful*. Initially, the Tibetan Ruler Miwang Gyurmé Sönam Tobgyé [Polhané] and the Lhagyari Zhabdrung Chakdor Wangchen had supplicated at the feet of my excellent Lama [and requested a *namtar* of her]. Then, a year before she passed into the Great Expanse of Peace, I asked twelve times for it, and she granted [permission]. "A lama's *namtar* should be written by their disciple, so it should come from you." Again, she exhorted me with the words, "Compose it!" Although I began, demons interfered and I abandoned [the project]. Then from the direction of Yeru, in Tsang, the ears of Deden Dorjé's mendicant student Gyurmé Chöpel were continually oppressed [meaning unclear]. [Then there was the birth of] the lineage son of that lord of all beings Rigdzin Pemalingpa, the incarnation of the renowned victorious dharma master [Terdak Lingpa], the one called Rigdzin Pema Wangyel Dorjé Pel Zangpo, gift of the gods. His speech urged me on. In particular, this aroused in me undivided scorching faith to plant seeds of faith for the sake of distant future generations, so that they could hold this immutable illustration of Mingyur (Peldrön) in their minds.³⁹

In describing his reasons for writing *Dispeller*, Gyurmé Ösel first invokes the names of Polhané and a member of the Lhagyari family.⁴⁰ Although

Polhané (here referred to by his full name, Miwang Gyurmé Sönam Tobgyé) had died in 1747, Gyurmé Ösel references him as one of the influencing forces behind the hagiography's completion. This final reminder of Polhané's relationship to Mingyur Peldrön reinforces Gyurmé Ösel's assertions that he was important in her life and in the creation of her hagiography. In reading it, one wonders whether one of Polhané's living family members—perhaps his daughter or another family member—had urged Gyurmé Ösel to write the *Life*. This final reference also suggests that Polhané's role as a legitimating supporter of Mingyur Peldrön continued to be important long after both of them had died. In the colophon Gyurmé Ösel outlines his reasoning for not completing *Dispeller* until thirteen years after her death. He explains that a variety of difficulties kept him from composing it, even after many years of discussing it with her during her lifetime and working to earn her definitive permission to write it the year before she died.

While the role of prominent politicians and their aristocratic families is clear, it seems that the preservation of lineage memory was Gyurmé Ösel's impetus for finishing *Dispeller*, and the person who inspired the composition of the hagiography was a boy who was likely an infant or young child when the book was completed. Gyurmé Pema Wangyel was the son of the Fifth Trichen, Gyurmé Trinlé Namgyel (1765–1812), and Mingyur Peldrön's grand-nephew. He would ultimately be identified as an incarnation of Terdak Lingpa and would go on to become the Sixth Trichen of Mindröling in his adulthood.[41] It is possible that the year 1782 coincided with the baby's birth, although this is not stated directly. In any event Gyurmé Ösel mentions that he hoped writing the hagiography would mean that the next generation of Mindröling would have access to the stories of their ancestors and that these stories would serve as an inspiration for future generations. If we also take into consideration his insistence that her next birth would be male for one generation in order to better serve the Mindröling cause, we might surmise that Gyurmé Ösel was hoping for the boy to be identified as her reincarnation. In the end Gyurmé Pema Wangyel was the newest member of the family in 1782, and the boy's arrival prompted Gyurmé Ösel to write about the *Life* of the child's deceased great-aunt. Some years later his sister, Trinlé Chödrön, would be born. Her role at Mindröling has been likened to that of Mingyur Peldrön's.

What little we know about Trinlé Chödrön echoes similarities with her great-aunt. Like Mingyur Peldrön, Trinlé Chödrön was the daughter of a trichen. She was born to the Fifth Trichen and an unnamed mother sometime in the late eighteenth century. Her dates are unclear, although she finished one of her works in 1825 and was said to have died young. In *A Festival of Victorious Conquerors* she is remembered for having dedicated her short life wholly to the dharma.[42] According to the modern-day narrative of Mindrolling Monastery in India, Trinlé Chödrön was an ordained nun who was known to be a great teacher and in particular a Dzogchen master. She reportedly acted as a teacher to Jamyang Khyentse Wangpo and Jamgön Kongtrul Lodrö Thaye and wrote at least one ritual text for the *sevasadhana* of Vajravarahi Kalikruddha, one instruction manual for the practice of Transference of Consciousness, or Powa, and an explanation of Anuyoga. She is also mentioned as part of the Mindröling lineage of Atiyoga in Dudjom Rinpoche's *The Nyingma School of Tibetan Buddhism*.[43] According to the *Lives of the Mindröling Succession Lineages*, "After Jetsün Mingyur Peldrön, she is the Mindröling Jetsünma to whom [Mindröling is] most indebted."[44] This text lists three women among its thirty-seven figures. One of them is Mingyur Peldrön. The others are her grandmother Yangchen Drölma and her grandniece Trinlé Chödrön. Other than this, I have found no Tibetan-language accounts of Trinlé Chödrön's life, and she has no namtar. It seems that her brother's namtar was destroyed by a "barbarian force" at an undisclosed time, and it is possible that any *Lives* about her might have met the same fate, if they had ever been written at all.[45] From what little we know of her, Trinlé Chödrön's trajectory was similar to Mingyur Peldrön's. She was educated alongside her elder brother, bestowed with kama and terma teachings at Mindröling, and eventually became a nun. She wrote several texts and was reportedly a teacher herself, and who knows what kind of impact she might have made had she lived longer. The existence of Mingyur Peldrön's namtar could have served as an example for her as she was growing up. Today she is still considered to be second only to Mingyur Peldrön as an important woman for their institution.

In spite of the clear importance of Mingyur Peldrön, Yangchen Drölma, and Trinlé Chödrön in the development of Mindröling as a viable religious institution, no formal reincarnation lineage has ever been established there that is filled exclusively by women. The women of the family all receive the title of jetsünma, but this serves more as a mark of respect, rather than identification with a specific set of responsibilities or forms of engagement with institutional stewardship. In contradistinction, there are expectations that come along with being named trichen or khenchen, both positions that have always been occupied by men. Mindröling's jetsünmas are nevertheless treated as a lineage of sorts and the third most important Mindröling line after the trichens and the khenchens. Mingyur Peldrön is considered the first in the jetsünma lineage and therefore very important indeed.[46] With the jetsünmas the tradition of strong female leadership has persisted at Mindröling, as most recently embodied in the lives and works of Jetsün Khandro Rinpoche and her sister, Jetsün Dechen Paldron. Born in India in 1967, Khandro Rinpoche has continued in Mingyur Peldrön's footsteps by becoming a nun and has been an active proponent of religious practice throughout her adulthood. In addition to founding and directing the Samten Tsé retreat center for nuns and international practitioners in Mussoorie, India, she maintains the Lotus Garden Retreat Center in Stanley, Virginia. While not identified as an incarnation of Mingyur Peldrön,[47] Khandro Rinpoche is certainly carrying on the traditions of women's education, dedication to monastic life, and female leadership at Mindröling. In 2012 or 2013 Dechen Paldron gave birth to the eldest in the next generation, a baby girl named Gautami Thrinley Choedron, currently the youngest Mindröling jetsünma. Hopefully, these traditions will continue.

The writing of a *Life* is always necessarily an act of creation. There are details that are included and omitted, communiqués that do and do not land for different audiences, and the inherent biases of both the author and the subject. This is true for Gyurmé Ösel's *Dispeller* and for this book. In the words of musician Ani DiFranco: "A life, anyone's life, is vast and uncontainable and I've discovered that you can make a whole book full of people and things and still there will be that much left over. . . . Let the record show that there are, in fact, whole other girls with the same face and the same name, who lived concurrently to this one in this story, but that this is the one that got written down. . . . History is not only a story told but a story *chosen*."[48]

I assuredly have omitted some aspects of Mingyur Peldrön's literary and historical existences. That said, as a story chosen, this study has had several goals. First, it has sought to bring forth the story of Mingyur Peldrön's life in as full a light as possible, as it is presented in the hagiography penned by Gyurmé Ösel. Also, in analyzing the narrative of this *Life* as a literary and historical creation, I have worked to discover what hagiography can tell us about the lives of historical women of privilege and about the Mindröling community in the eighteenth century. As an unusually long example of a woman's life story that adheres to a strict chronology and includes biographical accounts, the hagiography shows us a bit more about what life was like for one privileged Tibetan woman. While we cannot generalize based on a single narrative, Mingyur Peldrön's case offers a counterpoint to more frequent accounts of overt gendered oppression, familial ostracization, and related struggles that were frequently faced by women seeking the life of the religious practitioner. Instead, we see the ways that privilege and gender interact in her life, the actions she took in a variety of challenging contexts, and the ways that her hagiographer leverages all of these parts of her story when presenting the narrative of his beloved teacher.

Dispeller gives us a rare literary example of a privileged and highly educated woman in Tibetan history who advocated for the survival of her tradition and asserted monasticism-centered ideals. Hers is among a handful of such *Lives*, although others exist that have not yet been explored by scholars in the twenty-first century. Based on what is found in *Dispeller*, we can assume that socioeconomic and cultural privilege determined one's access to religious education alongside the strictures of gender and other factors. One's ability to participate in institutional development or to access systems of education, for example, is influenced by a host of intersectional factors that play upon a personal and communal experience. Mingyur Peldrön's story reminds us that sexual virtue (here in the form of abstinence) and a strong inclination for female religious leadership can indeed coexist within one personality.

Mingyur Peldrön's role in her religious community was that of eminent teacher of the masses, of other religious and political leaders, and of individual men and women of the aristocracy. Her position as a religious educator imbued her with an influence akin to leadership, which she exercised by asserting her ideals for proper conduct and dedication to the Great Perfection. She furthered her monastic mission and urged women to take positions of leadership. Gyurmé Ösel's hagiography of her is as much an exploration of his perceptions of the religious tensions of the mid-eighteenth century as it is a description of her life. The emphases in *Dispeller* suggest that he was concerned with asserting monasticism among the Nyingma and portraying the personality of his beloved and compassionate teacher. It is understood that any literary work will reflect the views of its author, and Gyurmé Ösel's representation of non-monastic tantric communities suggests that he was involved in disagreements about proper conduct and practice during his lifetime. While the true extent of these conversations remains unknown, his message to the next generation is clear: be like Mingyur Peldrön. And what did that mean, according to Gyurmé Ösel? In a quickly changing world, she worked with single-pointed focus to further her soteriological goals and did so in a way that allowed for her practical survival. She actively urged other community members to adhere to the rules of celibacy and chastised those who consumed any amount of alcohol. Gyurmé Ösel's anachronistic representation of the Fifth Lelung suggests a tension within the community to the point that an otherwise respected—if somewhat controversial—figure is presented as a charlatan and playboy in Mingyur Peldrön's namtar. Afforded many of the tools to participate in the maintenance of attendant goals and traditions, Mingyur Peldrön published several ritual texts and used her religious and aristocratic connections for the sake of her community and herself, and as a result she was able to rebuild Mindröling after its decimation. Her texts are evidence of her contribution to and effective support of Mindröling. Paired with *Dispeller*, her works suggest an institutional influence that likely contributed to the continued support of female leadership in Mindröling's education. Like her stone throne at Pemayangtsé, they have persisted through the generations to bring us a piece of the work of her lifetime.

Rather than a wholly deified Mingyur Peldrön, the nun of Gyurmé Ösel's hagiography had strong opinions regarding the public religious establishment and her role within it as a teacher and representative of monastic ideals. Her humanity is conveyed through her experiences with the religious and political instabilities of her time and accounts of her frustration with disciples who stray from her ideal path. The result of the combined presentation of her as perfected master and concerned teacher is an active interplay in the construction of public identity that takes into account both the subject's and narrator's intentions for the Mindröling audience. What emerges is a dialogue about how best one might create the public persona of an influential religious leader who also happens to be a woman. The presence of her own voice emphasizes the dialogic potential of Tibetan *Life* writing. The miraculous aspects of the narrative inform a sense of how one mid-eighteenth-century devotee sought to successfully glorify his master to the extent that she and her teachings would be remembered. Looking at Mingyur Peldrön's *Life* brings us one step closer to a critical mass of women's *Lives*, the analysis of which could eventually lead to broad conjectures about religious women and their educational, spiritual, and economic opportunities throughout Tibetan history.

As a "bridge" between two previously studied time periods (that is, the long seventeenth and early nineteenth centuries), Mingyur Peldrön's hagiography presents an interim in which many things were changing in the political, social, and religious landscapes of the Nyingma world. During the transition from the rise of the Ganden Podrang and the founding of Mindröling in the seventeenth century to the nonsectarian (rimé) developments of nineteenth-century Kham, leaders continued to argue questions of proper conduct and the interpretation of doctrine. Gyurmé Ösel's placement of Mingyur Peldrön within a larger historical context is significant for our understanding of her but also adds to our historical understanding of the period in which they both lived. By tying her to widespread sociopolitical events, he gives the reader a new perspective of the time period. By placing her at the forefront of the Nyingma struggle for survival, she and her family members become symbols of the changing tradition itself. By emphasizing her support of monasticism, he also reveals his own late-eighteenth-century concerns.

The historical memory of women such as Mingyur Peldrön can shift how we think about women's lives in the present and future as well as the past. This was clear to Gyurmé Ösel when he wrote *Dispeller* for the youngest generation of Mindröling. Mingyur Peldrön's life story and those of other historical Buddhist women continue to offer inspiration and advice for those living in the twenty-first century. Historical memory has persisted among the active community of Mindröling descendants living today at Mindrolling Monastery in Dehradun, India, which includes three living jetsünmas. Jetsün Khandro Rinpoche and her sister, Jetsün Dechen Paldron, hold leadership positions there. Khandro Rinpoche is a nun and has an active teaching career that has often meant world tours, during which she spent significant time in Singapore, Eastern Europe, and North America.[49] A charismatic teacher, she has been written about in several popular contexts.[50] Dechen Paldron is a laywoman who has directed a project collecting and distributing information about Mindröling's history. Her daughter, Gautami Thrinley Choedron, who was born in the winter of 2012–13, is currently the youngest living Mindröling jetsünma. If we ask whether Gyurmé Ösel was effective in solidifying his master's authenticity, the roles of Jetsün Khandro Rinpoche, her sister, and niece, and the continuing prevalence of the jetsünma tradition of Mindröling, are an indication that he was indeed effective in helping to cement women's importance in the tradition. There is no plaque at the throne at Pemayangtsé Monastery, but Mindrolling is currently directing a reconstruction of Mingyur Peldrön's former retreat on a nearby mountaintop. The fact that she is remembered today by modern female religious leaders as an important teacher and practitioner and that her memory remains alive at Pemayangtsé and Mindrolling suggests that her impact was far-reaching in the long eighteenth century. Her *Life* depicts a woman who lived through a very difficult historical moment and managed to benefit the world through her teachings.

Tibetan Glossary

A Note on the Transliteration of Phoneticized Tibetan Terms

Generally, Tibetan terms are rendered in this book according to the Tibetan and Himalayan Library's Extended Wylie transliteration (of spelling in written Tibetan) and phoneticization (of spoken Tibetan) systems and are shown in phonetic form throughout the main text. The exception is for terms for which the original Tibetan is informative for the discussion at hand. This glossary includes terms that are frequently used in the book, first with their phonetic romanized spelling, followed by the transliteration. Please note that the phonetics generally reflect a Lhasa dialect and so are not comprehensive in their depiction of accurate pronunciation across Tibetan cultural regions. For words for which other conventions are in use (such as when people have determined the phoneticization of their own name according to a different system), individuals' preferred spelling has been retained. When more than one spelling is used in the book, they are separated by a comma, and short forms appear in parentheses. The glossary includes the names of people, places, and other terminology that appear regularly in the book.

Personal Names

Changkya Rölpé Dorjé	lcang skya rol pa'i rdo rje
Chökyi Drönma	chos skyi sgron ma
Chökyi Gyatso	chos kyi rgya mtsho
Chökyi Wangchuk	chos kyi dbang phyug
Dechen Peldrön	bde chen dpal sgron
Deden Drölma	bde ldan sgrol ma

Desi Sangyé Gyatso	sde srid sang gye rgya mtsho
Dingri Lodrö Tenpa	ding ri blo gros brtan pa
Dokharwa Tsering Wangyel	mdo mkhar ba tshe ring dbang rgyal
Dorje Pakmo	rdo rje phag mo
Drimé Özer	dri med 'od zer
Dudjom Jikdrel Yeshé Dorjé	bdud 'joms 'jigs bral ye shes rdo rje
Dudjom Lingpa	bdud 'joms gling pa
Gesar	ge sar
Guru Rinpoche	gu ru rin po che
Gyurmé Chödron	'gyur med chos sgron
Gyurmé Namgyel	'gyur med rnam rgyal
Gyurmé Pagsam Trinlé	'gyur med dpag bsam phrin las
Gyurmé Pema Chogdrup	'gyur med pad+ma mchog grub
Gyurmé Pema Tenzin	'gyur med pad+ma brtan 'dzin
Gyurmé Pema Wangyel	'gyur med pad+ma dbang rgyal
Gyurmé Samten Chogdrup	'gyur med bsam gtan mchog grub
Gyurmé Trinlé Namgyel	'gyur med 'phrin las rnam rgyal
Jagöpa Chökyong Gyeltsen	bya rgod pa chos skyong rgyal mtshan
Jamgön Kongtrül Lodrö Thayé	'jam mgon kong sprul blo gros mtha' yas
Jamyang Khyentse Wangpo	'jam dbyangs mkhyen brtse'i dbang po
Jetsün Sherab Drönma	rje btsun shes rab sgron ma
Jigdrel Yeshé Dorjé	'jigs bral ye shes rdo rje
Jigmé Dorje	'jigs med rdo rje
Jigmé Lingpa Khyentse Özer	'jigs med gling pa mkhyen brtse 'od zer
Ju Mipam Gyatso (Mipam)	'ju mi pham rgya mtsho (mi pham)
Katok Rigdzin Tsewang Norbu	kaH thog rig 'dzin tshe dbang nor bu
Kelsang Gyatso	skal bzang rgya mtsho
Khandro Rinpoche	mkha' 'gro rin po che
Khandro Tāre Lhamo (Tāre Lhamo)	mkha' 'gro tA re lha mo (tA re lha mo)
Khangchenné	khang chen nas
Khyungpo Repa Gyurmé Ösel (Gyurmé Ösel)	khyung po ras pa 'gyur med 'od gsal ('gyur med 'od gsal)
Kunzang Drönma	kun bzang sgron ma
Lady Drung	lcam drung
Lady Peldzin	lcam dpal 'dzin
Lelung Jedrung Losang Trinlé	sle lung rje drung blo bzang 'phrin las

Lhatsun Chenpo Dzogchen Jigmé Pawo	lha btsun chen po rdzog chen 'jigs med dpa' bo
Lochen Dharmaśrī	lo chen d+harma shrI
Longchen Rabjampa (Longchenpa)	klong chen rab byams pa (klong chen pa)
Losang Chökyi Nyima	blo bzang chos kyi nyi ma
Machik Labdrön	ma gcig lab sgron
Milarepa	mi la ras pa
Mingyur Peldrön	mi 'gyur dpal sgron
Nangsa Öbum	snang gsal 'od 'bum
Ngawang Losang Gyatso	ngag dbang blo bzang rgya mtsho
Ngödrup Namgyel	dngos grub rnam rgyal
Nyangrel Nyima Özer	nyang ral nyi ma 'od zer
Orgyan Chökyi	o rgyan chos skyid
Orgyen Dorjechang	o rgyan rdo rje 'chang
Pema Gyurmé Gyatso	pad+ma 'gyur med rgya mtsho
Phuntsok Peldzöm	phun tshogs dpal 'dzoms
Polhané Sönam Tobgyé (Polhané)	po lha nas bsod nams stobs rgyas (po lha nas)
Rigdzin Pelden Tashi	rig 'dzin dpal ldan bkra shis
Rinchen Namgyel	rin chen rnam rgyal
Sakya Pandita	sa skya paNDita
Samten Gyatso	bsam gtan rgya mtsho
Sera Khandro	se ra mkha' 'gro
Shugsep Jetsün Rinpoche	shug sep rje btsun rin po che
Situ Penchen Chökyi Jungné	si tu paN chen chos kyi 'byung gnas
Sönam Peldren	bsod nam dpal 'dren
Tashi Gyatso	bkra shis rgya mtsho
Tenpé Drönmé	bstan pa'i sgron me
Tenzin Norbu	bstan 'dzin nor bu
Terdak Lingpa Gyurmé Dorjé (Terdak Lingpa)	gter bdag gling pa 'gyur med rdo rje (gter bdag gling pa)
Trinlé Chödrön	'phrin las chos sgron
Trinlé Lhundrup	'phrin las lhun grub

Tsewang Norbu	tshe dbang nor bu
Tsewang Rabten	tshe dbang rab brtan
Tsultrim Kelzang	tshul khrims skal bzang
Yangchen Drölma	dbyang can sgrol ma
Yeshé Tsogyel	ye shes mtsho rgyal
Yizhin Lekdrup	yi bzhin legs grub
Zhenpen Thayé Özer	gzhan phan mtha' yas 'od zer

Place Names and Institutions

Ardok Gönsar	ar dog dgon gsar
Dakpo	dwags po
Dargyé Chöding	dar rgyas chos gling
Drachi	gra phyi
Dranang	grwa nang
Drepung	'bras spungs
Dorjé Drak	rdo rje brag
Golok	mgo log
Katok	kAH thog
Kham	khams
Kongpo	kong po
Lhasa	lha sa
Mindröling, Mindrolling	smin sgrol gling
Mön	mon
Namdröl Yangtsé	rnam grol yang rtse
Pelyül	dpal yul
Pemayangtsé	pad ma dbyang brtse
Samding	bsam sding
Samten Tsé	bsam gtan rtse
Samten Chöling	bsam gtan chos gling
Sangnak Choeling	gsang sngags chos gling

Sera	se ra
Shauk Taggo	sha 'ug stag sgo
Tsang	gtsang
Tsangpo	gtsang po
Tsetang	rtse thang
Ü	dbus
Yorpo	g.yor po

Other Terms

chayik	bca' yig
chidar	phyi dar
Chöd	gcod
delok	'das log
Dorsem	rdor sems
Drepu	bras phu
düngyü	gdung rgyud
Dzogchen	rdzogs chen
Ganden Podrang	dga ldan pho brang
Gelongma	dge slong ma
Geluk	dge lugs
Gelukpa	dge lugs pa
geshe	dge bshes
gur	mgur
Jangter	byang gter
jetsün	rje btsun
jetsünma	rje btsun ma
kama	bka' ma
karchak	dkar chag
khenchen	mkhan chen
lama	bla ma
logyü	lo rgyus
Longdé	klong sde

Menakdé	man ngag sde
nakpa	sngags pa
namtar	rnam thar, rnam par thar pa
Neljorma	rnal 'byor ma
Nyingma	rnying ma
Nyingmapa	rnying ma pa
Nyingtik	snying thig
Nyö	gnyos, myos
Powa	'pho ba
rikné	rig gnas
rimé	ris med
Sakya	sa skya
Semdé	sems sde
senyik	gsan yig
Srémo	sras mo
sungbum	gsung 'bum
tertön	gter ston
terma	gter ma
Thögel	thod rgal
Three Vows	sdom gsum
Topyik	thob yig
Trekchö	khregs chod
trichen	khri chen
Tröma Nakmo	khros ma nag mo
tsünma	btsun ma
tulku	sprul sku
wang	dbang

Notes

Introduction

1. Thanks to Amy Holmes-Tagchungdarpa and Kalzang Dorjee Bhutia for telling me about the throne in the first place.
2. Khenpo Wangyal Dorjee, personal communication, May 2016.
3. A hallmark of Tibetan hagiography is to show the subject as enlightened while simultaneously conveying the challenges that that person faced in their lifetime. In connection with how we depict Tibetan life stories, Bessenger addresses the conundrum of whether or not to use the term *saint* in this context. She asks whether a person who is identified as always already enlightened can still be described as someone "who achieves his or her community's estimation of holiness in a lifetime." Following her, I apply the term *saint* to this context, as Mingyur Peldrön's hagiography does offer "a perhaps partially historical record of the difficult existence of a ... Tibetan woman attempting to create a religious identity." Bessenger, *Echoes of Enlightenment*, 24–25.
4. Tib. *rje btsun mi 'gyur dpal gyi sgron ma'i rnam thar dad pa'i gdung sel/*.
5. The calculation is taken from Bessenger, *Echoes of Enlightenment*, 129, which also borrows from Schaeffer, *Himalayan Hermitess*, 4; and Jacoby, *Love and Liberation*, 13.
6. Tib. *bod kyi sems chen ma dag gi rnam thar.*
7. I refer to the modern-day instantiation of the monastery, constructed in India in the twentieth century, as "Mindrolling." This is in keeping with how monastery inhabitants spell the name of their institution. Conversely, that which was founded by Terdak Lingpa and Lochen Dharmaśrī in central Tibet is identified as "Mindröling," the phoneticization of the Tibetan *smin grol gling* according to the Tibetan and Himalayan Library's Wylie phoneticization standards.
8. *Dispeller* ms.1, 118b–119a. That is, on the third day of the tenth month of the water tiger year.

9   Tib. *rdzogs chen a ti zab don snying po.*
10 Tib. *rdzogs chen a ti zab don snying po'i rig pa'i rtsal dbang skur thabs lhan thabs kyi tshul du spros pa.*
11 Quintman, *Yogin and the Madman*, 7.
12 Tib. *rnam par thar pa.*
13 For example, the work of DiValerio, Kragh, Quintman, and Willis.
14 For more on this, see the work of Ashton, Bynum, Coakley, Geary, Heffernan, Mooney, Renevey and Whitehead, and Tylus.
15 Taylor, "Hagiography and Early Medieval History," 7.
16 For more on the genre, see Bessenger, *Echoes of Enlightenment*, 3; Diemberger, *When a Woman Becomes a Religious Dynasty*, 17; Quintman, *Yogin and the Madman*, 7; Roberts, *Biographies of Rechungpa*, 4; Schaeffer, *Himalayan Hermitess*, 5; Willis, *On the Nature*, 304.
17 Geary, *Living with the Dead*, 28.
18 In the tripartite taxonomy of namtar (that is, outer, inner, and secret), Mingyur Peldrön's *Life* most closely resembles the ideal "outer" namtar, although it is not explicitly described as such. The tripartite taxonomy is as follows: outer namtar (*phyi'i rnam thar*), inner namtar (*nang gi rnam thar*), and secret namtar (*gsang ba'i rnam thar*) (Quintman, *Yogin and the Madman*, 8). Thus far, no inner or secret namtars are known for Mingyur Peldrön, nor have I found any explanation as to why there is only an outer namtar for her.
19 Geary, *Living with the Dead*, 13, see also 14–15, 17.
20 Schulenburg, *Forgetful of Their Sex*, 17.
21 Ashton, *Generation of Identity*, 3.
22 Bynum, *Holy Feast*, 149.
23 Dalton, *Gathering of Intentions*, 100 (see also 98–99); and Dalton, "Recreating the Rnying ma School," 92.
24 Regarding Terdak Lingpa as the son of Yangchen Drolma, see Jigdrel Yeshé Dorjé et al., *Nyingma School*, 496; and Lochen Dharmashrī, *Lha 'dzin dbyangs can sgrol ma'i rnam thar*, 2b–3a.
25 Lochen Dharmaśrī, *Lha 'dzin dbyangs can sgrol ma'i rnam thar*, 9b.
26 Lochen Dharmaśrī's works are compiled into a nineteen-volume collection, including his exegeses on the *Gathering of Intentions Sutra* (*dgongs pa 'dus pa'i mdo*). For more on this text, see Dalton, *Gathering of Intentions*; and Jigdrel Yeshé Dorjé et al., *Nyingma School*, 732.
27 Although their father was retroactively named the first trichen.
28 Dalton compares the projects of Mindröling and the Ganden Podrang: "Just as the nation of Tibet was gathered and symbolically arranged through these new public ceremonies [established by the Fifth Dalai Lama and Desi Sangyé

Gyatso], so too was the Nyingma School united by the new Mindröling rituals. The scale of Terdak Lingpa and Lochen Dharmaśrī's work was similarly large" (*Gathering of Intentions*, 98, see also 98–100).

29 This required "in-depth historical research, the systematization of the Spoken Teachings canon, and the creation of new, large-scale public rituals." Dalton, *Gathering of Intentions*, 99. For more on the invention of tradition during this period, see the discussion of Eric Hobsbawm in Cuevas and Schaeffer, *Power, Politics, and the Reinvention of Tradition*, 1.

30 See Jigdrel Yeshé Dorjé et al., *Nyingma School*, 898.

31 Bessenger, "I Am a God," 86.

32 Bessenger, *Echoes of Enlightenment*, 86–87.

33 Bessenger, *Echoes of Enlightenment*, 58–59. The comparison of these two texts raises a larger question about the important distinction between multivocality and multiple authorship. In particular, Gyurmé Ösel's assertions about single authorship, coupled with his reassurances that Mingyur Peldrön contributed by making suggestions for what topics he should cover, are useful for engaging in a discussion about the two concepts. In *Dispeller* multivocality is used as a means to convey tensions in Gyurmé Ösel's world, and his direct quotations of Mingyur Peldrön are representative of how he hoped his audience would perceive her.

34 Schaeffer, "Autobiography," 92.

35 Schaeffer, "Autobiography," 87.

36 I occasionally use the term *auto/biographical* to reference the various forms of life writing that include, but are not limited to, autobiography, biography, and hagiography.

37 Schaeffer, "Autobiography," 87, 107, 109.

38 Jacoby, *Love and Liberation*.

39 Dates tentative as per Schaeffer "Autobiography," 85.

40 Regarding Chökyi Drönma's aristocratic heritage, see Diemberger, *When a Woman Becomes a Religious Dynasty*, 116. Regarding Sera Khandro's heritage, see Jacoby, *Love and Liberation*.

41 Diemberger, *When a Woman Becomes a Religious Dynasty*.

42 Gayley, *Love Letters*, 38.

43 Gayley, *Love Letters*, 44.

44 For more on the hierarchical gendering and typology of terms relating to women and men, see Bessenger, *Echoes of Enlightenment*, 132–33. For connections between women's bodies, suffering, the Tibetan literary context, and the rest of the Buddhist world, see Schaeffer, *Himalayan Hermitess*, 92–94. Scholars focusing on historical moments and geographic regions

beyond the Tibetan cultural regions of the Buddhist world have also looked at relationships drawn between the experience of suffering, living as a woman, and karma, but they are too numerous to recount in full here.

45 According to Gyatso and Havnevik, the "damning moniker of the 'low birth (*skye-dman*)'" has been "used since at least the eleventh century and in the last several hundred years the standard word in both writing and speech for 'women,' often invoked by both men and women as a way of letting etymology prove the fact of a matter" (*Women in Tibet*, 9). See also Bessenger, *Echoes of Enlightenment*, 132; Jacoby, *Love and Liberation*, 133.

46 Diemberger, *When a Woman Becomes a Religious Dynasty*, 127.

47 For a more detailed exposition on how karma, rebirth, and gender are conceptualized within the context of Tibetan Buddhism, see Makley, "Body of a Nun," 268–70. See also Schaeffer, *Himalayan Hermitess*, 94; and Jacoby, *Love and Liberation*, 133.

48 Schaeffer, *Himalayan Hermitess*, 8 and 91.

49 Jacoby, *Love and Liberation*, 133.

50 Jacoby, *Love and Liberation*, 133.

51 For more on this phenomenon and how various women responded to and incorporated it in their *Lives*, see Schaeffer's chapter on "Women, Men, Suffering" in *Himalayan Hermitess*; Bessenger's chapter on "Low Birth but High Thought" in *Echoes of Enlightenment*; and relevant sections in Diemberger, *When a Woman Becomes a Religious Dynasty*; and Jacoby, *Love and Liberation*.

52 Schaeffer, *Himalayan Hermitess*, 69, 91–96. Unlike the current moment, in this period of Tibetan history *sex* and *gender* are treated as nearly synonymous terms. In keeping with the conventions of the time, I talk about sex and gender interchangeably. Please note that this interchangeability is historically positioned and reflective of the temporal moment of eighteenth-century central Tibet.

53 McIntosh, "White Privilege," 194, 203–4.

54 Coston and Kimmel, "Seeing Privilege Where It Isn't," 97.

55 This term is here used to include both emanation (for example, of a bodhisattva) and incarnation (of an individual), two ways of identifying a living person as the embodiment of another being that can lend weight to their individual authority (religious, political, or otherwise).

56 Langenberg, *Birth in Buddhism*, 15.

57 Padma'tsho and Jacoby, "Gender Equality," 4.

58 Bessenger, *Echoes of Enlightenment*, 63.

59 Jacoby, *Love and Liberation*, 17.

60 For more on auto/biographical voice in Tibetan *Life* writing, see the work of Gyatso and Jacoby.
61 See Gayley, *Love Letters from Golok*.

1. A Privileged Life

Epigraph: *Dispeller* ms. 1, 25b; *Dispeller* ms. 2, 19.

1   Pomplun, *Jesuit on the Roof*, 106.
2   Crossley, Köhle, and Petech have all addressed these developments in detail.
3   Pomplun, *Jesuit on the Roof*, 103 (see also 12).
4   Geary, *Living with the Dead*, 13–17.
5   *Dispeller* ms. 1, 21b. It was a ḍākinī day. Tibetan Phugpa Calendar Calculator, accessed January 12, 2013, DigitalTibetan.org. http://digitaltibetan.org/cgi-bin/phugpa.pl?year=1699.
6   *Dispeller* ms. 2, 16; *Dispeller* ms. 1, 21a.
7   See, for example, Conze, "Legend of the Buddha Shakyamuni," 1959.
8   Buswell and Lopez, *Dictionary of Buddhism*, 986; Jigdrel Yeshe Dorje et al., *Nyingma School*, 296.
9   *Dispeller* ms. 1, 22a–b.
10 *Dispeller* ms. 1, 22b–23a; *Dispeller* ms. 2, 16–17.
11 Tib. *rgyal sras rin chen rnam rgyal gyi rnam thar skal bzang gdung sel*.
12 *Rinchen Namgyel Namtar*, 64, 70.
13 *Dispeller* ms. 1, 30a–b, 74b–75a; *Rinchen Namgyel Namtar*, 64, 70.
14 Tib. *'bras ljongs dgon sde'i lo rgyus*.
15 *Dispeller* ms. 1, 23a–23b; *Dispeller* ms. 2, 17.
16 Tib. *re ba chen po*.
17 Orgyen Dorjechang—that is, Vajradhara, Padmasambhava.
18 *Dispeller* ms. 1, 24a–b; *Dispeller* ms. 2, 8. I have not yet located sources that mention Mingyur Peldrön's name prior to receiving the name by which she is now known.
19 Tib. *don gyi slad*.
20 Tib. *snying po'i bstan pa*.
21 *Dispeller* ms. 1, 25a–b; *Dispeller* ms. 2, 18.
22 *Dispeller* ms. 1, 25b; *Dispeller* ms. 2, 19.
23 *Dispeller* ms. 1, 35a.
24 Tib. *re ba chen po*.
25 "List of gsan yigs," Institute for Indology and Tibetan Studies, Ludwig-Maximilians-Universität München, accessed May 4, 2020, https://www.indologie.uni-muenchen.de/personen/2_professoren/kramer_jowita/projekte_kramer/gsan-yig/liste_gsan-yig/index.html.

26 *Dispeller* ms. 1, 34b.
27 *Dispeller* ms. 1, 35a and 29a–37a, Tib. *bi ma snying tig*.
28 *Dispeller* ms. 1, 34b–35b.
29 Jigdrel Yeshé Dorjé et al., *Nyingma School*, 734.
30 *Dispeller* ms. 1, 33b–34a; *Rinchen Namgyel Namtar*, 3, 63.
31 *Rinchen Namgyel Namtar*, 3–6.
32 Tib. *bzo rig pa, gso ba rig pa, sgra rig pa, gtan tshigs rig pa, nang don rig pa*. See Cabezón and Jackson, "Editor's Introduction," *Tibetan Literature*, 17.
33 Cabezón and Jackson, "Editor's Introduction," 18.
34 *Rinchen Namgyel Namtar*, 3.
35 Townsend, personal communication, August 29, 2019.
36 Gayley, *Love and Liberation*, 35–36.
37 *Dispeller* ms. 1, 8a.
38 Tib. *gter gsar*.
39 *Dispeller* ms. 1, 36b; *Dispeller* ms. 2, 2. *The Lives of the Mindröling Succession Lineages: A Festival of Victorious Conquerors* repeats some phrasing in its brief biography of her, including "bar skabs lo chen dhar+ma shrI las rab tu byung ste" (83).
40 *Dispeller* ms. 1, 23b, emphasis added; *Dispeller* ms. 2, 17. sku chung du nas sdom gsum 'gal med du dril nas bstan 'gro'i dpung gnyen dam par lung gi zin.
41 Anna Johnson, personal communication, April 14, 2020.
42 Tib. *'og min o rgyan smin grol gling gi gdan rabs mkhan brgyud rim par byon pa rnams kyi rnam thar g.yul las rnam par rgyal ba'i dga' ston/*.
43 *Festival of Victorious Conquerors*, 81. sku nar son pa nas sdom gsum 'gal med du dril nas thugs nyams su bzhes.
44 For a detailed discussion of the accessability of the non-tantric path of the *sngags pa* for women in the modern day, see Joffe, "White Robes, Matted Hair."
45 *Dispeller* ms. 1, 105b, "bsnyen par rdzogs."
46 While one might initially think that this is a short form of *jetsünma* (*rje btsun ma*), which can be used for both monastic and non-monastic women, the particular use of *btsun ma* in *Dispeller* is in reference to nuns. For example, there are references to "tsünmas and other renunciates" (*Dispeller* ms. 1, 87b) and discussions of large groups of nuns and monks (*btsun ma* and *gra pa* [*Dispeller* ms. 1, 71b]). Also, while Mingyur Peldrön's sister and mother might have been likewise referred to as "tsünmas" if it were a short form of *jetsünma*, they are instead referred to as "lcam" and "yum" and never "tsünma."
47 Starling, "Neither Nun," 278.
48 For more information on the question of women's ordination and the impact of ordination on women's lived experience in Buddhist communities, see

Diemberger, *When a Woman Becomes a Religious Dynasty*; Kawahashi, "Women Challenging the 'Celibate' Order"; Langenberg, "On Reading Buddhist Vinaya"; Mrozik, "Robed Revolution"; among others.

49 For more on the monastic-lay divide in Tibetan Buddhism, see Jacoby, "To Be or Not to Be Celibate." On the religious path of the non-celibate tantric practitioner, see Joffe, "White Robes, Matted Hair," chap. 2.

50 To be clear, the term *neljorma* can be applied to monastic and non-monastic women alike. But its applicability for those women who were not ordained, and the connections with consort practice, are the focus here.

51 Diemberger, *When a Woman Becomes a Religious Dynasty*, 132–38.

52 Gyatso and Havnevik, *Women in Tibet*, 15.

53 Makley, "Body of a Nun," 283–84 and elsewhere.

54 For a thorough exposition on twenty-first-century discussions about ordination among Tibetan Buddhist communities in the diaspora, see Schneider, "Ordination of the *dge slong ma*."

55 Gyatso and Havnevik, *Women in Tibet*, 16. See also Makley, "Body of a Nun." While focusing on a twentieth- and twenty-first-century context, Makley's observations are pertinent for our understanding of premodern and early modern Tibetan historical contexts.

56 In the fifteenth century Chökyi Drönma was fully ordained and sought to help other women also move toward full ordination. Chökyi Drönma also thought the path of the nun was most ideal for women who sought the life of a religious practitioner. Likewise, Dan Martin has found evidence of full ordination among nuns in the eleventh and twelfth centuries. See Diemberger, "First Samding Dorje Pakmo"; Martin, "Woman Illusion" (66 and elsewhere); and Gyatso and Havnevik, *Women in Tibet*, 15.

57 Diemberger, *When a Woman Becomes a Religious Dynasty*, 130.

58 Diemberger, "First Samding Dorje Pakmo." It is likely that there were other women with similar trajectories, but their lives have yet to be studied in detail.

59 Havnevik, "Autobiography of Jetsun Lochen Rinpoche."

60 According to Petech, having kept the death of the Fifth Dalai Lama secret for so long exacerbated argumentation and doubt about the validity of the recognized Sixth Dalai Lama, once he was revealed. Throughout the life of the Sixth Dalai Lama, political uncertainty and infighting developed unchecked both within and beyond the Geluk leadership. Petech, *China and Tibet*, 9–14.

61 Crossley, Petech, Pomplun, Köhle, and others have written extensively on the political strife of this period. What follows here is a very brief summary

of the political-historical events that were most influential for Mingyur Peldrön's experience.

62 Different scholars name different dates for Tsewang Rabten's ascension to rule. For further discussion, see Crossley, *Translucent Mirror*, 318–19; Petech, *China and Tibet*, 25. The Dzungars were a subgroup of the larger Oyirod federation, based in Ili, in modern-day Turkestan. Tsewang Rabten sought to influence the political atmospheres of western Mongolia, Turkestan, and Central Tibet. See Crossley, *Translucent*, 314, 319, 320. I rely on Crossley's spelling of *Oyirod*. For a discussion of spelling variance and historical representation of the Oyirod group, see Crossley, *Empire*, 81; and Petech, *China and Tibet*, 9.

63 Unhappy with the choice of the Sixth Dalai Lama and the Desi's handling of the Fifth Dalai Lama's death, Lhazang Khan marched to Lhasa in 1705 and executed the Desi but stopped short of dethroning the Sixth Dalai Lama for fear of instigating unrest. He established rule in Lhasa and was supported by the Qing imperium. The Sixth Dalai Lama would die under mysterious circumstances while on his way to Beijing in November 1706, making way for a new Dalai Lama and further unsettling the religiopolitical order. For further discussion, see Petech, *China and Tibet*, 9–14; Pomplun, *Jesuit on the Roof*, 69, 109–10.

64 Shakabpa, *One Hundred Thousand Moons*, 374.

65 Petech, *China and Tibet*, 44–45.

66 Sweet and Zwilling, *Mission to Tibet*, 138; Pomplun *Jesuit on the Roof*, 138; Petech, *China and Tibet*, 25, 27–29, 38. Tsering Döndrup was the brother of the "Dzungar King," Tsewang Rabten, and leader of the Dzungar expedition into central Tibet. Shakabpa, *One Hundred Thousand Moons*, 418. It is unclear how involved Tibetans actually were in the sack of the region that followed the Dzungar occupation of Lhasa. See Pomplun, *Jesuit on the Roof*, 112–14, 116, for discussion.

67 Shakabpa, *One Hundred Thousand Moons*, 423; Petech, *China and Tibet*, 42–45.

68 Petech, *China and Tibet*, 53, 65–66; Shakabpa, *One Hundred Thousand Moons*, 431.

69 *Dispeller* ms. 1, 39b; Shakabpa, *One Hundred Thousand Moons*, 420–21.

70 *Dispeller* ms. 1, 40a.

71 *Dispeller* ms. 1, 41a–43a; *Dispeller* ms. 2, 30–31.

72 *History of Sikkimese Monasteries*, 127.

73 khrag 'thung dpa' bo 'jigs med rdo rjes, sometimes referred to as "the Sikkimese Dzogchenpa" in *Dispeller*. First mention of him is in the list of teachings Mingyur Peldrön received from various people. Jikmé Dorjé is mentioned in *Dispeller* ms. 1, 37b.

74 *'bras ljongs rgyal rabs*, 86.

75 See Gyurmé Namgyel's namtar, in 'bras ljongs rgyal rabs, 86. See also *History of Sikkimese Monasteries*, 127; and Mullard, *Opening the Hidden Land*, 170.
76 *'bras ljongs rgyal rabs*, 86. This is described as "phar gsan tshur gsan."
77 *Dispeller* ms. 1, 46b; and personal communication with Wangyal Bhutia, May 2016. I later learned from Dominique Townsend that Mindröling Monastery's monastic code of conduct (*chayik*) strictly bars all women—including family members—from entering monastery grounds. Thus, Mingyur Peldrön's refusal to enter Pemayangtsé is in keeping with the rules of her home monastery. Personal communication, August 29, 2019.
78 I visited this site in May 2016. Nothing currently remains of Mingyur Peldrön's original residence, but new construction is underway for a meditation center associated with Mindrolling Monastery, India.
79 *'bras ljongs rgyal rabs*, 87. According to Gyurme Namgyel's *rnam thar*, this was on the twenty-fifth day of the seventh month.
80 Dudjom Rinpoche corroborates this commonly held notion: "Mingyur Peldron was largely responsible for the restoration of Mindroling following the Dzungar invasion of 1717. A brilliant teacher, she authored several important meditation manuals" (Jigdrel Yeshé Dorjé et al., *Nyingma School*, 81).
81 Tib. *zhabs rim pa*. This can be translated literally as "virtuous ones" but can also refer to servants.
82 Tib. *sman brjid*. The name and location of this institution is unclear. It does not seem to be a short form of *Mindröling* (*smin grol gling*), as the monastery is referenced in long form elsewhere in the text. Moreover, the spelling is consistent throughout all three of the manuscripts of *Dispeller* that I reference, which is not the case for other misspellings. With that said, it is potentially just a short form of *Mindröling* or might refer to a different site altogether.
83 In terms of detail, what could have been a protracted physical illness is glossed over briefly. These health concerns were not nearly as prominent in Gyurmé Ösel's mind as the religiopolitical dangers that Mingyur Peldrön faced. In comparison, her escape from the Dzungars takes some ten pages, including how they evaded the army at each turn as well as vivid descriptions of Mingyur Peldrön's emotional experience and the divine intervention that protected her. The result of this treatment is that we have little information about what might have been a continuing health factor throughout Mingyur Peldrön's life.
84 *Dispeller* ms. 1, 52b.
85 *Dispeller* ms. 1, 52b; *Dispeller* ms. 2, 38.
86 *Dispeller* ms. 1, 30b; *Dispeller* ms. 3, 179.
87 Tib. *na rag dong sprugs*.
88 Mingyur Peldrön, "na rag," 1a; Dudjom, *Nyingma*, 731; Ronis, *Celibacy*, 233.

2. Authorizing the Saint

Epigraphs: Lochen Dharmaśrī, *Dispeller* ms. 1, 31b; Gyurmé Ösel, *Dispeller* ms. 1, 2a.

1. Tib. *skyed dman*; Benard "Born to Practice," 6. See also Bessenger, *Echoes of Enlightenment*, 132.
2. Jacoby, *Love*, 143.
3. See Jacoby, "This Inferior," 145; and Schaeffer, *Himalayan Hermitess*.
4. Here I follow Severs, Celis, and Erzeel, who further an ontology of power based upon "a relational conception of political power that locates the constitution of power relations within social interactions, such as political representation" ("Power, Privilege, and Disadvantage," 346).
5. The self-humbling references were of course funneled first through the pen of Gyurmé Ösel.
6. Havnevik and Gyatso, "Introduction"; and Bessenger, *Echoes of Enlightenment*, 148.
7. Gyurmé Ösel uses variations of the Tibetan *sprul* (e.g., *emanated*, *emanation*).
8. For a detailed discussion, see Bessenger, "'I am a god.'"
9. Bessenger, *Echoes of Enlightenment*, 148.
10. Gayley, *Love Letters*, 50.
11. Diemberger, *When a Woman*, 241.
12. For example, Sangyé Gyatso's *Life* of the Fifth Dalai Lama begins with a detailed description of the subject's previous lives; see Ahmad, *Life of the Fifth Dalai Lama*, 43–126 (with a summary on 126). Although the tradition goes much further back, the hagiography of the Fifth Dalai Lama likely served as a timely representative model for authors writing in the mid- to late eighteenth century, and it is likely that Gyurmé Ösel was at least familiar with Sangyé Gyatso's work.
13. Weber, *Economy and Society*, 241 and 247. It is worth noting that when Weber discusses routinized charisma, he points to the incarnation lineage of the Dalai Lamas, which was the most internationally famous of the tulku lines in the twentieth century.
14. Jacoby, *Love and Liberation*, 91.
15. Tib. *yum chen mo*; Tib. *rdo rje rnal 'byor ma*; Bessenger, *Echoes*, 25 and 148–49.
16. Diemberger, *When a Woman*, 239; and Jacoby, *Love and Liberation*, 80–91. While she was identified as other figures later in her life, these are not included in her namtar, and Diemberger does not think these additional associations had much impact on her lived experience. In comparison, Chökyi Drönma's reincarnation was more emphatically associated with additional historical women. Diemberger, *When a Woman*, 240.

17 Schaeffer, *Himalayan Hermitess*, 47.
18 Gayley, *Love Letters*, 35.
19 Jikdrel Yeshé Dorje et al., *Nyingma School*, 11. Regarding Samatabhadra, Gyurme Dorje further explains that "the Nyingmapa hold that buddhahood is attained when intrinsic awareness is liberated just where it is through having recognised the nature of Samantabhadra, the primordially pure body of reality. This buddhahood is endowed with the pristine cognition of the expanse of reality (*chos-dbyings ye-shes*, Skt. *dharmadhātujñāna*), for it is free from all conceptual elaborations, and the pristine cognition of sameness (*mnyam-nyid ye-shes*, Skt. samatājñāna) which remains pure through the extent of saṃsāra and nirvāṇa" (19). Moreover, "Samantabhadra is the teacher in whom both saṃsāra and nirvāṇa are indivisible, the antecedent of all, who holds sway over existence and quiescence in their entirety, and who is the expanse of reality and the nucleus of the sugata" (115–16). Samantabhadrī only appears in Tibetan contexts, whereas Samantabhadra is also prevalent in several East Asian Buddhist traditions; see Buswell and Lopez, *Princeton Dictionary of Buddhism*, 745.
20 *Dispeller* ms. 1, 3a–b.
21 Gyurmé Ösel furthermore specifies that Nangsa Öbum was a speech emanation (Tib. *gsung sprul*) of Yeshé Tsogyel. *Dispeller* ms. 1, 15b.
22 Melnick Dyer, "Female Authority," 218.
23 See the work of Cuevas, Pommaret, and Prude.
24 For examples, see Cuevas, *Travels in the Netherworld*; Pommaret, "Delok ('das log) Women"; and Prude, "Death, Gender, and Extraordinary Knowing."
25 Schaeffer, "Autobiography," 93–94, 107; and *Himalayan Hermitess*, 120.
26 *Dispeller* ms. 1, 51a.
27 See Bessenger, *Echoes of Enlightenment*, 163; Jacoby, *Love and Liberation*, 316; and Schaeffer, *Himalayan Hermitess*, 40.
28 Jacoby, *Love and Liberation*, 80, 87–89.
29 Gayley, *Love Letters*, 35.
30 Jacoby, *Love and Liberation*, 190; Gayley, *Love Letters*, chap. 3, "Inseparable Companions."
31 Jacoby, *Love and Liberation*, 96.
32 Jacoby, *Love and Liberation*, 96. See also 204–7, where Jacoby explains the "substantial connection between sex and text, more specifically between channel and wind practices involving sexuality and the revelation of scriptures and religious artifacts" (205).
33 Jacoby, *Love and Liberation*, 207, 213.
34 Jacoby, *Love and Liberation*, 191–92.
35 Gayley, *Love Letters*, 35 and 50.

36 Gayley, *Love Letters*, 50.
37 Gayley, *Love Letters*, 50. "I would aver that such appropriation allows Nyingma masters to make room for women who enter their circle of close relations as wife, consort, or daughter in order to constitute them as authorized participants in an otherwise male-dominated milieu."
38 Gayley, *Love Letters*, 160. See also 50: "It was also pivotal to her status as a tertön later in life, since those who reveal treasures necessarily trace their past lives to the imperial period as a direct disciple of Padmasambhava or a comparable master."
39 Gayley, *Love Letters*, 155.
40 *Dispeller* ms. 1, 8a–b; *Dispeller* ms. 2, 6. I have not yet located this quotation in the text to which he ascribes it.
41 *Dispeller* ms. 1, 10b, bdud 'dul drag mo rtsal/ ye shes mtsho rgyal/.
42 *Dispeller* ms. 2, 7.
43 For further discussion, see Jigdrel Yeshe Dorjé et al., 394; and Dowman, *Sky Dancer*, 4.
44 Jigdrel Yeshe Dorje et al., *Nyingma School*, 734; Jamyang Khyentse Wangpo, "sngon 'gro tshogs," 149.
45 *Rinchen Namgyel Namtar*, 3.
46 Weber, *Economy and Society*, 215.
47 Cooper, "Intersectionality," 392.
48 Dalton, *Gathering of Intentions*, 100.
49 Jacoby, *Love and Liberation*, 41–52.
50 The most salient comparison that I have found in the Tibetan tradition is with the Samding Dorje Phagmo; see Diemberger *When a Woman*.
51 Cooper, "Intersectionality," 398.
52 Weber, *Economy and Society*, 215.
53 Weber, *Economy and Society*, 215–16.
54 *Dispeller* ms. 1, 36b.
55 On Rinchen Namgyel's return, see *Dispeller* ms. 1, 52a.
56 This is not to deny the importance of mothers and wives in the functioning of the family. For example, while Yangchen Drölma was lauded for her role in maintaining the household prior to the founding of Mindröling, she did not further the family's goals by engaging in religious teaching, nor does her form of leadership appear to be focused on the spiritual or political realms. With that said, the role that Mingyur Peldrön would ultimately take is more reflective of the activities of her father, uncle, and brothers, rather than that of her grandmother, mother, or sisters.
57 Tib. *rje bla ma*.
58 Tib. *rje nyid*; Tib. *nga ba'i bla ma*; Tib. *rje bla ma mchog*.

59 See Martin, "Pearls from Bones," 301.
60 Tib. *rje bla ma dam pa dA ki'i gtso mo*. References include, for example: "Excellent Master, Supreme Blissful *Ḍākinī* Queen" (rje bla ma dam pa bde chen mkha' 'gro'i gtso mo). In other cases he uses the Sanskrit loan *dA ki'i* instead of *mkha' 'gro*. *Dispeller* ms. 1, 82b–83a.4b, 49a and b, 50a, 64a, 116b. For more on this loan word, see Gyatso, *Apparitions*.
61 Tib. *bla ma dam pa bde chen Da k+ki'i gtso mo*. *Dispeller* ms. 1, 4b.
62 *Dispeller* ms. 1, 49b.
63 In this case she is *skyabs rje bla ma dam pa bde chen dA ki'i gtso mo*. *Dispeller* ms. 1, 64a.
64 Again, in this case there is a slight variation, as she is described as "skyabs kyi mchog gyur rje bla ma dam pa bde chen DA ki'i gtso mo." *Dispeller* ms. 1, 116.
65 Tib. *bu mo, sras mo*.
66 *Dispeller* ms. 1, 31b.
67 I define this term according to Dan Martin: "'Lineage holder' is here defined not only as a person who holds the main teachings (secret precepts and the like) from a particular teacher, but one who also passed them on in a lineage significant for posterity." "Woman Illusion," 62–63.

3. MULTIVOCAL *LIVES*

1 For more on Sönam Peldren's multiauthored *Life*, see Bessenger, *Echoes of Enlightenment*; and for more on Sera Khandro's auto/biography, see Jacoby, *Love and Liberation*.
2 This brief piece is included in Lochen Dharmaśrī's collected works, or sungbum, in a section dedicated to Mindröling's history and hagiography. It appears chronologically after *Lives* of the brothers' contemporaries Jagöpa Chökyong Gyeltsen (1648–90), written in 1699, the year of Mingyur Peldrön's birth; and Dingri Lodrö Tenpa (1632–87), written in 1700; as well as the *Lives* of all those in Lochen Dharmaśrī's *vinaya* transmission lineage; and Lochen Dharmaśrī's namtar. The texts in this section are all ordered chronologically according to when they were written. Based on its placement in the sungbum, we can surmise that Yangchen Drölma's *Life* was written shortly after 1701, when Mingyur Peldrön was a toddler.
3 Dharmashrī, "yum," 2b, 6a–7a, 9b.
4 *Dispeller* ms. 1, 96b.
5 That is, the *Lives* of Christian saints between 1200 and 1500 CE.
6 Ashton, *Generation of Identity*, 2, 4–5, 12–15, 46, 103–4.
7 See Coakley, *Women, Men, and Spiritual Power*.

8   See Mooney, *Gendered Voices*.
9   Bakhtin, "Discourse in the Novel."
10 Jacoby, *Love and Liberation*, 13. Jacoby references Mary Mason and Estelle Jelinek in her development of this idea.
11 Jacoby, *Love and Liberation*, 15–16.
12 *Dispeller* ms. 1, 55a–b.
13 *Dispeller* ms. 1, 86a–b.
14 *Dispeller* ms. 1, 78b.
15 *Dispeller* ms. 1, 28b.
16 Respectively, Jackson, "Poetry," 369; Gyatso, *Apparitions of the Self*, 101; Ardussi, "Brewing and Drinking," 115; Quintman, *Yogin and the Madman*, 58. See also Jackson, "Poetry," 369, 381; and Sujata, *Tibetan Songs*, 116. Gur are written in many meters, including lines of anywhere between four and ten syllables per line and also with varied syllables per line.
17 Gyatso, *Apparitions*, 104.
18 Kvaerne, *Anthology*, 7–8. For more on the history of gur and its connections to traditional Tibetan and Indian Buddhist poetics, see Jackson, "Poetry," 368–72; Sørensen, *Divinity*, 14; Sujata, *Tibetan Songs*, 79, 84.
19 That is, the later diffusion of Buddhism (*chidar*, eleventh to fourteenth centuries).
20 Jackson, "Poetry," 369.
21 The form was used extensively by Sakya Pandita and Milarepa as well as being the most common meter for the Gesar epic. Sujata, *Tibetan Songs*, 123–25. Sujata goes so far as to refer to it as "the meter of Mi la ras pa."
22 *Chandaḥ*. I refer here to his *sdeb sbyor rin chen 'byung gnas kyi 'grel pa don gsal me long*.
23 Townsend, *Materials*, 125, 157.
24 Other well-known authors who lived during Mingyur Peldrön's lifetime include the Seventh Dalai Lama Kelsang Gyatso, and Changkya Rölpé Dorjé (1717–86). Sørensen, *Divinity*, 16; and Sujata, *Tibetan Songs*.
25 Thanks to participants of the 2018 Lotsawa Translation Workshop for their help in developing this translation.
26 *Dispeller* ms. 1, 45b.
27 Quintman, *Yogin and the Madman*, 59, 84; Jackson, "Poetry," 372–73.
28 Ardussi, "Formation of the State of Bhutan," 115. Ardussi explains that yogins were associated with the "great Tantric magician-saints (*siddhācārya*; Tib. *grub-thob*) of India."
29 See also Jackson, "Poetry," 374. Döndrup Gyel defines seven general goals for gur composition delineated as (1) remembering the guru's kindness, (2) indicating the source of one's realizations, (3) inspiring the practice of

Dharma, (4) giving instructions on how to practice, (5) answering disciples' questions, (6) urging the uprooting of evil, and (7) serving as missives to gurus or disciples.

30 Ardussi explains the connection thus: "Having gained control over their 'subtle physiology,' the *cakras* or mystical centers symbolically located along the axis of their bodies, and the 'winds' or forces which move along the mystical 'veins,' they are able to concentrate this force in the center located at their neck, usually identified with the *Sambhogakaya* (Tib. *longs-spyod-sku*) or 'Enjoyment Body' of the Buddha. The process is a meditative one, and the practitioner at this level is regarded as partaking of Buddhahood and becomes able to produce songs of the Absolute Truth spontaneously; they simply appear in his mind as mental experience (Tib. *nyams*) natural to one who has achieved the *longs-spyod* level of Buddhahood." Ardussi, "Formation of the State of Bhutan," 117.

31 Ardussi, "Formation of the State of Bhutan," 117.
32 Jigdrel Yeshe Dorje et al., *Nyingma School*, 81 n. 1137.
33 Tib. *rin chen gter mdzod*.
34 Mingyur Peldrön, *Ambrosial Feast*, 192–93.
35 Siddha Yolmowa is Tenzin Norbu, b. 1598.
36 Mingyur Peldrön, *Ambrosial Feast*, 193–94.
37 Tib. *'dam mkhan* (muck expert).
38 Tib. *thugs dpal be'u stim pa*.
39 *Dispeller* ms. 1, 62b–63a; *Dispeller* ms. 2, 46.
40 That is, the *mkha' 'gro gsang ba ye shes kyi khrid yig*. Elsewhere it is referred to as the *mkha' 'gro gsang ba ye shes kyi rnal 'byor rim bzhi'i lam zab mo nyams su len pa'i khrid yig man ngag gsal sgron/*, or simply as the *rim bzhi'i lam zab mo nyams su len pa'i khrid yig*. *Dispeller* ms. 1, 63a.
41 chos kyi dbang phyug, "tshe dbang nor bu'i," 74–75. For a brief discussion of Tsewang Norbu, see also Garry, "Rigdzing Tsewang Norbu," Treasury of Lives.
42 She appears multiple times in prayers and lineage lists found in the works of the nineteenth-century scholar Jamyang Khyentse Wangpo.
43 These are her "rdzogs chen a ti zab don snying po'i khrid dmigs zin bris su spel ba kun bzang dgongs rgyan" and "gar tshe'i brgyud 'deb ldeb." She is also listed in several lineages found in his *gdams ngag mdzod*.
44 *Dispeller* ms. 1, 47a.
45 Samten Gyatso, *'bras ljongs dgon sde'i lo rgyus*, 127–29.
46 *Dispeller* ms. 1, 59b, 67b, 71b, 92a, and elsewhere.
47 Khenpo Wangyel Dorjee and Tshering Bhutia, personal communication, May 2016.
48 Schaeffer, *Himalayan Hermitess*, 94.

49 In particular, Terdak Lingpa's revealed treasure cycles focusing on the Embodiment of All the Sugatas (*thugs rje chen po bde gshegs kun 'dus*).
50 *Dispeller* ms. 3, 62a.
51 *Dispeller* ms. 3, 124–25.
52 *Dispeller* ms. 3, 73a; *Dispeller* ms. 1, 95a–b.
53 *Dispeller* ms. 1, 85b.
54 *Dispeller* ms. 1, 60b–61a; *Dispeller* ms. 3, 80; *Dispeller* ms. 2, 44.
55 *Dispeller* ms. 2, 45.
56 *Dispeller* ms. 2, 45.
57 *Dispeller* ms. 2, 45.
58 See, for example, Tsultrim Kelzang, "bod kyi lo rgyus phyogs bsdus," 109; and Tukwan Losang Chokyi Nyima, "grub mtha' thams cad kyi khung," 79–80.
59 Ardussi, "Brewing and Drinking," 118.
60 *Dispeller* ms. 3, 55a; *Dispeller* ms. 1, 83a.
61 I have discussed this somewhat obtuse phrase with several scholars of Tibetan language and history, and the consensus is that the men who had been drunkards returned (or "circled back") to the proper forms of behavior. That is to say, they abandoned their wayward behavior and returned to the prescribed life of abstention from alcohol and sex and, in so doing, were able to become leaders at the retreat center.
62 *Dispeller* ms. 1, 83b–84a.
63 *Dispeller* ms. 1, 83a–b.
64 Khenpo Sherap Konchok, personal communication, April 2012.
65 *Dispeller* ms. 1, 94a.
66 *Dispeller* ms. 1, 94a.
67 *Dispeller* ms. 1, 94a.
68 *Dispeller* ms. 1, 84 a–b.
69 *Dispeller* ms. 1, 87b–88a.
70 Ashton, *Generation of Identity*, 4–5, 13–15, 46.

4. Mingyur Peldrön the Diplomat

Epigraph: *Dispeller* ms. 1, 54a.
1 Gyatso and Havnevik explain it thus: "There is a long history of the Buddhist monastic order (that is, despite its enduring androcentrism) and other renunciate communities serving as an alternative life-space for women, where they could escape their unhappy circumstances in society. The classic Pali collection *Therīgāthā* clearly connected the monastic life to deliverance from specifically female predicaments such as oppressive husbands and misogynistic disparagement. One finds similar aspirations among Tibetan nuns." *Women in Tibet*, 15.

2   Pomplun, *Jesuit on the Roof*, 103.
3   Shakabpa, *One Hundred Thousand Moons*, 634; Kapstein, "Seventh Dalai Lama."
4   Shakabpa, *One Hundred Thousand Moons*, 440.
5   Petech, *China and Tibet*, 21.
6   Shakabpa, *One Hundred Thousand Moons*, 459.
7   Shakabpa, *One Hundred Thousand Moons*, 431–32.
8   Not to be confused with the Sikkimese king of the same name.
9   Kapstein, "Seventh Dalai Lama."
10 Shakabpa, *One Hundred Thousand Moons*, 432–33. See also Kapstein, "Seventh Dalai Lama."
11 Duckworth, *Mipam on Buddha-Nature*, xx.
12 Stoddard, "Rig 'dzin dpal ldan bkra shis," 107.
13 *Rinchen Namgyel Namtar*, 18, 33, 113, and elsewhere.
14 Terdak Lingpa Gyurmé Dorjé, *o rgyan smin grol gling gi 'dus sde'i bca' khrims kyi yig blang dor gsal bar byed pa'i nyi ma*, 95.
15 Townsend, "How to Constitute a Field of Merit," 4.
16 Townsend, "How to Constitute a Field of Merit," 3–4, 11, and elsewhere.
17 Jigdrel Yeshe Dorje et al., *Nyingma School*, 731.
18 Ronis, "Celibacy, Revelations, and Reincarnated Lamas," 156.
19 He received teachings from Rinchen Namgyel when he fled to Kham during the civil war and also from Pema Gyurme Gyatso at some point. Ronis, "Celibacy, Revelations, and Reincarnated Lamas," 93.
20 Stoddard, "Rig 'dzin dpal ldan bkra shis," 97–100, 108, and elsewhere.
21 Stoddard, "Rig 'dzin dpal ldan bkra shis," 92.
22 Duckworth, *Mipam on Buddha-Nature*, xxii.
23 Duckworth, *Mipam on Buddha-Nature*, xxii–xxiii.
24 *'bras ljongs dgon sde'i lo rgyus*.
25 *rje btsun sku zhabs* ("jetsün of high family"); *History of Sikkimese Monasteries*, 127.
26 *History of Sikkimese Monasteries*, 127–28.
27 Shakabpa, *One Hundred Thousand Moons*, 403. Polhané put down an attempted rebellion by the Hor leader Uicing Taiji around 1714 and played an important role in Lhazang Khan's war against Bhutan in 1714. See also Petech, *China and Tibet*, 22.
28 Dr. Jampa Samten, personal communication, April 19, 2012.
29 Petech, *China and Tibet*, 92–96.
30 Jigdrel Yeshe Dorje et al., *Nyingma School*, 81 n. 1137.
31 *Dispeller* ms. 2, 38. See also Petech, *China and Tibet*, 110.
32 The phrase *a kha kha!* is difficult to translate. Here I have rendered it as well as possible in order to convey Polhané's shock and dismay.
33 *Dispeller* ms. 1, 53a–b; *Dispeller* ms. 2, 39; *Dispeller* ms. 3, 70–71.

34 *Dispeller* ms. 2, 38.
35 Tib. *zhabs rim pa* (virtuous ones). This term is intentionally left ambiguous, as it might be referencing a servant or another member of the household, but their virtue is emphasized elsewhere in this section of the text.
36 *Dispeller* ms. 1, 53b–54a.
37 Shakabpa, *One Hundred Thousand Moons*, 439.
38 Shakabpa, *One Hundred Thousand Moons*, 440.
39 *Dispeller* ms. 2, 41; *Dispeller* ms. 1, 56a–b.
40 *Dispeller* ms. 2, 42: de skabs o rgyan min grol gling gi zhig gso'i ar las tshugs pa'i mchod rten tsam ma gtogs grub nyer yod/: "At that time at Mindröling, all the construction repairs were accomplished, except for the construction of some stupas."
41 *Dispeller* ms. 2, 42; *Dispeller* ms. 1, 58a–b. The term *geshes (dge bshes)* refers to monks in the Geluk denomination who have proceeded through the monastic education system and have undertaken their final examinations, somewhat akin to a doctor of philosophy or doctor of theology degree in the United States. For more on the geshe system of monastic education in the Geluk denomination, see Dreyfus, *Sound of Two Hands Clapping*.
42 *Dispeller* ms. 2, 46–47.
43 *Dispeller* ms. 1, 49a.
44 *Dispeller* ms. 2, 67.
45 According to Gene Smith's introduction to the *Autobiography of the First Panchen Lama*, "Tibetan sectarian and political rivalries were increasingly aired to Mongol patrons; and, in turn, these princes implored manifestations of the magical powers of their favored lamas, sometimes against their enemies, more often against their closest kin" (2).
46 Shakabpa, *One Hundred Thousand Moons*, 432.
47 Shakabpa, *One Hundred Thousand Moons*, 432.
48 For more on Polhané's two sons, Gung Gyurmé Tseten and Gyurmé Namgyel, see Shakabpa, *One Hundred Thousand Moons*, 463.
49 *Dispeller* ms. 1, 91b; *Dispeller* ms. 3, 120.
50 Petech, *Aristocracy*, 54.
51 *Secret Wisdom Ḍākinī Instruction Manual*, Tib. *rim bzhi'i lam zab mo nyams su len pa'i khrid yig*; *Dispeller* ms. 1, 63a.
52 Tib. *tshe dbang drag dmar*.

5. THE DEATH OF MINGYUR PELDRÖN

Epigraph: *Dispeller* ms. 1, 81b.
1 *Dispeller* ms. 1, 81b.

2   In other words, that the mind has an adamantine nature.
3   *Dispeller* ms. 1, 82a–83a; *Dispeller* ms. 3, 134–36.
4   Geary, *Living with the Dead*, 2.
5   Tib. *sku gdung 'bar ba* (Blazing Remains Tantra). Martin, "Pearls from Bones," 281–82. Atmospheric phenomena include "rain, storms, hail, wind, mist, fog, rings around the moon." As an aside, the Blazing Remains Tantra is a Precepts Class, or *menakdé*, text of Atiyoga.
6   *Dispeller* ms. 1, 47b–48a.
7   Tib. *nges gsang rdo rje snying po'i bstan*.
8   *Dispeller* ms. 1, 84b–85b.
9   *Dispeller* ms. 1, 86b.
10 *Dispeller* ms. 1, 88a.
11 *Dispeller* ms. 1, 87a.
12 Tib. *mkha' 'gro snying thig* (Khandro Nyingtik); Tib. *zab lam bde gshegs kun 'dus* (Zaplam Deshek Kündü), *Dispeller* ms. 1, 87a–b; Tib. *nyang gter drag dmar* (Nyangter Drakmar). *Dispeller* ms. 1, 70a, 99b, and elsewhere. For more on Adon, see Dalton, *Gathering of Intentions*, 154.
13 *Dispeller* ms. 1, 99b.
14 *Dispeller* ms. 1, 83b.
15 *Dispeller* ms. 1, 81b.
16 Tib. *gdung mchod*.
17 *Dispeller* ms. 1, 81b–82a.
18 *Dispeller* ms. 1, 84a–b.
19 *Dispeller* ms. 1, 85b.
20 *Dispeller* ms. 1, 84a–85b.
21 *Dispeller* ms. 1, 82b, 84a–b. At the time of her cremation, miraculous events were reported from Chöding hermitage and at Kachö Dechen Ling.
22 *Dispeller* ms. 1, 85a.
23 *Dispeller* ms. 1, 85b.
24 Martin, *"Pearls from Bones,"* 281.
25 *Dispeller* ms. 1, 84b–85a.
26 Martin, *"Pearls from Bones,"* 282.
27 *Dispeller* ms. 1, 81b.
28 *Dispeller* ms. 1, 81b.
29 *Dispeller* ms. 1, 83a–b.
30 See Tenpé Drönmé, *gsang chen*; and *Festival of Victorious Conquerors*, for descriptions of commemoration days.
31 *Dispeller* ms. 1, 85b–86a.
32 Tenpé Drönmé, *gsang chen*, 205–7.
33 Tib. *dbus gtsang gnas yig*.

34 Chökyi Gyatso, *Pilgrimage Guide to Ütsang*, 202 and 354.
35 Thanks to Natasha Kimmet for discussing some of these images.
36 Martin, *"Pearls from Bones,"* 290.
37 *Dispeller* ms. 1, 83a–b.
38 *Dispeller* ms. 1, 89a.
39 *Dispeller* ms. 1, 87b, 88a.
40 His title suggests that he was a person of importance from Lhagyari, although his specific station remains unknown.
41 *Festival of Victorious Conquerors*, 109–10.
42 *Festival of Victorious Conquerors*, 112.
43 Jigdrel Yeshe Dorje et al., *Nyingma School*, 734.
44 *Festival of Victorious Conquerors*, 112.
45 Tib. *klo klo'i dpung* (barbarian force). *Festival of Victorious Conquerors*, 110.
46 Jetsün Khandro Rinpoche, personal communication, September 2011.
47 Rather, she is considered to be an incarnation of Urgyen Tsomo (1897–1961), who was herself identified as an incarnation of Yeshé Tsogyel.
48 DiFranco, *No Walls and the Recurring Dream*, 302.
49 Jetsün Khandro Rinpoche was enthroned in 1976 at the age of nine, in Kalimpong. There was discussion about whether she should be enthroned in the Mindröling (Nyingma) or Karma Kagyu lineages. Ultimately, she was enthroned thrice, which leads to further questions about sectarian differentiations, even in the present day. Simmer-Brown, *Dakini's Warm Breath*, 183 and 399.
50 For example, see Haas, *Dakini Power*; and Chodron, *Blossoms of the Dharma*.

Bibliography

Abbreviated Translated Titles Used in Citations

A Festival of Victorious Conquerors. See Minling Editorial Committee, ed. *'Og min o rgyan smin grol gling gi gdan rabs mkhan brgyud rim par byon pa rnams kyi rnam thar g.yul las rnam par rgyal ba'i dga' ston/*.

Ambrosial Feast. See Mi 'gyur dpal sgron, "Dri lan bdud rtsi'i dga' ston le tshan ldeb/."

Dispeller ms. 1. See Khyung po ras pa 'gyur med 'od gsal, *Rje btsun mi 'gyur dpal gyi sgron ma'i rnam thar dad pa'i gdung sel/*.

Dispeller ms. 2. See *Rje btsun mi 'gyur dpal sgron gyi gsung rnam*, Gangs can skyes ma'i dpe tshgos, vol. 5.

Dispeller ms. 3. See "Rje btsun mi 'gyur dpal gyi sgron ma'i rnam thar dad pa'i gdung sel/."

Dredging the Depths of Hell. See Smin gling rje btsun mi 'gyur dpal sgron, and rGyal sras gzhan phan mtha' yas, "Na rag dong sprugs kyi dbang gi cho ga mtshams sbyor gyis brgyan pa bde chen lam bzang."

History of Sikkimese Monasteries. See Bsam gtan rgya mtsho, *'Bras ljongs dgon sde'i lo rgyus 'Bras ljongs dgon sde'i lo rgyus/*.

Rinchen Namgyel Namtar. See 'Bar bla bkra shis rgya mtsho, "Rgyal sras rin chen rnam rgyal gyi rnam thar skal bzang gdung sel/."

Tibetan-Language Sources

'Bar bla bkra shis rgya mtsho. "Rgyal sras rin chen rnam rgyal gyi rnam thar skal bzang gdung sel." In *Sngags mang zhib 'jug (7)*, edited by Lce nag tshang hūṃ chen he ru ka, Ye shes sgrol ma, and Lce nag tshang nyi zla he ru ka, 7–125. Spyi'i 'don thengs bdun pa/. Zi ling: mTsho sngon zhing chen nang bstan rig gnas zhib 'jug lte gnas, 2003. [*Rinchen Namgyel Namtar.*]

Bdud 'joms gling pa. *Gnas lugs rang byung gi rgyud rdo rje'i snying po.* Pe cin: Mi rigs dpe skrun khang, 2004.

Bdud 'joms 'jigs bral ye shes rdo rje. *Bdud 'joms chos 'byung.* Khreng Tu'u: Si khron mi rigs dpe skrun khang, 1996.

Brag dkar rta so sprul sku chos kyi dbang phyug. "Gter gnas de nyid nas spyan drangs pa'i rdzogs chen a ti zab don snying po'i skor yongs rjogs thob pa." In *Gsung 'bum chos kyi dbang phyug*, 2:330–44. Swayambhunath, Kathmandu: Khenpo Shedup Tenzin, 2011.

Bsam gtan rgya mtsho. *'Bras ljongs dgon sde'i lo rgyus.* Gangtok, Sikkim: Namgyal Institute of Tibetology, 2008. [*History of Sikkimese Monasteries.*]

Bstan pa'i sgron me. *Gsang chen rnying ma'i 'dus sde 'og min o rgyan smin grol gling nges pa don gyi dka' ba'i tshal chen po'i dkar chag rang bzhin bden brjod ngo mtshar shel gyi a dar+sha/.* Pe cin: Krung go'i bod kyi shes rig dpe skrun khang, 1992.

Gter bdag gling pa 'gyur med rdo rje. *Na rag dung sprugs kyi cho ga 'khor ba kun sgrol.* [No additional publication information.]

———. "O rgyan smin grol gling gi 'dus sde'i bca' khrims kyi yi ge blang dor gsal bar byed pa'i nyi ma." In *gSung 'bum 'gyur med rdo rje*, 16:127–96. Dehra Dun: D. G. Khochhen Tulku, 1998.

'Jam dbyangs mkhyen brtse'i dbang po sogs bla ma kha shas kyi gsung phyogs bsgrigs. 18 vols. [No additional publication information.]

'Jam mgon kong sprul blo gros mtha' yas, ed. "rDzogs pa chen po man ngag snying thig gi bla ma brgyud pa'i rim pa mchod pa'i cho ga kun bzang rnam par rol pa'i rgyan." In *gDams ngag mdzod*, 2:445–86. Delhi: Shechen Publications, 1999.

———, ed. *Rin chen gter mdzod chen mo.* New Delhi: Shechen Publications, 2008.

Kaḥthog rig 'dzin tshe dbang nor bu. "Rdzogs pa chen po yang zab bla sgrub dkon mchog spyi 'dus kyi khrid yig gu ru'i dgongs rgyan nyin byed snying po las rdzogs rim khrid yig khams gsum yongs grol." In *Gsung 'bum tshe dbang nor bu*, 3:537–68. Pe cin: Krung go'i bod rig pa dpe skrun khang, 2006.

Kaḥthog rig 'dzin tshe dbang nor bu, and Brag dkar rta so sprul sku chos kyi dbang phyug. "Tshe dbang nor bu'i zhabs kyi rnam thar brjod pa ngo mtshar dad pa'i rol mtsho." In *gSung 'bum tshe dbang nor bu*, 1:35–192. Pe cin: Krung go'i bod rig pa dpe skrun khang, 2006.

Kaḥthog si tu 03 chos kyi rgya mtsho. "Ru lu sgang dpal chen lha khang." In *Dbus gtsang gnas yig*, 376–79. Khreng Tu'u: Si khron mi rigs dpe skrun khang, 2001.

———. "U rgyan smin grol gling." In *Dbus gtsang gnas yig*, 221–39. Khreng Tu'u: Si khron mi rigs dpe skrun khang, 2001.

Khang dkar tshul khrims skal bzang. *Bod kyi lo rgyus phyogs bsdus bod dang bod mi.* New Delhi: Western Tibetan Cultural Association, 1980.

Khyung po ras pa 'gyur med 'od gsal. *rJe btsun mi 'gyur dpal gyi sgron ma'i rnam thar dad pa'i gdung sel.* Thimphu: National Library of Bhutan, 1984. [*Dispeller* ms. 1.]

Mdo mkhar zhabs drung tshe ring dbang rgyal. *Mi dbang rtogs brjod.* Par gzhi dang po. Khreng Tu'u: Si khron mi rigs dpe skrun khang, 1981.

Mi 'gyur dpal sgron. "bLa ma drag po'i dkyil 'khor du bdag nyid 'jug pa'i cho ga nag 'gros su bkod pa dbang drag sgrub pa'i lam bzang ldeb." In *gSung 'bum*, vol. 1. [Unpublished volume compiled by Sean Price at Mindrolling Monastery, Clement Town, India.]

———. "Dri lan bdud rtsi'i dga' ston le tshan ldeb/." In *rJe btsun mi 'gyur dpal sgron gyi gsung rnam/*. [Unpublished text compiled by Sean Price for the Tsadra Foundation, 159–202.] [*Ambrosial Feast*.]

Minling Editorial Committee, ed. *'Og min o rgyan smin grol gling gi gdan rabs mkhan brgyud rim par byon pa rnams kyi rnam thar g.yul las rnam par rgyal ba'i dga' ston*. Clement Town: Ngagyur Nyingma College, 2002. [*Lives of the Mindröling Succession Lineages: A Festival of Victorious Conquerors*.]

Mkhan chen 'jam dbyangs rgyal mtshan, ed. "Sdom 'bul." In *Bka' ma shin tu rgyas pa (kaḥthog)*, 1:365–68. Chengdu, China: KaH Thog Mkhan Po 'jam Dbyangs, 1999.

Mkhyen brtse'i dbang po, and Klong chen rab 'byams pa dri med 'od zer. "Sngon 'gro tshogs bsags kyi dmigs rim ngag 'don mdor bsdus pa gdod ma'i gseng lam." In *Gsung 'bum dri med 'od zer (dpal brtsegs mes po'i shul bzhag)*, 4:142–49. Pe cin: Krung go'i bod rig pa dpe skrun khang, 2009.

Rje btsun mi 'gyur dpal sgron gyi gsung rnam. Gangs can skyes ma'i dpe tshgos, vol. 5. Khren tu'u: Si khron dus deb tshogs pa si khron mi rigs dpe skrun khang, 2015. [*Dispeller* ms. 2.]

Rje btsun mi 'gyur dpal sgron gyi gsung rnam. [Unpublished text compiled by Sean Price and given to me by Marcus Perman of the Tsadra Foundation.] [*Dispeller* ms. 3.]

Smin gling lo chen dharma shrī. "Rab byung gi gzhi'i cho ga rin chen them skas." In *bKa' ma shin tu rgyas pa (kaḥthog)*, edited by mKhan chen 'jam dbyangs rgyal mtshan, 1:279–362. Chengdu, China: KaH Thog Mkhan Po 'jam Dbyangs, 1999.

———. "Yum chen lha 'dzin dbyangs can sgrol ma'i rnam thar." In *gSung 'bum dharma shrī*, 2:695–722. Dehradun, India: D. G. Khochen Tulku, 1999.

Smin gling rje btsun mi 'gyur dpal sgron. *Zab lam bde gshegs kun 'dus las mkha' 'gro gsang ba ye shes kyi rnal 'byor rim bzhi'i lam zab mo nyams su len pa'i khrid yig man ngag gsal sgron*.

Smin gling rje btsun mi 'gyur dpal sgron, and rGyal sras gzhan phan mtha' yas. "Na rag dong sprugs kyi dbang gi cho ga mtshams sbyor gyis brgyan pa bde chen lam bzang." In *bKa' ma shin tu rgyas pa (kaḥthog)*, edited by mKhan chen 'jam dbyangs rgyal mtshan, 18:265–342. Chengdu, China: KaH Thog Mkhan Po 'jam Dbyangs, 1999. [*Dredging the Depths of Hell*.]

Thu'u bkwan 03 blo bzang chos kyi nyi ma. *Grub mtha' shel gyi me long*. Lan kru'u: Kan Su'u Mi Rigs Dpe Skrun Khang, 1984.

English-Language Sources

Ardussi, John. "Brewing and Drinking the Beer of Enlightenment—the Doha Tradition in Tibet." *Journal of the American Oriental Society* 2 (1997): 115–24.

———. "Formation of the State of Bhutan ('Brug gzhung) in the 17th Century and Its Tibetan Antecedents." In *The Relationship between Religion and State (chos srid zung 'brel) in Traditional Tibet*, edited by Christoph Cüppers. Lumbini, Nepal: Lumbini International Research Institute, 2004.

Ashton, Gail. *The Generation of Identity in Late Medieval Hagiography: Speaking the Saint*. New York: Routledge, 2000.

Bakhtin, Mikhail M. *The Dialogic Imagination*. Austin: University of Texas Press, 1981.

Benard, Elisabeth. "Born to Practice: The Sakya Jetsunma Phenomenon." *Revue d'Études Tibétaines* 34 (2015): 1–20.

Bessenger, Suzanne M. *Echoes of Enlightenment: The Life and Legacy of the Tibetan Saint Sönam Peldren*. New York: Oxford University Press, 2016.

———. "'I am a god, I am a god, I am definitely a god': Deity Emanation and the Legitimation of Sönam Peldren." *Revue d'Études Tibétaines* 38 (2017): 84–103.

Buswell, Robert E., Jr., and Donald S. Lopez Jr. *The Princeton Dictionary of Buddhism*. Princeton: Princeton University Press, 2014.

Bynum, Caroline Walker. *Holy Feast and Holy Fast: The Religious Significance of Food to Medieval Women*. Berkeley: University of California Press, 1987.

Cabezón, José, and Roger Jackson, eds. *Tibetan Literature: Studies in Genre*. Boulder: Snow Lion, 1996.

Chodron, Thubten, ed. *Blossoms of the Dharma: Living as a Buddhist Nun*. Berkeley: North Atlantic Books, 1999.

Coakley, John Wayland. *Women, Men, and Spiritual Power: Female Saints and Their Male Collaborators*. New York: Columbia University Press, 2006.

Collins, Patricia Hill. "Toward a New Vision: Race, Class, and Gender as Categories of Analysis and Connection." In *Privilege: A Reader*, edited by Michael S. Kimmel and Abby L. Ferber, 240–57. Boulder: Westview Press, 2010.

Conze, Edward. *Buddhist Scriptures*. London: Penguin Books, 1959.

Cooper, Brittney. "Intersectionality." In *The Oxford Handbook of Feminist Theory*, edited by Lisa Disch and Mary Hawkesworth. New York: Oxford University Press, 2016.

Coston, B. M., and Michael Kimmel. "Seeing Privilege Where It Isn't: Marginalized Masculinities and the Intersectionality of Privilege." *Journal of Social Issues* 68, no. 1 (2012): 97–111.

Crossley, Pamela Kyle. *Empire at the Margins: Culture, Ethnicity, and Frontier in Early Modern China*. Berkeley: University of California Press, 2006.

———. *A Translucent Mirror: History and Identity in Qing Imperial Ideology*. Berkeley: University of California Press, 1999.

Cuevas, Bryan J. *Travels in the Netherworld: Buddhist Popular Narratives of Death and the Afterlife in Tibet*. New York: Oxford University Press, 2008.

Cuevas, Bryan J., and Kurtis R. Schaeffer, eds. *Power, Politics, and the Reinvention of Tradition. Tibet in the Seventeenth and Eighteenth Centuries*. Leiden: Brill, 2006.

Dalton, Jacob. *The Gathering of Intentions: A History of a Tibetan Tantra*. New York: Columbia University Press, 2016.

———. "Recreating the Rnying ma School: The mDo Dbang Tradition of sMin grol gling." In *Power, Politics, and the Reinvention of Tradition: Tibet in the Seventeenth and Eighteenth Centuries*, edited by Bryan Cuevas and Kurtis Schaeffer, 91–102. Leiden: Brill, 2006.

Diemberger, Hildegard. "The First Samding Dorje Pakmo, Chokyi Dronma." Treasury of Lives. Accessed May 7, 2020. http://treasuryoflives.org/biographies/view/First-Samding-Dorje-Pakmo-Chokyi-Dronma/13205.

———. *When a Woman Becomes a Religious Dynasty*. New York: Columbia University Press, 2007.

DiFranco, Ani. *No Walls and the Recurring Dream*. New York: Viking, 2019.

Dowman, Keith. *Sky Dancer: The Secret Life and Songs of the Lady Yeshe Tsogyel*. London: Routledge & Kegan Paul, 1984.

Dreyfus, Georges. *The Sound of Two Hands Clapping; The Education of a Tibetan Buddhist Monk*. Berkeley: University of California Press, 2003.

Duckworth, Douglas S. *Mipam on Buddha-Nature: The Ground of the Nyingma Tradition*. Albany: State University of New York Press, 2008.

Garry, Ron. "Rigdzin Tsewang Norbu." Treasury of Lives. Accessed May 16, 2020. http://treasuryoflives.org/biographies/view/Rigdzin-Tsewang-Norbu/9372.

Gayley, Holly. *Love Letters from Golok: A Tantric Couple in Modern Tibet*. New York: Columbia University Press, 2017.

Geary, Patrick. *Living with the Dead in the Middle Ages*. Ithaca: Cornell University Press. 1994.

Goodman, Steven D. *Tibetan Buddhism: Reason and Revelation*. Albany: State University of New York Press, 1992.

Gyatso, Janet. *Apparitions of the Self: The Secret Autobiographies of a Tibetan Visionary; a Translation and Study of Jigme Lingpa's Dancing Moon in the Water and Dakki's Secret Talk*. Princeton: Princeton University Press, 1997.

Haas, Michaela. *Dakini Power: Twelve Extraordinary Women Shaping the Transmission of Tibetan Buddhism in the West*. Boston: Snow Lion, 2013.

Havnevik, Hanna. "The Autobiography of Jetsun Lochen Rinpoche: A Preliminary Research Report." In *Tibetan Studies: Proceedings of the 7th Seminar of the International Association of Tibetan Studies, Graz 1997*, edited by Helmut Krasser et al.,

1:355–67. Vienna: Verlag der Österreichischen Akademie der Wissenschaften, 1997.

Havnevik, Hanna, and Janet Gyatso. "Introduction." In *Women in Tibet: Past and Present*. edited by Janet Gyatso and Hanna Havnevik, 1–28. New York: Columbia University Press, 2005.

Heffernan, Thomas J. *Sacred Biography: Saints and Their Biographers in the Middle Ages.* New York: Oxford University Press, 1988.

Heller, Natasha. "Zhongfeng Mingben and the Case of the Disappearing Laywomen." *Chung-Hwa Buddhist Journal*, no. 26 (2013): 67–88.

Jacoby, Sarah. *Love and Liberation: Autobiographical Writings of the Tibetan Buddhist Visionary Sera Khandro.* New York: Columbia University Press, 2014.

———. "'This Inferior Female Body': Reflections on Life as a Tibetan Visionary through the Autobiographical Eyes of Se ra mkha' 'gro (Bde ba'i rdo rje, 1892–1940)." *Journal of the International Association of Buddhist Studies* 32 (2009): 115–50.

———. "To Be or Not to Be Celibate: Morality and Consort Practices According to the Treasure Revealer Sera Khandro's (1892–1940) Auto/biographical Writings." In *Buddhism beyond the Monastery: Tantric Practices and Their Performers in Modern Tibet*, edited by Sarah Jacoby and Antonio Terrone, 37–71. Leiden: Brill, 2009.

Jigdrel Yeshe Dorje, Dudjom, Gyurme Dorje, and Matthew Kapstein. *The Nyingma School of Tibetan Buddhism: Its Fundamentals and History.* Boston: Wisdom Publications. 1991.

Joffe, Ben. "White Robes, Matted Hair: Tibetan Tantric Householders, Moral Sexuality, and the Ambiguities of Esoteric Buddhist Expertise in Exile." PhD diss., University of Colorado, 2019.

Johnson, Allan. "Privilege, Power, Difference, and Us." In *Privilege: A Reader*, edited by Michael S. Kimmel and Abby L. Ferber, 59–68. Boulder: Westview Press, 2010.

Kapstein, Matthew. "The Seventh Dalai Lama, Kelzang Gyatso." Treasury of Lives. Accessed June 15, 2020. http://treasuryoflives.org/biographies/view/Seventh-Dalai-Lama-Kelzang-Gyatso/3107.

Kawahashi, Noriko. "Women Challenging the 'Celibate' Buddhist Order: Recent Cases of Progress and Regress in the Sōtō School." Special issue, "Gendering Religious Practices in Japan." *Japanese Journal of Religious Studies* 44, no. 1 (2017): 55–74.

Köhle, Natalie. "Why Did the Kangxi Emperor Go to Wutai Shan? Patronage, Pilgrimage, and the Place of Tibetan Buddhism at the Early Qing Court." *Late Imperial China* 29, no. 1 (June 2008): 73–119.

Kvaerne, Per. *An Anthology of Buddhist Tantric Songs: A Study of the Caryāgīti.* Bangkok, Thailand: Orchid Press, 2010.

Langenberg, Amy Paris. *Birth in Buddhism: The Suffering Fetus and Female Freedom.* New York: Routledge, 2017.

———. "On Reading Buddhist Vinaya: Feminist History, Hermeneutics, and Translating Women's Bodies." *Journal of the American Academy of Religion* 88, no. 4 (December 2020): 1121–53.

Makley, Charlene. "The Body of a Nun: Nunhood and Gender in Contemporary Amdo." In *Women in Tibet: Past and Present,* edited by Janet Gyatso and Hanna Havnevik, 259–84. New York: Columbia University Press, 2005.

Martin, Dan. "Pearls from Bones: Relics, Chortens, Tertons, and the Signs of Saintly Death in Tibet." *Numen* 41 (1994): 273–324.

———. "The Woman Illusion? Research into the Lives of Spiritually Accomplished Women Leaders of the 11th and 12th Centuries." In *Women in Tibet: Past and Present,* edited by Janet Gyatso and Hanna Havnevik, 49–82. New York: Columbia University Press, 2005.

McIntosh, Peggy. "Reflections and Future Directions for Privilege Studies." *Journal of Social Issues* 68, no. 1 (2012): 194–206.

———. "White Privilege and Male Privilege: A Personal Account of Coming to See Correspondences through Work in Women's Studies." In *Privilege: A Reader,* edited by Michael S. Kimmel and Abby L. Ferber, 15–27. Boulder: Westview Press, 2010.

Melnick, Alison. "Mingyur Peldron." Treasury of Lives. 2015. Accessed January 9, 2016. http://www.treasuryoflives.org/biographies/view/Mingyur-Peldron/9394.

Melnick Dyer, Alison. "Female Authority and Privileged *Lives*: The Hagiography of Mingyur Peldrön." *Journal of International Association of Buddhist Studies* 41 (2018): 209–34.

Mizzi, Robert. "Unraveling Researcher Subjectivity through Multivocality in Autoethnography" *Journal of Research Practice,* 6, no. 1 (2010): art. M3. Accessed July 11, 2019. http://jrp.icaap.org/index.php/jrp/article/view/201/185.

Mooney, Catherine M., ed. *Gendered Voices: Medieval Saints and Their Interpreters.* Philadelphia: University of Pennsylvania Press, 1999.

Mrozik, Susanne. "A Robed Revolution: The Contemporary Buddhist Nun's (Bhikṣuṇī) Movement." *Religion Compass,* June 2009.

Mullard, Saul. *Opening the Hidden Land: State Formation and the Construction of Sikkimese History.* Leiden: Brill, 2011.

Padma'tsho (Baimacuo) and Sarah Jacoby. "Gender Equality in and on Tibetan Buddhist Nuns' Terms." *Religions.* October 2020.

Petech, Luciano. *Aristocracy and Government in Tibet, 1728–1959.* Rome: Instituto Italiano per medio ed estremo oriente, 1973.

———. *China and Tibet in the Early 18th Century: History of the Establishment of Chinese Protectorate in Tibet.* Westport, CT: Hyperion Press, 1973.

Pommaret, Françoise. "Delok ('das log) Women on the Fringes of Buddhism." *SSEASR Journal* 6 (2012): 56–64.

Pomplun, R. Trent. *Jesuit on the Roof of the World: Ippolito Desideri's Mission to Eighteenth-Century Tibet.* New York: Oxford University Press, 2010.

Prude, Alyson. "Death, Gender and Extraordinary Knowing: The Delog ('das log) Tradition in Nepal and Eastern Tibet." PhD diss., University of California, Santa Barbara, 2011.

Quintman, Andrew. *The Yogin and the Madman: Reading the Biographical Corpus of Tibet's Great Saint Milarepa.* New York: Columbia University Press, 2014.

Renevey, Denis, and Christiania Whitehead, eds. *Writing Religious Women: Female Spiritual and Textual Practices in Late Medieval England.* Cardiff: University of Wales Press, 2000.

Roberts, Peter Alan. *The Biographies of Rechungpa: The Evolution of a Tibetan Hagiography.* New York: Routledge, 2010.

Ronis, Jann. "Celibacy, Revelations, and Reincarnated Lamas: Contestation and Synthesis in the Growth of Monasticism at Katok Monastery from the 17th through 19th Centuries." PhD diss., University of Virginia, 2009.

———. "The Prolific Preceptor: Si tu paṇchen's Career as Ordination Master in Khams and Its Effect on Sectarian Relations in Sde dge." *Journal of the International Association of Tibetan Studies* 7 (August 2013): 49–85.

Sangs rgyas rgya mtsho (sde srid). *Life of the Fifth Dalai Lama.* Translated by Zahiruddin Ahmad. New Delhi: International Academy of Indian Culture and Aditya Prakashan, 1999.

Schaeffer, Kurtis R. *The Culture of the Book in Tibet.* New York: Columbia University Press, 2009.

———. *Himalayan Hermitess: The Life of a Tibetan Buddhist Nun.* New York: Oxford University Press, 2004.

Schneider, Nicola. "The Ordination of *dge slong ma*: A Challenge to Ritual Prescriptions?" In *Revisiting Rituals in a Changing Tibetan World*, edited by Katia Buffetrille, 109–35. Leiden: Brill, 2012.

Schulenburg, Jane Tibbetts. *Forgetful of Their Sex: Female Sanctity and Society, ca. 500–1100.* Chicago: University of Chicago Press, 2001.

Severs, Eline, Karen Celis, and Silvia Erzeel. "Power, Privilege, and Disadvantage: Intersectionality Theory and Political Representation." *Politics* 36, no. 4 (2016): 346–54.

Shakabpa, Tsepon W. D. *One Hundred Thousand Moons.* Translated by Derek F. Maher. Leiden: Brill, 2010.

Simmer-Brown, Judith. *Dakini's Warm Breath: The Feminine Principle in Tibetan Buddhism*. Boston: Shambala, 2002.

Smith, E. Gene. "Introduction." *The Autobiography of the First Panchen Lama Blo-bzang-chos-kyi-rgyal-mtshan*. New Delhi: Ngawang Gelek Demo, 1969.

Starling, Jessica. "Neither Nun nor Laywoman: The Good Wives and Wise Mothers of Jōdo Shinshū Temples." *Japanese Journal of Religious Studies* 40, no. 2 (2013): 277–301.

Stoddard, Heather. "Rig 'dzin dpal ldan bkra shis (1688–1743); the '1900 Dagger-Wielding, White-Robed, Long-Haired Yogins' (sngag mang phur thog gos dkar lcang lo can stong dang dgu brgya) & the Eight Places of Practice of Reb kong (Reb kong gi sgrub gnas brgyad)." In *Monastic and Lay Traditions in North-Eastern Tibet*, edited by Yangdon Dhondup, Ulrich Pagel, and Geoffrey Samuel, 89–116. Leiden: Brill, 2013.

Sweet, Michael J., trans., and Leonard Zwilling, ed. *Mission to Tibet: The Extraordinary Eighteenth-Century Account of Father Ippolito Dsideri, S.J.* Boston: Wisdom, 2010.

Taylor, Anna. "Hagiography and Early Medieval History." *Religion Compass* 7, no. 1 (2013): 1–14.

Townsend, Dominique. "How to Constitute a Field of Merit: Structure and Flexibility in a Tibetan Buddhist Monastery's Curriculum." *Religions* 8 (2017): 174.

———. "Materials of Buddhist Culture: Aesthetics and Cosmopolitanism at Mindroling Monastery." PhD diss., Columbia University, 2012.

Tylus, Jane. *Reclaiming Catherine of Siena: Literacy, Literature, and the Signs of Others*. Chicago: University of Chicago Press, 2009.

Weber, Max. *Economy and Society: An Outline of Interpretive Sociology*. Edited by Guenther Roth and Claus Wittich. Berkeley: University of California Press, 1978.

Weber, Max, and S. N. Eisenstadt. *Max Weber on Charisma and Institution Building: Selected Papers*. Chicago: University of Chicago Press, 1968.

Willis, Janice D. "On the Nature of rnam thar: Early dGe Lugs pa *Siddha* Biographies." In *Soundings in Tibetan Civilization*, edited by Barbara Nimri Aziz and Matthew Kapstein, 304–19. New Delhi: Manohar Publications, 1985.

Index

Adon instructions, 165
alcohol consumption, 127–30, 131, 132, 135, 176
Anuyoga (Subsequent Yoga), 4, 44, 173. *See also* Atiyoga
appellations and pronouns, 95–99; authorizing referents, 69; "unwanted daughter," 35, 96, 99–100
Ardussi, John, 199n30
Ashton, Gail, 107–8, 137
Atiyoga (Highest Yoga), 4, 44, 62–63, 98, 173
authority: "charismatic" (Weber), 74, 92, 194n13; and gender, 68, 103, 111, 139; "legal" (Weber), 91–92; and privilege, 25, 88–89, 101, 102–3; three modes of, 25–26, 71, 95, 98, 100–101, 103; Weber's divisions, 71, 87. *See also* educational authority; emanation authority; institutional authority
autobiography: "auto/biography," 17, 28–29, 187n36; *Lives*, 17, 18, 74, 81; self-humbling strategies 29, 67–68, 194n5

Bakhtin, Mikhail, 109
beer. *See* alcohol consumption
Bessenger, Suzanne, 16, 185n3
bhikṣuṇī, 50, 51. *See also* nuns
biography, 6–7. *See also* autobiography; hagiography; *Lives*
Blazing Remains Tantra, 163, 203n5

buddhavacana (Buddha's word), 14
Bumrap Jampa Orgyen Kelsang, 56

Cabezón, José, 45
celibacy: and Geluk norms, 135, 147, 148; as Mingyur Peldrön's ideal, 49, 135, 147, 148; and Mingyur Peldrön's previous lives, 48, 83–84; non-celibate religious paths, 12, 50, 129, 142; theme in *Dispeller*, 27, 48, 147; and women's autonomy, 64, 82–83, 142–43. *See also* monasticism; non-monastic practice communities; nuns; *and under* Mingyur Peldrön
Celis, Karen, 23, 194n4
Chakdor Wangchen, 171
Changkya Rölpé Dorjé, 198n24
charlatans, 128, 130–31, 176
Chöding hermitage, 203n21
Chökyi Drönma, 2, 191n56; compared with Mingyur Peldrön, 18, 52, 53, 89; *Life*, 18; past lives, 75, 194n16
Chökyi Gyatso: *Pilgrimage Guide to Ütsang*, 169
Chökyi Wangchuk, 122
Churner of the Depths of Hell (text and ritual), 44, 62
civil war (1717–18), 53–59; deaths, 35–36, 54, 57, 92, 114, 153; and the Dzungar Mongols, 31, 54–56, 143, 150, 192n66, 193n83; and intersectarian tensions,

215

civil war (1717–18) *(continued)*
   53–54, 112; flight and exile of Mingyur Peldrön, 3, 37–38, 55–59, 93, 114–16, 193n83; and Mindröling Monastery, 35, 55, 59, 78–79, 88, 93, 151–52, 155, 160, 193n80; presented in *Dispeller*, 29. *See also* Tibet in the eighteenth century
Cixous, Hélène, 107
Coakley, John, 108
Columbel, Eric, 3
commemoration rites, 168–69
consort relationships, 18, 19; and alcohol, 127; Mingyur Peldrön's rejection of, 27, 52, 143; offer by Fifth Lelung, 156–57; Padmasambhava and Yeshé Tsogyel, 80, 81, 82, 84; religious benefits of, 142, 157; Samantabhadra and Samantabhadrī, 76; of treasure revealers, 81–82, 129, 142
Cooper, Brittney, 87
Coston, Ethan M., 23
Crenshaw, Kimberlé, "intersectionality," 23. *See also* intersectionality

Dajin Badur, 153
ḍākinīs, 14, 97, 100; Venerable Master, Excellent Queen of the Ḍākinīs title, 97–98, 102, 155
Dalai Lamas, incarnation lineage, 194n13
Dalton, Jacob, 11, 13, 186–87n28
Dargyé Chöding lineage, 12, 100, 106, 133
Dechen Paldron (Jetsün Dechen Paldron), 174, 177
Deden Drölma, 159, 168
Definitive Secret Vajragarbha, 39, 165
deloks, 77–79
Depa Wangdu, 55
Dharmavajra, 40, 41
dialogue, 28–29, 96, 105, 107, 111–12, 136–37, 139
Diemberger, Hildegard, 18, 73
DiFranco, Ani, 174

Dingri Lodrö Tenpa, 197n2
Dispeller: account of Mingyur Peldrön's death and funerary arrangements, 162–68; account of sectarian violence, 55–56; author's agenda, 136–38, 177; author's self-presentation, 70, 110; authorship of, 16, 104, 187n33; birth story, 32, 39; as bridge between time periods, 177; on childhood and religious education, 43, 45–46; closing colophon, 33, 171–72; date of, 8–9; description of institutional relationships, 89–90, 141; descriptions of previous incarnations, 7, 72–75, 76, 78, 82–83, 86–87, 101; dialogue and quotations, 28–29, 70, 96, 105, 108, 111–12, 130–31, 134, 135, 136–37, 139, 187n33; editions, 3; format, 22, 69–71; as hagiography, 6–7, 163–64; historical events in, 10, 19, 29, 177; literary style and linguistic conventions, 28–29, 70, 97–100, 111; on Mingyur Peldrön as nun, 50, 52, 190n46; on Mingyur Peldrön as teacher, 105, 120–23, 128–31, 137; miraculous accounts in, 7, 163–64, 167–68, 170; multivalent approach to, 68–69; as multivocal narrative, 28, 105, 108, 109, 117, 136, 138, 187n33; as "outer" namtar, 186n18; poetic verse attributed to Mingyur Peldrön, 70, 111–12, 114–17; on Polhané, 151, 154–55; portrayal of Mingyur Peldrön as emotional being, 79–80, 112–13, 115–16, 117, 135; presentation of Mingyur Peldrön's siblings, 93; rainbows and portents, 40, 41, 63, 164, 167–68; reflection of Gelukcentrism, 31, 135; theme of monasticism and celibacy, 48, 118, 120, 123, 126, 131, 136–37, 148, 177; themes of privilege, authority, gender, and dialogue, 9, 22, 25–26, 29, 68–69, 72, 95, 98–99, 100–101, 102; treatment of gender, 2, 10, 19, 20, 21, 26–27,

66–69, 71–72, 73, 95–101, 103, 138–39; use of appellations and pronouns, 95–99, 155; use of senyik style, 42, 43, 49, 70, 92, 165; wide range of presentations, 112. *See also* Gyurmé Ösel
Döndrup Gyel, 198–99n29
Dorjé Drak Monastery, 11, 13
Dorje Pakmo, 75, 196n50
Dredging the Depths of Hell, 44, 62
Drepu retreat center, 128–29, 200n61
Drikung Kagyu denomination, 45
Drimé Özer, 18
Duckworth, Douglas, 146
Dudjom Lingpa, 122
Dudjom Rinpoche, 84, 118, 145, 173, 193n80
Dzogchen. *See* Great Perfection teachings
Dzungar Mongols, 192n62; and the civil war of 1717–18, 31, 54–56, 143, 150, 192n66, 193n83; destruction of non-Geluk sites, 112; Gyurmé Namgyel and, 144, 159; harassment of Nyingma women, 69; occupation of Lhasa, 54, 55, 192n66; violence against Mindröling Monastery, 55–56, 114

educational authority, 71, 90–95, 98, 102, 111, 125; and Weber's "legal authority," 91–92
emanation authority, 71, 72–87, 98, 101, 188n55; case of Nangsa Öbum, 77–79; case of Samantabhadrī, 76–77; case of Yeshé Tsogyel, 80–85; and religious authority, 85
empowerments (*wang*), 25, 42, 43, 44, 121, 135, 159; and authority 89, 90, 91, 92, 93, 98; Four Empowerments, 40; long-life, 164; Precious Word, 48; wrathful, 165
Erzeel, Silvia, 23, 194n4
esoteric texts, 13–14, 62, 159. *See also* terma

factionalism, 30–31, 54, 144
Festival of Victorious Conquerors, 49, 106–7, 173, 190n39
Fifth Dalai Lama (Ngawang Losang Gyatso): death of, 30, 54, 191n60, 192n63; and the Ganden Podrang government, 11; initiation of Rinchen Namgyel, 45; and intersectarianism, 11, 30, 54; *Life* by the Desi Sangyé Gyatso, 194n12; patronage of Mindröling and relations with Terdak Lingpa, 15, 55, 88, 113, 154; tomb of, 153
Fifth Lelung. *See* Jedrung Losang Trinlé
five sciences (rikné), 15, 45–47, 64

Ganden Podrang government: cabinet after civil war, 144, 150, 153; and death of the Fifth Dalai Lama, 30, 53–54; factions of, 54; under the Fifth Dalai Lama, 15, 55, 88; founding of, 11; under Polhané, 144; relationship with Dzungars, 54, 159; relationship with Mindröling, 63, 88. *See also* Fifth Dalai Lama
Garchen Rinpoche, 85
Gautami Thrinley Choedron, 174, 177
Gayley, Holly, 19
Geary, Patrick, 8, 31
Gegen Rabten Gyau, 156
Gelongma Palmo, 74, 75
Geluk order: after civil war, 63, 143; competing factions, 31, 144; dominance of, 30, 31, 135; Dzungar forces backed by, 54 112; geshe system, 202n41; persecution of non-Geluk communities, 30; relations with Nyingma, 11, 144–47, 148, 152–56, 155
gender: advice to women and men, 131–32, 139; appellations and pronouns, 95–100; and authority, 68, 85, 89–90, 103, 111, 125, 136, 139; and author-saint relationship, 107–8; in *Dispeller*, 2, 10, 19, 20, 21, 26–27, 66–69, 71–72, 73,

INDEX 217

gender *(continued)*
    95–101, 103, 138–39; in eighteenth-century Buddhist context, 26; in hagiography, 108; and monasticism, 51, 123–26, 131, 200n1; and official lineage at Mindröling, 140; and privilege, 2, 69, 101, 102–3, 175; and rebirth, 85–86, 134; and religious education, 38, 46–47, 105, 112, 136; and sex, 20, 26, 188n52; as theme in the life of Mingyur Peldrön, 2–3, 9, 20, 26–28. *See also* "lesser female birth"; nuns
Gendun Tsampel, 57
Gesar epic, 198n21
Great Master of Oddiyana. *See* Padmasambhava
Great Perfection teachings (Dzogchen), 2, 40, 49; Atiyoga and Anuyoga, 4, 44, 62–63, 98, 173; experts in, 58; Instruction category (Menakdé), 33, 44; Mingyur Peldrön's works, 60, 105, 118; Nyingtik genre, 33; Samantabhadra and Samantabhadrī as progenitors, 41, 76–77; secret Vajragarbha, 39, 40, 165; Thögel, 33; Three Classes, 33, 42, 44; transmission of, 46–47; Trekchö, 32, 33
Gung Lumpawa, 144
gur (metered verse), 112–17, 134, 198nn16,18,21; and realization, 117, 199n30; seven goals of, 198–99n29
Guru Rinpoche. *See* Padmasambhava
Gyatso, Janet, 51, 112
Gyurmé Chödron, 32, 34, 57, 151, 156
Gyurmé Chöpel, 171
Gyurmé Namgyel (king of Sikkim), 58, 157
Gyurmé Namgyel (son of Polhané), 144, 159
Gyurmé Ösel (Khyungpo Repa Gyurmé Ösel): counseled about drinking, 129–30; and the death of Mingyur Peldrön, 166; as disciple of Mingyur Peldrön, 4, 7, 8, 17, 29, 106, 110, 129–30, 171; on *Dispeller*, 133, 171–72; first meeting with Mingyur Peldrön, 109–10; life of, 4; relationship with Mingyur Peldrön, 104–6, 137, 138; self-presentation, 70, 110; views on monasticism, 175–76. *See also Dispeller*
Gyurmé Pema Tenzin, 35
Gyurmé Pema Wangyel, 133–34, 171, 172
Gyurmé Samten Chogdrup, 105, 121, 159
Gyurmé Tharchin, 121
Gyurmé Trinlé Namgyel (Fifth Trichen), 172, 173
Gyurmé Yangdzöm, 57, 151–52, 156
Gyurmé Zangpo, 159
Gyurrme Zhenpen Wangpo, 56

hagiography: authorizing referents in, 69; author-saint relationship, 107–8, 137–38, 170; definition, 5; dialogic potential of, 28–29, 136–39, 176; *Dispeller* as, 9–10; of the Fifth Dalai Lama, 194n12; gender in, 108; and history, 8, 31; medieval European, 4–7, 107–8, 137; modes of authentication, 71; and namtar, 3–7, 69; as propaganda, 8. *See also Dispeller*; *Lives*; namtar
Havnevik, Hanna, 51
Heart Essence of Vimilamitra, 44
histories (*logyü*), 7, 10
History of Sikkimese Monasteries, 57
Hong Taiji, 34
Hor, 48, 55–56, 201n27. *See also* Dzungar Mongols
householder life, 51–52, 120

incarnation lineage: and gender, 85–87, 133–34; of Dalai Lamas, 194n13
Indian poetry, 113
Institut für Indologie und Tibetologie collection of senyik, 43

institutional authority, 71, 87–90, 102; and gender, 89–90, 125; and social privilege, 88–89; terminology used for, 98–99
intersectionality, 23, 67, 87, 90, 101, 103
invention of tradition, 13, 187n29
Irigaray, Luce, 107

Jackson, Roger, 45
Jacoby, Sarah, 18, 26, 74; "relational selfhood," 109
Jagöpa Chökyong Gyeltsen, 197n2
Jamgön Kongtrul Lodrö Thayé, 173; *Great Collection of Precious Treasure*, 118, 122
Jamyang Khyentse Wangpo, 84, 122, 173, 199n42
Jara Taiji, 144
Jedrung Losang Trinlé (Jedrung Rinpoche, Fifth Lelung): brokered peace between Geluk factions, 156, 157; connection with Mindröling, 157; love for women and alcohol, 127–28; relationship with Mingyur Peldrön, 49, 62, 98, 127, 135, 143, 156–58; representation in *Dispeller*, 49, 126–28, 158, 176
jetsünma title, 140–41, 173–74, 177, 190n46
Jigmé Dorjé, 58–59, 192n73
Jigmé Lingpa, 105
Jigmé Pawo (Lhatsun Chenpo Dzogchen Jigmé Pawo), 150

Kachö Dechen Ling, 162, 203n21
kama tradition, 14, 62
Kangxi emperor, 54
Karma Kagyu lineage, 204n49
Katok Monastery (Kham), 62
Kelsang Gyatso. *See* Seventh Dalai Lama
Kham, 11, 62, 177
Khandro Nyingtik, 165
Khandro Rinpoche (Jetsün Khandro Rinpoche), 174, 177, 204n49

Khandro Tāre Lhamo (Tāre Lhamo): compared with Mingyur Peldrön, 2, 19, 24, 53, 75–76, 89; *Life*, 73, 75, 76; past lives, 75, 81, 82
Khangchenné (Khangchenné Sönam Gyelpo), 144, 150, 154
Khyungpo Repa Gyurmé Ösel, *The Life of Mingyur Peldrön: A Dispeller of Distress for the Faithful. See Dispeller*; Gyurmé Ösel
Kimmel, Michael, 23
Kongpo, 59–60, 90, 151–52
Kristeva, Julia, 107
Kunkyen Drimé Özer. *See* Longchenpa
Kunkyen Longchen Rabjampa. *See* Longchenpa
Kunzang Drönma, 126

Lady Drung, 37–38, 55, 58
Lady Peldzin, 37–38, 55; education of, 37, 47, 64, 93–94; as incarnation of her grandmother, 37, 106; marriage alliance with king of Sikkim, 37, 38, 58, 64, 149–50, 157–58
lama: translation of, 96; use of term *jé lama*, 96–97, 98
Langenberg, Amy, 26
laywomen, 21, 50, 169, 177; and "harlots," 129, 132
Lelung Jedrung Losang Trinlé. *See* Jedrung Losang Trinlé
Lelung Monastery, 53
"lesser female birth," 20–21, 67, 68–69, 123, 133, 134, 188n45
Lhadzin Yangchen Drölma. *See* Yangchen Drölma
Lhakyi Peldzöm, 32
Lhasa: as center, 10; during civil war of 1717–18, 54, 55, 192n66; under Gelukpa control, 152–54; murder of Han Chinese, 159
Lhatsun Chenpo Dzogchen Jigmé Pawo. *See* Jigmé Pawo

Lhazang Khan, 31, 54, 150, 192n63, 201n27; successors of, 158
Life of Shakyamuni, 52
lineage holders, 34, 49, 122; defined, 197n67; Mingyur Peldrön as, 25, 63, 83, 93, 102, 141, 160
lineage systems, 12, 91; *tulku*, 73
Lingza Chokyi, 75
Lives: auto/biographical, 17, 18, 28–29, 74, 81, 187n36; European and North American medieval, 4–7, 107–8, 137; as hagiographies, 6, 29; male authorship of, 107, 137; related to Mindröling Monastery, 106–7; stylistic patterns, 22; of Tibetan Buddhist women, 16, 24, 176; treatment of gender, 2, 24–27, 67–68, 86, 101–2. See also *Dispeller*; hagiography; namtar
Lives of the Orgyen Mindröling Lineage Succession: A Festival of Victorious Conquerors, 49, 106–7, 173, 190n39
Lochen Dharmaśrī: arrest and execution in civil war, 55, 57, 114, 153; and birth of Mingyur Peldrön, 32; closeness to Fifth Dalai Lama, 15; and education of Mingyur Peldrön, 1, 15, 43, 45, 48–49, 92, 99, 100; establishment and leadership of Mindröling Monastery, 12, 30, 55, 140, 185n7; family of, 12; *Life* of his mother, 106–7, 197n2; and Mindröling's Nyingma practice, 13, 62, 187n28; and monastic ordination, 12–13, 145; namtar, 197n2; quoted in *Dispeller*, 99–100, 139; works, 113, 186n26, 197n2
"long eighteenth century," 10–11, 19, 31, 178
Longchenpa (Kunkyen Drimé Özer/Kunkyen Longchen Rabjampa), 33, 34; commentary on *The Heart Essence of Vimilamitra*, 44
Lotus Garden Retreat Center (Stanley, Virginia), 174

Losang Kalsang Gyatso. *See* Seventh Dalai Lama

Machik Jomo, 74, 75
Machik Labdrön, 74, 75; *Severance (Chöd)*, 44
Machik Zurmo, 74, 75
Makley, Charlene, 51
Manchus, 31, 159. *See also* Qing dynasty
Martin, Dan, 191n56; on "lineage holder," 197n67
McIntosh, Peggy, 22–23
meditation caves, 80
Menji Monastery, 56
Menji nunnery, 60–61, 193n82
Milarepa, songs of, 112, 198n21
Mindröling Monastery: association with Great Perfection teachings, 33, 77; as center for Lhasa elite and "mother monastery," 15; code of conduct, 145, 193n77; curriculum, 14–15; descendants at Mindrolling in India, 177; founding, 12–13, 30, 140, 185n7; histories of, 10; inclusiveness, 13, 186–87n28; intersectarian engagements, 13, 155, 161; invention of tradition at, 13, 187n29; kama and terma traditions, 13–14, 62; leadership of, 55, 94; lineage holders, 25, 34, 49, 63, 83, 93, 102, 122, 160, 186n27; lineage systems, 12–13, 140, 172–74, 177, 204n49; *Lives* of lineage holders, 49, 106–7, 173, 190n39; location of, 1; and Mingyur Peldrön's institutional authority, 87–90, 102; monasticism and ordination, 145–46, 147; non-monastic practitioners, 131, 141–42; nunnery, 60, 193n82; reputation in Sikkim, 57–58; restoration of, following invasion, 59, 78–79, 88, 151, 152, 155, 156, 160, 193n80; sectarian violence against, 55, 57, 114; spelling of name, 185n7; survival of teachings after civil war, 92–93; ties with Fifth

Dalai Lama, 15, 88; visitors to, 121–22, 146; women's roles, 46, 47, 142; in the year 1699, 30, 32

Mindrolling Monastery (India), 3, 59, 145, 169, 173, 177–78, 193n78; jetsünmas, 177; spelling of name, 185n7

Mingyur Dechen Leytroling center, 59

Mingyur Peldrön: alignment with Geluk culture, 135; arranged marriage of her sister, 58, 64, 149–50; audience with Seventh Dalai Lama, 153; birth story, 32–33, 39; celibacy, 49, 64, 82–84, 135, 142–43, 147, 148, 157–58; cremation, 167–68, 203n21; decline and death, 63, 163–67; as diplomat, 141, 143, 149, 160; early years, 31, 32–35, 36–37; educational authority, 90–95; emanation authority, 72–87; empowerments and teachings, 60, 61, 121, 149, 150, 159, 164; engagements with political and religious leaders, 149–50, 152–53, 158–61; exile in Sikkim, 34–35, 37–39, 55–59, 64, 78–79, 88, 114–16, 164, 193n83; family, 1, 35–39, 106, 149; final teachings, 164–66; future birth as a man, 49–50, 52, 68, 132–34, 172; gender and authority, 21–22, 65–66, 68, 103, 136, 139; health, 61, 63, 193n83; institutional authority, 87–90; instruction of nuns, 112, 123–26, 134; involvement in her namtar, 110–11; memorials and images, 168–70; and monasticism, 63, 118–20, 123, 134, 146, 147; moral advice, 118–19; names and titles, 40, 97–98, 102, 153, 155, 189n18; as nun, 21–22, 47–53, 91, 92, 94, 125, 148, 169, 190n46; ordered to Kongpo, 59–60, 90, 151–52; ordination, 48–49, 52–53; previous lives, 7, 14, 33, 48, 70, 72–75, 80–86, 132–33, 170–71; privilege, 2–3, 9, 24, 25, 63–65, 84, 87–88; profound compassion, 33; quoted in *Dispeller*, 105, 111–12, 130–31, 133, 134, 135; references to, in collections, 121–22, 199nn42–43; refuge ceremony, 40–41, 48, 111; rejection of consort relationships, 27, 52, 143; relationships with religious and political leaders, 60, 63, 65; relationship with father, 39–42; relics, 167–68, 170; religious training, 1, 15, 38–39, 41–46, 48–49, 64, 90–91, 92, 103, 159, 165; roles and status at Mindröling, 47, 90, 94, 140–41; sainthood, 163, 168, 170; sense of humor, 110; stone throne outside Pemayangtsé, 1, 59, 122, 176, 177; supernatural abilities, 33–34, 35, 40–41, 158, 164; tantric practice, 49, 169; teaching activities, 2, 61–62, 102, 122–24; teaching career in Sikkim, 58–59, 93, 98, 122; travels, 60–62; as "unwanted daughter," 35, 96, 99–100

Mingyur Peldrön, works of, 2, 3, 60, 62, 105, 117–20, 134–35, 136, 176; *Ambrosial Feast of Questions and Answers*, 118–20; *Elaborations on the Awareness-Empowerment Methods for the Ati Zabdön*, 4; instruction manuals for rituals and praxis, 62–63, 122; literary style, 113; poetic verse, 112–15, 117, 134; *Secret Wisdom Ḍākinī Instruction Manual*, 121, 159

Mipam, 146

miracles, 7, 163–64, 167–68, 170

Miwang Gyurmé Sönam Tobgyé. *See* Polhané Sönam Tobgyé

monasticism: as escape from women's circumstances, 51, 200n1; Geluk and Nyingma approaches, 147–48; and gender, 51, 123–26, 131, 200n1; Mingyur Peldrön's approach to, 118–20, 132, 147–48; Nyingma approaches to, 145–46; tensions between monastics and non-monastics, 146; theme in *Dispeller*, 48, 118, 120, 123, 136–37, 148, 177; wayward behavior of monks, 126–29, 132, 135, 200n61. *See also*

monasticism (continued)
    non-monastic practice communities; nuns; ordination
Mongols, 202n45. See also Dzungar Mongols
Mooney, Catherine, 108
multivocality, 109, 187n33. See also *Dispeller*: as multivocal narrative

nakpas (non-celibate teachers), 12, 147
Namdra Pendé Leksheling Monastery, 153
namtar: contrasted with histories (*logyü*), 7–10; death narrative, 170; format, 7, 69–71, 72–73; genre of, 4–5; and hagiography, 4–7, 69; as literary works, 9, 70; of Lochen Dharmaśrī, 197n2; master-disciple relationships in, 104; of Rinchen Namgyel, 10, 36–37, 86–87, 92, 94; stylistic practices, 33, 35; systems of authority, 71; tripartite taxonomy of, 186n18. See also *Dispeller*; hagiography
Namtar of the Bodhisattva Rinchen Namgyel, Dispeller of Longing for the Fortunate, The, 36. See also namtar: of Rinchen Namgyel
Namtrul Rinpoche, 19, 81, 82
Nangsa Öbum, 74, 75, 77–79, 195n21
Ngawang Losang Gyatso. See Fifth Dalai Lama
Ngödrup Namgyel, 159
non-monastic practice communities, 128–29, 130–31, 132, 142
Northern Treasure tradition (Jangter), 44
nuns, 20–22; with *Lives*, 53; material concerns of, 124–26, 132, 143; at Mindröling, 141; Mingyur Peldrön as, 21–22, 47–53, 91, 92, 94, 125, 148, 169; Mingyur Peldrön's instruction of, 123–26, 134; monastic hierarchy, 20–21; ordination, 48, 50–53, 191n56; reference to, in *Dispeller*, 190n46; women's decisions to become, 49,

200n1. See also celibacy; Chökyi Drönma; monasticism; ordination
Nyangral Nyima Ozer, hagiography of Padmasambhava, 123
Nyangter Drakmar, 165
Nyingma religious order, 1–2, 34; community in Sikkim, 58; division of kama and terma texts, 13–14; Dodrup tradition, 146; as ecumenical tradition, 13, 30, 145; under the Fifth Dalai Lama, 11, 30; lineages, 34, 204n49; monasticism, 145–46; postwar revival, 60; relations with Geluk order, 11, 30–31, 145, 146–47; six "mother monasteries," 15. See also Great Perfection teachings; Mindröling Monastery; treasure revelation tradition
Nyö clan, 12, 34

ordination: Chökyi Drönma, 52, 191n56; at Mindröling, 12–13, 145–46, 147; women and, 48, 50–53, 191n56
Orgyan Chökyi, 24, 27, 53, 78; compared with Mingyur Peldrön, 16–17, *Life*, 17, 75
Orgyen Rabten, 56, 151
Orgyen Tenzin Dorje, 165
Oyirod federation, 192n62. See also Dzungar Mongols

Padmasambhava (Guru Rinpoche), 33, 40, 56; hagiography, 123; Mother-Father Union practice, 126; Terdak Lingpa as, 41, 115–16; and treasure revelation, 14, 34, 196n38; and Yeshé Tsogyel, 80, 81, 82–84
Padma'tsho, 26
Pelchen temple (Rulugang), 169
Pema Gyurmé Gyatso, 35–36, 43, 45, 55, 57; training of Situ Penchen, 146, 201n19
Pema Katang, 82–83
Pemalingpa (Rigdzin Pemalingpa), 171
Pema Tenzin Rinpoche, 165

Pemayangtsé Monastery (Sikkim), 38, 148, 149–50, 177–78; instruction by Mingyur Peldrön, 59, 64, 122; Mingyur Peldrön imagery, 169; Mingyur Peldrön's refusal to enter and her stone throne outside gates, 1, 59, 122, 176, 177, 193n77

Pesé Ngapö, 144

Petech, Luciano, 54, 159, 191n60

Phuntsok Peldzöm 1, 99, 142; accidental mention to Dzungars, 55, 57; and birth of Mingyur Peldrön, 32; exile in Sikkim, 58; quoted in *Dispeller*, 139; in Samten Gyatso's *History of Sikkimese Monasteries*, 38

poetic verse. *See* gur

Polhané Sönam Tobgyé (Polhané), 36, 201n27; and the hagiography of Mingyur Peldrön, 171–72; ordered Mingyur Peldrön to Kongpo and Lhasa, 60, 90; as political leader of central Tibet, 144; relationship with Mingyur Peldrön, 60, 63, 88, 150–56, 158–59, 160

Pomplun, Trent, 31

Precious Word Empowerment, 48

previous lives, 48; of Mingyur Peldrön, 7, 14, 33, 48, 70, 72–75, 80–86, 132–33, 170–71; of Rinchen Namgyel, 86; of Sönam Peldren, 75; of Tāre Lhamo, 76

Price, Sean, 3

privilege: application to Tibetan Buddhist history, 23–24; and authority, 3, 25, 87–89, 101, 102–3; education and, 15, 24, 38, 39, 94; and gender, 2, 9, 69, 101, 102–3, 175; in the life of Mingyur Peldrön, 2–3, 9, 24, 25, 63–65, 84, 87–88; of monks and nuns, 131; religious affiliation and, 23; scholarship on, 22–23; social, 24, 88–89; use of term, 24–25

Qing dynasty, 54, 144, 150–51, 159, 192n63

Ratna Biza. *See* Rinchen Namgyel

rebirth: buddha/bodhisattva vs. human, 72, 73; and gender, 85–86, 134. *See also* previous lives

relational selfhood (Jacoby), 109

Revealed Treasure of the Empty Plain, 40

Rigdzin Pelden Tashi, 146

Rigdzin Tuktik, 40

rikné (five sciences), 15, 45–46, 64

Rinchen Namgyel (Ratna Biza): coleader of Mindröling, 2, 36–37; depictions in *Dispeller*, 36, 93; exile of, 55, 57, 94; namtar of, 10, 36–37, 86–87, 92, 94; previous lives, 86; as proponent of nonsectarianism, 145; references to, in collections, 122; relations with Mingyur Peldrön, 43, 60; relations with Polhané, 151, 154; religious education, 38, 41, 44–45, 64; return to Mindröling, 59, 152; training of Situ Penchen, 146, 201n19; and the transmission of Mindröling-specific teachings, 92–93, 122; as trichen of Mindröling, 46

sainthood, 163, 170; signs of saintly death, 163–64, 167–68, 203n5; use of term "saint," 185n3

Sakya denomination, 43, 45

Sakya Pandita, 198n21

Samantabhadra, 41, 195n19; paired with Samantabhadrī, 76

Samantabhadra palace, 40, 41, 156

Samantabhadrī, 76–77, 195n19; as previous life of Mingyur Peldrön, 74, 75, 76–77

Samding Dorje Phagmo, 75, 196n50

Samding Nunnery, 18

samsara, 4, 73, 83, 115, 116; and gender, 20, 21, 68; and nirvana, 34, 76, 195n19

Samten Gyatso, *History of Sikkimese Monasteries*, 37, 38, 150

Samten Tsé retreat center, 60–61, 174

Sangnak Choeling Monastery (West Sikkim), 57, 59, 149, 169, 171

Sangyé Gyatso (Desi Sangyé Gyatso), 11, 13, 31, 192n63; *Life* of the Fifth Dalai Lama, 194n12
Schaeffer, Kurtis, 17
Schulenburg, Jane Tibbetts, 8
senyik (lists of teachings): for nine Sakya practitioners, 43; used in *Dispeller*, 42, 43–44, 49, 70, 92, 165; used in Rinchen Namgyel's hagiography, 92
Sera Khandro: compared with Mingyur Peldrön, 2, 17–18, 27, 53, 88–89; consort relationships, 18, 81; *Life*, 18, 104, 109; as past life of Tāre Lhamo, 82; past lives, 74, 75, 81, 194n16; privilege in the life of, 24; as treasure revealer, 81
Serzang Drupchen Gyurmé Longdröl, 121
Seventh Dalai Lama (Kelsang Gyatso): composed gur, 198n24; enthronement, 143; and the Gandren Podrang government, 54, 144; Mingyur Peldrön's relationship with, 60, 63, 88, 151, 153, 154
Severs, Eline, 23, 194n4
sex and gender, 20, 26, 188n52
Shakabpa, 153, 159
Shakyamuni Buddha, 32
Shauk Taggo, 126, 129; Terdak Lingpa's *Shauk Treasures*, 121
Shugsep Jetsün Rinpoche, 53
Siddhartha Gautama, 32
Siddha Yolmowa (Tenzin Norbu), 119, 199n35
Sikkim: exile of Mingyur Peldrön, 34–35, 37–38, 55–59; histories, 10; king of, 37, 38; Mingyur Peldrön's connections with aristocracy, 149; Mingyur Peldrön's retreat center, 93, 149
Situ Penchen, 146, 201n19
Sixth Dalai Lama, 30, 191n60, 192n63
Sönam Peldren: compared with Mingyur Peldrön, 16, 27, 53; *Life*, 16–17, 73, 104; previous lives, 75; privilege in the life of, 24
sorcery, 158

speech emanation, 195n21
Spiraling Vine of Faith, 75, 76. *See also* Khandro Tāre Lhamo
Spoken Teachings, 13, 187n29
srémo, 99
Starling, Jessica, 50
Sukhasiddhi, 74

tantrism, 12, 28, 117, 128, 153, 175, 198n28; of Mingyur Peldrön, 49, 105, 169; tantric consorts, 14; texts, 145; of Sera Khandro, 18; of Sönam Peldren, 16
Tārā, 74, 76
Tāre Lhamo. *See* Khandro Tāre Lhamo
Tashi Wangchuk, 57, 151
Taylor, Anna, 5
Tenzin Norbu (Siddha Yolmowa), 119, 199n35
Terdak Lingpa (Terdak Lingpa Gyurmé Dorjé): appellations of, 40, 114; closeness to Fifth Dalai Lama, 15, 88, 113; code of conduct for Mindröling Monastery, 145; as Dharmavajra and Padmasambhava, 40, 41, 83–84, 115–16; disciples of, 121; in *Dispeller*, 98, 139; establishment of Mindröling Monastery, 12–13, 30, 140, 185n7, 187n28; family of, 12, 32; as Great Tertön, 39, 40, 124, 150, 157; gur of, 113; heritage of, 34; illness and death, 35, 40, 41, 42–43, 48, 55, 61; instruction of Mingyur Peldrön, 1, 39–42, 44, 45–46, 92; naming of Mingyur Peldrön, 40; references to, in collections, 122; reincarnations of, 133, 172; reputation in Sikkim, 58; and treasure revelation, 4, 12, 14, 34, 36, 44, 48, 60, 62, 92, 123, 142, 165, 200n49; treasure revelation at Shauk Taggo, 126, 129; as trichen, 12; verse addressed to, 114–16; and women's training, 46
terma (hidden treasure texts), 12, 13–14, 62, 122, 129. *See also* treasure revelation tradition

tertöns, 12, 39, 40, 82, 84, 124, 150, 157, 196n38. *See also* treasure revelation tradition
Three Jewels, 56
Three Vows, 39, 49
Tibetan Buddhist women, 15; consort relationships, 18, 19; *Lives* of, 16, 20, 21; scholarship on, 17, 18, 19, 20. *See also* Chökyi Drönma; Khandro Tāre Lhamo; Orgyan Chökyi; Sera Khandro; Sönam Peldren
Tibet in the eighteenth century, 143–44, 153–54; factionalism, 30–31. *See also* civil war; Polhané Sönam Tobgyé; Seventh Dalai Lama
Tobgyé, 129
Townsend, Dominique, 46, 145
Transference of Consciousness (Powa), 173
treasure revelation tradition: association with Padmasambhava, 14, 196n38; connection with Nyingma school, 34; consort relationships in, 81–82, 195n32; Mingyur Peldrön's training in, 44; and Mingyur Peldrön's works, 62, 118, 122, 134; Northern Treasure tradition, 44; pacification rituals, 155; Yeshé Tsogyel and, 14, 74, 80, 81. *See also* Terdak Lingpa; terma
Trewang, 156
trichen and khenchen, 12–13, 35, 36, 43, 46, 140, 173–74
Trinlé Chödrön, 122, 172–73
Trinlé Lhundrup (Sangdak Trinlé Lhundrup), 12, 33, 34
Tsadra Foundation, 3
Tsering Döndrup, 54, 55, 192n66
Tsewang Norbu, 121–22
Tsewang Rabten, 54, 192nn62,66
tsünma (nun), 50, 190n46. *See also* nuns
tulku lineage system, 73; of the Dalai Lamas, 194n13. *See also* rebirth

Uicing Taiji, 201n27
Ü region, 1, 12, 22, 29, 113, 135, 144, 168. *See also* Mindröling Monastery
Urgyen Tsomo, 204n47

Vajrasattva, 163
Vajravarahi Kalikruddha, 173
Vajrayana Buddhist tradition, 50, 62
Vajrayogini, 75
Venerable Master, Excellent Queen of the Ḍākinīs, 97–98, 102, 155

Wangchuk Gyurmé Nangdrol, 121
water offerings, 130
Weber, Max: "charismatic authority," 74, 92, 194n13; "legal authority," 91–92; "traditional authority," 87; types of authority, 71

Yangchen Drölma, 12, 37, 140, 142, 173, 196n56; *Life*, 106–7, 197n2
Yellow Hats. *See* Geluk order
Yeshé Tsogyel: association with treasure revelation, 14, 80, 81, 82; as celibate student of Padmasambhava, 83–84; as consort of Padmasambhava, 80, 81, 82; depiction in *Dispeller*, 80–81, 82–83; incarnations of, 74, 75, 81, 76, 82, 204n47; in other women's *Lives*, 81; pilgrimage sites, 80; as previous life of Mingyur Peldrön, 48, 68, 74, 76, 82, 163, 170–71; visions of, in gur of Mingyur Peldrön, 115–16
Yizhin Lekdrup, 35, 45
yogini (*neljorma*), 50, 52, 191n50. *See also* tantrism
Yongzheng emperor, 144

Zaplam Deshek Kündü, 165
Zhenpen Wangpo, 56
Zhunggyu Dumpo Tashi, 56
Zukyi Nyima, 74
Züngharia, 31

www.ingramcontent.com/pod-product-compliance
Lightning Source LLC
Chambersburg PA
CBHW030620230426
43661CB00053B/2085